MY ESTONIA

3

JUSTIN PETRONE

My Estonia 3

WHAT HAPPENED?

PETRONE PRINT

Editors: Mike Collier, Epp Petrone
Cover design: Madis Kats
Cover photo: Remo Savisaar
Back cover photo: Kaari Saarma
Photo gallery: Justin Petrone and his friends
352 pages + 16 pages of photos

Printed by: OÜ Greif

ISBN 978-9985-9996-7-7 (Entire Series)
ISBN 978-9949-556-10-6 (Part 3)
ISBN 978-9949-479-30-6 (Entire Series: epub)
ISBN 978-9949-556-11-3 (Part 3: epub)

PETRONE PRINT

www.petroneprint.ee

To Epp

TABLE OF CONTENTS

WHERE THERE'S FIRE, THERE'S SMOKE

First there is fire and then there is smoke. Like clockwork.

I've seen it over and over again with my own eyes. You leave the old wood in the same spot through the seasons until it at last arrives, the long-awaited event: Midsummer, Saint John's Day. Then you stuff it with newspapers, cardboard, douse it with gasoline, oil, some leftover moonshine, whatever you like. Strike the match and with a pull of the wind it erupts, like your own personal volcano.

After the fire catches, you have to wait a bit. Then you hear the squeaking and croaking and tra-la-la-ing of all the little creatures who have made their homes in the pile. Mice, toads, and newts come scampering and hustling out of that miniature hell. Running for their lives, literally. They rush to the forest or to the barn, to the meadows and streams, to the neighbor's house, where they remember there is a safe hollow behind the walls. The Estonians call this inferno the *jaani-tuli* – Saint John's Fire. There is shared knowledge about these holy flames. The people say that if you run and leap over the fire, you will have good luck for the next year. The Estonians really believe this. They may not believe in humdrum things, but they believe in the power of fire.

I enjoy the fires as well. I like to get bundled up close to them, to listen to the tinder as it cracks and splinters from the heat, so near that I lose sensation in the tip of my nose and the skin over my cheeks. It's an invigorating flush, a rechristening by blaze. I like to study the colors of the flames, too, how they hue from yellow to blue, blood orange to green. There is a lot going on in just one bonfire.

My life in Estonia has been like a *jaanituli*. It's been one passionate and roasting mess. I came here many years ago knowing nothing about what was about to happen, then I got married, had a kid, left for New York for a while, and then came back because I felt it calling me. I thought I might make it as an academic in Estonia, or enter the world of diplomacy, or up my journalism game and write for some famous international newspaper. Instead I wound up writing some entertaining books about Estonia. Then something strange happened. I had to go away again. Now I'm back.

My books are like the smoke from this flame of life. They smell of the thing, but are not the thing itself. They curl up and sail away pleasantly toward the stars, or linger along foggy country lanes and city streets, thick and sinister, making it hard for you to breathe.

That's all this book is. Smoke. The smoke of fiery years spent in this windswept peninsula land.

Justin Petrone,
Back in Estonia,
April 2015

THAT HOLE

It was easy to get distracted in the toilet of Cafe Fellin because of the words on the inside of the door.

The words told about the origins of the name Viljandi, the picturesque and peculiar small town in Estonia where we lived. They were written by a local historian and typed below an old photograph of the lake front and its many villas. It was framed and covered in glass. In the cafe with its white wooden furniture and pleasant spirals of floral-printed wallpaper, you could hear the people bustling and glasses clinking, the fidgeting of a jazz guitarist, and maybe somebody waiting on the other side of that toilet door, turning the knob to remind one of the urgency of the situation. But that was too bad. I was still reading.

The *Vi* was an older form of *vee*, water in Estonian, the historian had written. The *Ljandi* brought to mind the ancient name of Tallinn, *Lindanisse*, which meant a town or stronghold. And so, there it was: Viljandi, the town on the water. It was still true in part. In old illustrations and wood carvings, you could see that the lake beside this town was higher, and the rivers were higher, too. I had heard that one could *sail* to

Viljandi with the right kind of boat, navigating down long-lost waterways. Back then, Viljandi was a Hanseatic merchant town, connected to the outside world by its waters.

Nowadays, it felt more like a backwater. To get anywhere from Viljandi, you needed to drive. A trip to the capital, Tallinn, and back could take five hours out of your day. The second biggest city, Tartu, with our publishing house, was an hour to the east. The beach and spa resort Pärnu was an hour to the west. And I didn't even bother taking note of how long it took to get to our farm house in Setomaa on the Russian border. On those long days, I just drove and drove.

Some people didn't think Viljandi was a backwater though. For these self-electing few, Viljandi was a bohemian jewel sparkling with artists and activists and eccentrics, hidden away from the crass commercialism that had afflicted the rest of the country, a respite for those who preferred to see their children fingering zithers and playing among castle ruins rather than sitting behind a computer.

There were also those who condemned the so-called "city" of Viljandi as a depopulated outpost of alcoholics and pensioners. A friend, who had left Viljandi, referred to his hometown as "That Hole."

"How can you stand living in that hole?" this Estonian friend would ask me. He had left "That Hole" when he was eighteen and never looked back. Now I wasn't even sure what to call him. His mother had named him Priit, but after he moved to Hollywood and started a career in music and film, he started calling himself "Brad." Brad Jurjens, you know, like Brad Pitt. Each year, he returned to visit his mother in "That

11

Hole" for a few weeks, then he was gone again, back to the City of Angels. When he did come to visit he would invite me out to a pub, where he would guzzle beers, check out girls from behind his shades, and ask me awkward questions.

"You've got to explain it to me. How can an American guy like you stand to live in a hole like this?"

"You really think your hometown is a hole?"

"Of course it is! Why do you think I left?"

The same question was more or less posed to me by my new acquaintance Diego when he stopped by during the Viljandi Folk Music Festival, and asked in a low and weary voice, "How can a guy from New York like you stand to live here?"

"You mean in this hole?"

"*Si.*"

Diego didn't ask me this question in front of our Estonian wives. No, he decided to wait until we were out in the street to spring it on me. It still wasn't much of a street. Sepa, or Smith Street, was more of a dirt path when our family moved in. There were some remnants of cobblestones, but most had been dug up and sold by some entrepreneurial Viljandier in the past, and what was left was so mottled that I had even come to fear it, mostly in autumn and spring when the rains came or when the snows melted, because deep puddles would hide amongst the muck and your car would hit them hard and get stuck. Whenever it did, I would think of my Estonian friend in Hollywood and chuckle about "That Hole."

The street that day though was still under construction, full of mud and sand and new pipes sticking out at strange angles.

There was also hope. For a long time, I had feared that nothing in Viljandi would change. And yet it *had* changed in my few years spent there, mostly for the better. It just took longer for the change to arrive to Viljandi than it did in the bigger Estonian towns. I was sure that Sepa Street would once again be proud. Perhaps most of the city would follow. A fully functional cinema would open one day, maybe even a spa.

But that would take more time. On that day there were still rotting planks over the stagnant puddles. The faint musk of dog feces snaked through the air and into the nostrils, and since you could never seem to *see* the source of the stink, you just had to wonder if it was new excrement or perhaps older, medieval, archaeological scat, that had been unearthed by a workman.

I had taken Diego out into the street to show him the steps to the ancient cellar that had been found.

But the steps were not the only thing. There had been other interesting finds.

When they had pulled up the street, or what had been left of it, the archaeologists went to work with surveying tools and shovels. They were led by Andres, a former neighbor of ours from Tartu. He was another one of those mythical Estonian men who carried around with him a big personality and yet communicated very little.

Andres was about a decade older than me, a dark-haired, sturdy guy with a square chin. His wife Kärt was a petite woman with a terrific laugh. I would make a droll comment now and then and then she would cackle with her entire body, leaving me to wonder if what I had said had actually been funny or if Kärt was just a bit insane.

Kärt was a brunette, and similar enough in coloring that she could have been Andres' midget sidekick. But Kärt had an Estonian last name. Andres had a strange last name that had some T's and V's in it, and I had heard that his father had been Ossetian, a little nationality wedged in the Caucasus. Andres also had fathered about seven children, three of them with Kärt, but despite this obvious source of stress, he seemed entirely relaxed, and kept a number of pot-bellied pigs in his backyard. During 'white night' grilling parties in June, he would take the pigs out and stroke their bellies and grin. That was back in those Tartu days. Sometimes in Viljandi, I did wonder why we had ever left.

Once I had proofread an academic article for Andres. It involved discoveries found in an ancient latrine located just across from the main building of the University of Tartu. Old toilets, as I learned, are goldmines for archaeologists. One can imagine how some Estonian court jester in the Hanseatic days went to relieve himself after a night of dancing and debauchery and dropped his flute into the toilet's hole. Bloop! Centuries later, Andres showed up with his own gang of merry men and women and found the same instrument encased in the orange-colored clay of the ancient dumping site. According to the article, the flute they found in that old toilet still played. I imagined how Andres had held the precious find aloft in triumph, and then cleaned it out a bit with his muddy fingers, placed it to his lips, and started to play it. When I described this scene, Kärt cackled insanely and said that it didn't happen exactly that way.

Andres loved his job and I envied him for that. He spent those weeks in our mud hole of a street in Viljandi scurrying back and forth and taking measurements. Each time he passed, I would ask if they had found any skeletons. I was convinced that there had to be dead people under our street. It just seemed like that kind of place.

"So, Andres, have you found any Teutonic knights?"

He shook his head. No knights yet.

"Any Swedish soldiers?"

"Not yet," he said and trudged on.

I was cautioned by a neighbor about this morbid interest. "God forbid those people find a skeleton," she had said. "In that case the archaeologists will be digging here for a year! The street will never get done."

But they did not find any human bones on Sepa Street. There was plenty of trash though. It made Andres' eyes brighten. There was fog and delirium behind his glasses. And every once in a while, he would come to me to share his special treasures.

"Do you see this beaker shard?" he would hold out a sliver of ancient blue glass in his palm. "This was made in Venice!"

I stared at the shard, trying to imagine how a tiny piece of such a great city could wind up in a hole in Viljandi.

And around the corner, at the end of Munga or Monk Street, Andres said they had found the remains of a potter's shop. The style of the earthenware matched ceramic shards found in Pskov, a Russian city of 200,000 located 20 km southeast of the Estonian border. It seemed that the potters in Viljandi, the water city, had been trading with the Slavs of Pskov long before any marauding Teutonic crusaders arrived on horseback. Or perhaps a potter from Pskov had gotten in trouble with the local authorities and fled his home to set up shop in quiet Viljandi, a place where it was certain that nobody would ever find him.

There were other curious finds on our street. Some coins, a horse shoe, a stone pendant. And plenty of animal bones.

Even I had my little discovery. I had been raking out a plot of dirt when I turned up a very human-looking jawbone. This led me to all kinds of uncomfortable hypotheses about my neighbors, until Andres came and calmed me and said that it had probably belonged to a sheep.

But the day after brought something truly sinister to the surface – an unexploded mine that had been dug up right next to our barn! You can imagine how happy I was that I had never done any renovation work around there. The newspaper said it had been lying there since the Second World War, and a special bomb unit had been called in to take it away and detonate it. I asked all the old neighborhood ladies I knew, but nobody could remember hearing of any battles on my home street.

Andres didn't bother himself with such things anyway. They weren't old enough. But he did find some ancient cellar steps that led straight across Sepa Street. They were formed by huge, rounded boulders, stacked on top of each other by God-knows-who, hundreds, or even a thousand years ago. They went down into the ground and then rose up again on the other side. The archaeologists had marked off the site with a metal fence. They had even brought a video camera to record the dig. Andres said he had been studying maps of the site, drawn by cartographers in the employ of the Polish crown, to which Viljandi and much of southern Estonia had been subject between the 1560s and 1620s. It was one of those periods that only historians bothered to recall, but the oldest, most accurate maps of old Viljandi made by Polish cartographers were actually kept in Moscow, Andres said.

Andres and the archaeologists abandoned their camp when the Viljandi Folk Music Festival came around. But I was impressed enough with the cellar to show it to Diego, my new Chilean friend, that day when he came to visit. And while we were standing there, gazing down into the ancient hole, he had to ask:

"Don't you go out of your mind with boredom in this hole, man?"

Poor Diego. He was like me. He had come to Tallinn on a whim and met his future wife by chance. Any rational man would have gone back to Santiago and married a local girl named Violeta or Veronica. But Diego was different. He was a romantic. It had been the night before he had to leave and yet

17

he couldn't forget that Estonian maiden, even in Chile. So he had to marry her and move to Estonia after that.

And so here he was, staring down into some crypt, grateful that he lived up in Tallinn and not down on Sepa Street.

"When you have three kids, you don't have time to go out to bars or the movies anyway," I told Diego. "And this place is good for raising kids. I can walk them to school, bike to the shop to pick up some groceries. Our daughters can run to their friends' houses to play. You can't do that in Tallinn. Or in New York."

Diego nodded a bit as if he almost believed me.

"And, I mean, the view of the lake is beautiful," I added.

"Sure, it is. But do you really want to look at it every damn day?"

A mutual friend told me Diego was having a hard time adjusting to life in Estonia. I knew he had quit working at a graphic design firm, not because of pay or disappointment with the work given him, but because he could not connect with his co-workers for some reason. I bet it wasn't anything they said or did, but the silence that had gotten into his bones and irritated him from the inside out. Why else would Diego have pulled me aside earlier that summer and whispered, "All the people from this country should be removed and replaced by Brazilians"?

Elias, my Swedish-Estonian chef friend, had stopped working at a local restaurant for much the same reason. He complained how his fellow cook, an Estonian, would say nothing to him during the work days.

"Nothing, not a word. You ask him a question and he shrugs." It drove Elias to take up work on a cruise ship.

"You still didn't answer me," Diego said and put a hand on my shoulder. "How do you cope, man?"

It seemed Diego wanted a longer answer from me. "Look, don't get me wrong, it's been really hard," I confessed.

"What's been hard?"

"Oh, living here. Everything. You know, I really started to hate the Estonians in my heart. I started to think that they were all just a bunch of Nazis and I didn't want to have anything to do with them."

Diego took off his sunglasses and looked up at me. "Man, that is exactly how I feel," he stammered. "And I thought I was alone. And I've had nobody talk to."

"You can't exactly tell your wife that her people are a bunch of Nazis."

"No, I don't think that would go over too well."

"But, hey, not all of them are like that, and, whatever, you've just got to accept them. I've learned that I am who I am and they are who they are, and I might as well just live my life and be happy."

I didn't tell Diego that I had been seeing a psychiatrist for years. And whether the emotional temperament of some Estonians had been connected with my depression or not, they had not made my life any easier. Little things would set off my rage. The sight of an alcoholic rummaging through a trash can. The impatience of a person standing behind me in line at the grocery store. I could hear those tight breaths, feel them on my neck because I had bought enough food and drink to last a week, and that person just wanted to buy his ham and cigarettes. Those clicks of the tongue, that nettled sigh that said, "You are inconveniencing me." In Viljandi, a man would bump into you on a sidewalk, clip you on the shoulder, nearly knock you down, and then grunt and keep on walking, as if nothing had happened. It was all, as they said, *normaalne.*

Ninety-seven out of a hundred Estonians would be fine to me. But it was those three Estonians, those garbage-picking drunks and pushy shoppers and rude pedestrians, whom I loathed. I knew it was wrong to hate a whole nation just because of the pitfalls of a few bad characters. Estonia had given me everything: a lovely and loving wife, three children, a writing career, a charming house in a rambling old town, stunning lake views, fun anecdotes about medieval toilets, unearthed mines, and sheep bones. On warm summer afternoons in Pärnu the car would cruise down the streets past the most golden, beautiful women you ever saw. You'd go to "Supelsaksad," the 1920s-style cafe and eat the best meal you ever ate, sit on the most comfortable camel-humped couch you ever sat on, and then head over to the beach to swim in the warmest water you had ever touched and to breathe in the freshest air your lungs ever savored and roll amongst the soft, wonderful sands.

And yet I had grown wary of Estonians, even those ones in Pärnu. Every zombie drunk forager, every heel-clicking bureaucrat. My distaste ran so dark and deep that I eventually determined the only way out was either to run away and desert my family or to succumb to tolerance and accept the locals for being who they were, not because they all deserved it, but because not accepting them was unhealthy and could drive me to do dangerous and unreasonable things.

The way I had come to see it, Estonia wanted you to change. It wanted you to speak its language and think its thoughts. It wanted you to ignore those drunks in the park, and to be more efficient with your shop transactions. It wanted you to grunt and keep on walking when a fellow pedestrian slammed his shoulder into you. And, above all, it insisted that you would never complain about its weather. Even a "Kind of cold today, isn't it?" would earn you another lecture about wearing warmer clothing.

In the end, to become an Estonian was to kill some Italian-American or Chilean part of yourself, if you had the fortitude or mental discipline to really do that. Most people didn't. Most foreigners who reached that point went running back to the mother country.

I remembered reading an interview with an American-Estonian businessman who had lived in Tallinn for years. I found it in a celebrity magazine shortly after we had moved back to Estonia. While we were unpacking our bags, the businessman's family was packing theirs. "Ten winters of this is enough," the guy said in the story. "We're moving to Hawaii!"

Back then, I thought Hawaii was for surfers and the weak of mind. I thought I would be tougher than that businessman and others like him.

By the time Diego had asked me his very big question, I thought I had graduated from the most painful parts of the adaptation process. It had been almost seven years since we had returned from New York with our six suitcases, and I thought that I had at last come to terms with Estonia and my relationship to it. I believed that I was emotionally prepared to spend a long time in Viljandi's watery embrace. The future, as far as I could see, would be more of the same.

Little did I know.

SIX SUITCASES

You should know that I returned to Estonia with only love in my heart.

In the cafes and arcades of lower Manhattan, which are haunted by eccentric and deranged characters, like the lady we used to call the "cat woman," because she was always stroking a feral cat, I felt the long-armed but loving embrace of Estonia, that land I had left behind. Even while the mountains of garbage piled up along the avenues, and the cat woman's dementia grew worse through the seasons, so that I once saw her with vomit all over her coat and the sidewalk before her, I had that extra bounce in my stride because I knew that I was one of the lucky ones, the ones with alternatives, the ones with another place to go.

In my New York office, I decorated my computer screen with an image of a lighthouse on Saaremaa, the largest Estonian island, and when I grew tired of sighing over the cool water and rocks, I changed it for an aerial view of Tartu's Supilinn area, those crooked roofs, the orange and red autumn leaves. I would ride satellite maps across the ocean, to see how close I could get to the cozy studio apartment in Tallinn's

Kalamaja district that we left behind when we moved to New York, and though we were so far away and someone else was living there, I would stare at the tiny red roof for a while, and imagine it was me standing in that sunny driveway beside it, and how I would walk down the road and pass the cats at the dumpster and then head on to the local corner shop, to buy a few boxes of tasty Georgian dumplings and a big bag of Kalev chocolates...

Some might have called it "homesickness" but, somehow, I was experiencing this longing in my country of birth.

When Supilinn's rooftops ceased to soothe me, to console me among the jackhammers and bleating cars and arrogant pedestrians, I found another image of Estonia, a photo of an old farmhouse nestled in green-yellow fields, and put that across my desktop. That farmhouse, the real one in the picture, was from Iceland or Greenland, and it had that Ilon Wikland illustration-like Swedish red, with the white trim around the windows, but in my mind that didn't matter, because it was my Imaginary Estonian Farmhouse, a place where I thought the greater me, the eternal soul of me, belonged.

One time, my boss Bernadette caught me staring at it.

"What's that?" she asked. Bernadette was anything you could ever want from an Irish woman, with the big hair and the big laugh and that bright, joyous, contagious sarcasm that all us New Yorkers seemed to have. Bernadette and I used to give each other updates not only on the latest biotech industry rumors but also on the cat woman's condition if we saw her, taking note of her general deterioration into madness, whether she looked clean or dirty, or if she had gotten sick again. And yet neither of us expressed any regret about her. We had to laugh about it because it was so awful.

"What's what?" I looked up, blushing.

"That," she pointed at the screen with a freckled finger. "You keep staring at it."

"Oh that. It's my Imaginary Estonian Farmhouse," I said. "See, there's the main house, and the barn."

"So, is that where you'll be doing your job for us next year?"

"What? Oh, yeah, sure," I pointed at the wooden dwelling. "I'll be writing about biotech from there."

People always want to know the "why" of things, why you did this or that, but the truest, most absolute answer is that we left New York because it was leading us around in circles, and something else was calling us from beyond the sea.

Estonia, Estland, population 1.3 million or so at that time. A speck of marshes and forests on the northern seas, with a few castles and apartment blocks and country estates thrown in for decorative purposes. It was calling us, the same way it had called me with its siren song many years before. Something was going to happen to us in Estonia, and so we had to go there.

But what was it?

We didn't know that part. Whatever it was, it was strong enough for us to endure the physical and emotional hardships of leaving America.

And that was a true hell. All of that furniture, all of those contracts that needed to be severed, telecommunications devices that needed to be returned, all of the family drama, the grief, the bitterness.

"How could you leave behind New York?"

"Why not? Should I spend the rest of my life renting the second floor of somebody else's house? And spend three hours every day in the dirty subway train, commuting?"

"You could look for a new job."

"I have looked for a new job, and all of the others pay less than the one I have."

"That just can't be. That just can't be…"

I have to look out the window now, to stare at a tree or a train, something to forget about the memories. When I think of those months toward the close of 2006 and beginning of 2007, I can only remember the darkness and the rain. Only one majestic moment stands out. That was the night I went for a walk beside the Atlantic Ocean, the night when I learned that we were expecting a new child. The sound of the waves was heavy, and there were a lot of stars in the sky, and it was moist and cool enough that you could see your breath. I stayed out on that ocean beach for a long time that night, staring up into the reassuring cosmos. There were forces in the universe greater than yourself. You just had to trust them. Somebody had told me something like that.

I heard footsteps approaching in rapid succession, the sound of shoes on sand, and then a late-night beach jogger ran past me. Out on the sea, I could see the glow from the ships. I thought about the ship that had run aground once out here, its hold full of illegal Chinese immigrants destined for sweatshops. That was their dream, though, to come here, to New York, the place to be. And I was one of the lucky few who were actually born here. Why did I need to leave?

The waves crashed on the shells, and I watched a plane come in to land at John F. Kennedy International Airport, which wasn't so far from our house. We had already bought the tickets. It was all done and set. All we would need to do is pack our suitcases. There were three of us and each of us could take two. Six suitcases for lugging one family's life across the ocean.

But there were actually four of us now, sort of. A new child. Epp wanted to call her Anna. The last time Epp had visited Estonia, she had interviewed her grandmother Laine, and heard more stories about Laine's mother Anna, a lady who lived in a big house by the sea a long time ago. Grandma Laine was not one to peddle sob stories, but she was not the most uplifting character either. Laine had very light blue eyes and an ancient face. It was a face of cataclysmic geology, that peak of a nose, those ravines of eyes, the patch of snowy white fuzz beneath the chin. She wore a blue handkerchief around her head, and asked you practical questions about the pluses and minuses of life.

But at least one time, Laine gave Epp the full story about what had happened to their family in 1949, how Anna and a teenaged Laine hid in the woods when the Soviet military

27

forces came to arrest them and send them to Siberia, surviving on ants during three long nights in March. So they escaped. A middle aged woman and a teenage girl managed to outwit one of the most bloodthirsty regimes in living memory. There were uglier things, too, but I won't go into those. What I will tell you is that Anna's story was a hero's story, and even when I was standing on that dark, foggy beach, I knew that a new heroic little Anna was coming.

But she wouldn't be born in New York. Not all children could be born there. Some children had to be born in other places and this child would be born in Tartu.

Tartu, where my sister-in-law and brother-in-law and little troublemaking niece Simona lived, Tartu, with its university where I could continue my studies, perhaps gaining skills that would bring in income, or maybe, if I was truly lucky, I could live the easy life of an academic myself, idling away the hours reading books and grading papers and thinking of ways to spend all of those free days in summer. Tallinn was full of bankers and politicians and professional celebrities who liked to have their personal lives chronicled in the tabloids, but Tartu! It was different. The academic, bohemian oasis was waiting for me.

And so, we put our most important possessions into six bags one night and boarded a plane to Warsaw, and from there to Tallinn, to take the train to Tartu.

VÄINO'S MAGIC TRICK

The first thing I remember about those Tartu days was the strange and metallic sound of two pieces of frozen firewood being struck against each other in the February night.

It was dark out in the yard beside the barn, and Väino was hitting the two pieces of wood together, gently. Väino, a middle aged man in a puffy insulated jacket. Average height and features, quick speaker, strutting posture. If I had to choose an animal or a bird that best represented Väino, it would be a rooster. He smiled at us as he hit the wood and his eyes lit up, as if he had just pulled a rabbit out of a hat, or made a pigeon disappear.

Kluck. Klick.

Back then, my Estonian wasn't good, so I couldn't understand most of what Väino was saying. But it involved the word *puu* (wood). We needed *puu* for heating the apartment we would rent from Väino, and Väino just happened to have a whole spare barn full of *puu* that could be had for a special discount price. And it was good dry *puu*, see? Väino hit the two pieces of frozen wood together again.

Kluck. Klick.

"Hey, I like this guy," Epp whispered into my ear. "He seems cool."

"Sure," I said. But that's not what I thought. What I thought was that my great intuition had led me to a driveway in Estonia watching a man play with wood. The jet lag from the journey still hadn't worn off, so I felt awful, and all of the caffeine from the bowls of cappuccinos we drank in Tartu's favorite place, Cafe Werner, made me feel even more dehydrated and apathetic. The ground was white, the air was cold, but the warm clothes you had to wear as you trudged about the city made you sweat, so you were never entirely at peace, whether indoors or out. Why had I forgotten about these things? Why hadn't I noticed how rundown some parts of Tartu were? The city had looked so nice in the pictures. And we still hadn't found a home since starting our search that morning.

But this one, Väino's one, was much better than the rest. The other ones were up creaking staircases, connected by dark corridors that smelled of wood smoke and cat urine. Väino's apartment was clean and new. We could move in tomorrow, if he agreed, and we could have that barn full of quality wood too.

After a day of walking around Tartu that was fine with me. All I wanted at that point was to give Väino the money for the apartment and the wood, go inside, take a shower, and sleep.

The house, what would become our home for some time, was on a crooked street at the mouth of a neighborhood of Tartu known as Karlova. As I later came to know, it was named after a German landowner named Karl. When this Karl, who I always imagined as a reclusive and eccentric count, had lived, no one told me. But his name stayed with the locals.

The name of every Tartu neighborhood meant something.

Supilinn, "Soup Town," for example, was the bohemian shanty town of dirt roads down by the river. It was a 19th century slum that had somehow made it into the 21st century, limping and bent, but still there, with funny street names that translated to Pea, Bean, Potato, Pumpkin, Celery, Melon, and Berry. They said it was called Supilinn because when the River Emajõgi overflowed, it turned the little neighborhood with its tasty street names into soup. The apartment we looked at there was housed in a hulk of splintered wood that looked like the Vasa after it had been lying on the bottom of Stockholm Harbor for a while. But it had potential! That was Supilinn.

Tucked beyond the railroad tracks was Tammelinn, "Oak Town." It was the resort of wealthier families, of proud, stately homes and new, shiny tin roofs and oak-lined streets. Prime Minister Andrus Ansip lived around there, it was said. We didn't bother looking for a place in Tammelinn. Too far from the center, we decided.

Karlova was something of a mix between Supilinn and Tammelinn, more crooked, ancient dwellings, like down by the river, but with cared-for, paved, tree-lined streets. Our new apartment was in an old wooden red house. It wasn't situated in a peaceful country field like the red house in my old New York computer desktop, but for now, it was close enough. And it was certainly respectable. Half of the homes on the street were still abandoned then.

Today, they have all been renovated, painted, and put into good use. I would stare at those broken windows and peeling paint back then, and imagine how it all could be. And now it has become what I prayed for.

Väino was a pioneer in this regard. He had renovated the house and lived in another house directly behind it. The two houses shared a yard between them, as well as the driveway. As the owner of everything, Väino was sort of like lord of the manor and we were his tenant farmers. But he worked too much for a lord. Late into the night, we could hear him renovating the apartment above ours, drills drilling, hammers hammering, portable radios playing at nine, ten, eleven o'clock. Sometimes I would wake up to the sound of a ghostly saw and my wife would sense my panic, reach out and touch my arm and say, "Don't worry, honey. It's only Väino, working."

Lord Väino dwelled with his young son and teenage daughter. His wife Ly was away in Germany studying international politics. The teenage daughter's name I don't remember, but the son was named Karl, "Like a Swedish king," as Väino had boasted, as if he was secretly loyal to the monarchy in Stockholm and kept a small Swedish flag on top of his dresser. The little King Karl was three, about the same age as our daughter Marta. Karl would play a lot in the mud in our yard and then come to our kitchen window and Epp would let him come inside and wash his hands and face and send him out to play again.

There was a familial relationship between us and our manor owner. When I burned through two computer adapters,

Väino took me to the electronics store so that I could obtain a third. And when we set about getting a car, Väino got down on his back and slid as far as he could beneath it, in the snow, to see if the engine was all right, because Väino knew cars as well as he knew houses.

Most of his words of wisdom were imparted to me via translation, so I began to feel as if I had entered a new reality, a dubbed film like *Seven Samurai*, starring Väino.

His manner was Japanese in a way, or at least how I imagined Japanese warriors to be. Austere. Controlled. His back was straight. His words were incontestable declarations. Even simple utterances like, "It seems to be a fine car," carried a certain weight with them because Väino had said them, and he knew.

Many of Väino's teachings were new to these ears. For example, he said that the three-year-old tires on my new car – which had been imported by some worldly and entrepreneurial Estonian from Staten Island in New York – were as good as one-year-old Estonian tires, "Because three years on the American roads are equal to one year on the Estonian roads."

I didn't understand how that could be possible then, but would understand soon enough.

Väino also took interest in our manner of heating the furnace. It was tiled in white, and looked almost too beautiful to touch.

But I had to touch it, I even had to start fires in it. The apartment was heated by wood, and it was the first time in my life using wood as an energy source. I brought it in and opened the furnace's door. Then I stacked the wood, two pieces on each side, then three across, and then three perpendicular to those on top. I twisted up a fresh copy of *Postimees** and put it at the base of this little construction, and set it alight with a match... The newspaper flared up and burned through, but the wood would not catch. Only the bark around its edges smoked a bit and Epp smelled it from the other room and came into see what was going on.

"Hey, it looks like you need a little help," she said.

"I don't get it! I just burned through a whole *Postimees* and still nothing."

"Don't be so frustrated!" she said. "You could use a few pieces of cardboard to get a fire started." She retreived a flap from a broken moving box and set it in the middle and lit another match. In a minute, the entire furnace was ablaze with fire and warmth.

"See," she said and shrugged proudly. "Just add some cardboard. No problem."

As a rule, I used ten pieces of firewood for any fire. Ten seemed like a good number as I had ten fingers, and the metal basket I used to transport the good, dry wood from the barn to our house could hold about ten pieces.

Sometimes it created just the right amount of heat. But other times, our kitchen became unbearably warm and sauna-like. It hurt to touch the walls of the furnace because they

---

*   An Estonian daily newspaper.

were so hot. I even feared that the walls might crack, they contained so much energy. On one of these occasions, Väino happened to enter the room, perhaps to do a little electrical work, and also began to sweat. "You are overheating," he pronounced and wagged a finger at me in his Samurai teacher way. "Overheating." He had a word for what I was doing, you see. It meant that ten pieces of wood weren't always the best way to go. Sometimes it would have to be twelve or other times five, depending on the temperature outside and inside and how long had it been since the last fire.

There was a measured art to wood heating that I would have to learn from men like Väino. I was a novice Estonian. He was a pro.

Väino was also always talking about someone named Endel. I didn't know who this Endel was. The reclusive neighbor next door was an older guy named Aadu. You might catch a glimpse of him and his old-fashioned flat cap if you happened to walk into the shared foyer at the same time. Maybe you might exchange a "*Tere*" *or* "Hello" with him, too. There was also Nils, the musician with the ponytail who lived upstairs. He also only said "Tere," but in a more alert and friendly manner, and you could hear his keyboard music at night.

But Endel? Who the heck was Endel?

What was more confusing, Väino said he had even made our apartment for Endel. It was a luxury apartment, he said proudly, *luksuskorter,* with tomato red painted walls and hound-tooth patterned Styrofoam moldings around the ceiling, plus that dreamy white-tiled furnace that looked as if he had brought it all the way to Karlova from Versailles. And it was all for Endel! "*Ma tegin Endlile*," Väino would repeat. I only nodded.

One day, I asked Epp out of curiosity about this mysterious Endel whom I had never seen but who was supposed to get this apartment before we showed up.

"What Endel?" she asked.

"You know, Endel. Väino is always saying, he made our luxury apartment for Endel. He says, '*Ma tegin Endlile*.'"

"Oh, no, Justin," she said. "He's saying, '*Ma tegin end-a-le*,'" Epp laughed. "It means: 'I made it for myself.'"

"Oh."

"And all this time you've been wondering about this non-existent person named Endel? Hahaha!"

That was the extent of her sympathy. After that day, whenever Daki, Tiina, Anna, the other Tiina, and all the other female visitors came to our home, I was instructed to repeat the, "*Ma tegin Endlile*" joke to their tea-spitting delight, and I always did it well, like a trained circus bear.

Väino's *luksuskorter* was a fine place to live. We managed to stay there for five months.

The couple that moved in after us was an American woman and a German man who were both teaching at the university and enjoyed ballroom dancing. They had no children, and so I assumed that those three luxury rooms would suit their needs for some time to come, and maybe they wouldn't mind Lord Väino's midnight drilling upstairs.

Väino's wife happened to be back in Tartu that week and negotiated the contract in German with the German man and they discussed utility bills and other interesting topics. We sold the transatlantic ballroom-dancing couple the kluck-klick wood we had bought from Väino for about the same price. It was July then, and there was no need to hit the pieces of wood together to show their quality.

They probably wouldn't have understood what that meant anyway.

Then, one hot summer night a week or so later, the young couple left the windows to the apartment open, and thieves climbed through them while they were asleep and stole most of their valuables. They were very upset and they asked me for advice about what they should do. I told them to just go and check the local *pandimaja* – I used this exact word – because the thieves might have tried to sell the stolen goods there. "Just go check the *pandimaja*. There's one on Tähe and Pargi Street around the corner."

"*Pandimaja*, what's that?" the American woman asked me.

"Oh, that's right, it's a pawn shop," I said. "It's just been a while since I've used that term in English."

That was when I knew that my Estonian had improved.

WOODSMAN MATS

*Our second home in Tartu was in the district of Täht-
vere, "the professors' quarter," as they called it.*

Tähtvere sat on another hill outside of the city center. This
neighborhood had larger, postwar dwellings with smooth,
plastered surfaces and big windows and balconies. On
occasion, you would see a house with round, porthole-like
windows, which gave the structure the appearance of a pas-
senger ship moored on land.

Some of the larger Tähtvere houses sat on well-tended
plots dotted with orchards and gardens, and were painted in
creamy, pleasant colors. Others were gray and crumbling and
circled by wraith-like trees. When we walked by these kinds
of houses, Epp would remind me that most professors were
paid little and couldn't afford renovations.

The streets in Tähtvere were planned, orderly and mostly
tidy. They were named after well-known Estonian National
Awakening figures from the 19th Century. Jakobsoni Street
was named for Carl Robert Jakobson, the writer, newspaper
publisher, and politician; Hurda was named for Jakob Hurt,
the folklorist, theologist, and linguist; Koidula for Lydia

Koidula, the romantic poet; Jannseni for Johan Voldemar Jannsen, the writer and poet (and father of Koidula); and Hermanni for Karl August Hermann, the composer.

Most of these people's faces were featured on Estonian bank notes, I learned. Though, at times, with all of those beards and spectacles, it was hard to tell who was who.

The neighborhood streets also had some mystical names. Taara Avenue, named after the Estonian pagan god, thought by some to be akin to the Viking Thor, ran straight through Tähtvere. Another street was called Hiie, named after the sacred forests of Estonia's pre-Christian belief system. And then there was Vikerkaare, Rainbow Street, so called because it was shaped like a Rainbow. It was easy to get lost on that street because you would follow the rainbow around and almost wind up back where you started.

Most of the houses in Tähtvere we came across were heated by wood and had long barns built alongside of them. It could take half a day to fill these barns with fresh stock, usually ordered in early autumn by calling numbers in advertisements for dry wood, at good prices, found in the backs of the local newspapers.

And so one day toward the middle of our first autumn back in Estonia, Epp came to the office upstairs in our house in Tähtvere to tell me that Woodsman Mats was downstairs waiting for me to come and help unload the wood. When I came outside in a t-shirt and jeans and shoes, Mats was waiting for me behind his truck. If Karlova Väino had been a rooster, then I would have to say that Woodsman Mats was a bear. Yet there was something gentle and un-bear-like about

Mats. Maybe he was more like a pine marten, a *metsnugis*. He certainly looked a bit like one. He had long, shoulder-length hair, which I found unusual for an older Estonian man, and those slanted Uralic eyes. Later, when I described Mats to my father, his hair, his manner of speech, he only said, "He's a Native American, Justin." – "No, he's an Estonian, Dad." – "No, Justin. He's a Native American."

The first thing I noticed that day about Mats, after we exchanged greetings, was his hands. Each one of his fingers was fat and swollen and calloused. It was as if he had only thumbs. My fingers were different. My fingers were long and smooth and lined. I had writer's hands, typist's hands. He had hands that could be applied to just about any kind of hard labor. I imagined how he could hammer a stake into the ground with his hand.

But the interesting thing was that, a few hours later, after Mats' shipment of wood had been unloaded, my hands looked a lot like Mats'. They were red and covered in blisters and a few splinters had been pulled from them. I know what you're thinking – Justin, why didn't you wear gloves? Would you think I was weird if I told you that I wanted to feel the wood I was loading into my barn? That I wanted to have that forest in my hands? As soon as Mats backed that truck up to the barn, I took down two pieces and banged them together, to see if they would make that magic sound.

Kluck? Klick?

But there was no kluck nor klick, because it was only October then and they weren't frozen, and so they made no sound at all.

"You're supposed to carry the wood, not hit it together," said Mats.

I said nothing and began loading the pieces into my arms, ten at a time.

Over the three winters that we lived in that house, Mats would come over many times and bring his truck full of wood. Through a few conversations, I came to know a little more about him. He lived out in Elva, a small town 20-minutes' drive from Tartu, he said. It seemed like a fitting home for a man like Mats.

Anyone who has been to Elva knows that the town is covered by a canopy of sky-tall thick pine trees that cast solemn green shadows on anyone and everything beneath them. I imagined Woodsman Mats out there in his log cabin near Elva, smoking his pipe, and occasionally felling trees that would be brought out to his reliable writer clients in Tähtvere.

Once, Mats even told us his last name – Talts. Mats Talts. This caused a bit of a stir on our front porch. Was this Mats Talts of the same family as the Estonian weightlifter Jaan Talts, who had competed at the 1968 Olympic Games in Mexico City? Epp had asked. Yes, indeed, said Woodsman Mats. Jaan Talts of Mexico City was in fact Mats Talts of Elva's brother.

It surprised me that Epp even knew what Estonians were on the Soviet team in Mexico City in 1968. She wasn't alive then. I didn't know which Americans were at the '68 games. But this was a common Estonian knowledge thing. All

Estonians had memorized their Olympic victors going back to the 1896 Games in Athens, I bet. There had been so few of them, so it was easy to remember who they were and if they had won anything.

Another time, Mats showed up to the house with his wife. This surprised me, because long-haired, slow-speaking, Big Indian Chief Mats Talts, brother of Jaan of Mexico City, had an average Estonian woman as a spouse. She was the type of woman you stood behind in the department store, or passed in open air markets. She sat in the front seat of the car lea-fing through a recent edition of *Kroonika* while Mats and I took care of the wood. I had been expecting Pocahontas, the Indian princess, but no: Mats' wife reminded me a tiny bit of Angela Merkel instead.

There was some sense to this though. There were different faces in Estonia. Some people, like Mats' wife, or Priit Pulle-rits, the ever youthful Godfather of Estonian journalism and *Postimees* editor, had what I thought of as the German face. His hair was parted on the side, and his mug reminded me of a lion, with a long nose that broadened at its base and a mouth that ran straight across. When he wore his mustache, Pullerits looked a bit like a 1970s soap opera star, and when he shaved the hair from his face, he looked all of 19 years old, even though he was in his 40s. Pullerits had told me once (in an interview for a book about Estonia that I never wrote) how he walked through a town on the French-German border, and everyone spoke to him in German, because they knew a German when they saw one.

Others, like our friend Airi from Hiiumaa or Taavi from Põlvamaa, had the long Scandinavian faces, with hair so blond it was almost white, and eyes so blue, they were almost white, too. These people were also exotic to me, but for other reasons. Both of them seemed to me like golden gods. Whether I was with Taavi in the sauna or with Airi at the beach, I would catch myself looking at them and wondering what it might feel like to be born into such a different body, not this hairy Mediterranean thing I had inherited. Whenever one of my American friends would come across Airi or Taavi in one of our pictures, she would gasp and touch her chest and say, "My God, they are all so damn... blond."

And then there were the Uralic-looking Estonians. Mats Talts was one of them. Epp was one of them, too. In some photos, especially where she was smiling, her eyes would curl up into tiny ribbon-like slits, as if there was another Asian face straining to break out from beneath her European one. Sometimes in public places like festivals or at the open-air produce markets, I would see people who I could swear were from the Far East. The eyelids were too narrow, the cheekbones too high. They were simply not Europeans, so they had to be tourists. Were they Yupik people or Aleut or Inuit? Maybe some Koreans had descended upon a Tartu tractor show? I would stray from my family and follow these curious people through the crowds, just to hear what language they were speaking. You can imagine how I felt each time when I saw a Korean woman's mouth open and heard Estonian come out.

My romantic image of Woodsman Mats crumbled one day. We had unloaded one truck-load of wood and Mats said that he would have to go pick up another to fulfill the order.

"What, drive all the way back to your cabin in Elva? And then chop a new truckload of wood by yourself?" I asked him. "Isn't that going to take a while?"

"What do you mean cabin in Elva, chop it myself?" said Mats, running his clubs of fingers through his hair. "I live in an apartment. I pick up the wood from a lot outside of Tartu. That's where I'm going."

On that day, Mats the Woodsman lost a bit of his exotic sheen and wild charm.

KEEPING THE FIRES LIT

Our place in Tähtvere had four neighbors and four furnaces.

Two neighbors were in the back, one was on either side of us. I met one of the back neighbors once when her cat got stuck in one of our trees and I helped to coax the lost feline down. She was an old lady, and seemed a little surprised when I asked her what her name was. Her name was Astrid, which I thought was a pretty name, but I didn't tell her that, which was a shame because after the incident with the cat, I never saw Astrid again.

That was one more time than the other neighbor behind us. In three years, I never saw that person or those persons once. I was sure someone was living there though, because on winter nights, when you could see through the bushes and trees that separated our yards, each evening one of the rooms was illuminated by the glow of a television set. Still, I never saw a shadow of a person pass in front of this spectral light. The TV was just on.

The inhabitants of the house to our right, if you looked from the street, were a man, woman, and son who looked as if they had stepped out of a local advertisement for grills or lawn mowers. On the weekends, they were always doing something around the house – raking leaves and picking apples from their trees in autumn, shoveling the snow from the front of their house in winter, burning leftover debris in spring, cutting the grass at 6 a.m. in summer. When we were out working and they were out working at the same time, we would greet each other with "*Jõudu tööle!*" which meant, literally, "Strength to work!" Then they would continue raking or plucking or burning and grunt back at us. "*Tarvis!*" – "Needed!"

I never knew any of their names during those three years I lived there. And I never got close enough to any of them to see what they really looked like. They were just blurry images. Only on the very day when we were moving out did the man come over to the fence and wish me "Strength to work!" with the move and I managed to worm his name out of him. It was Tõnu.

Fortunately, I did come to know one of my neighbors quite well, because he was my doctor. For months, when we first moved in, the house next door to us had been vacant. Major renovations were planned, I had heard, including large windows on the back to capture the light in the dreary winter months. When the renovations started and I saw the size of the windows, I shuddered a bit, because I knew how the heat had a tendency to escape from our home through the windows, and thought of how much wood the poor fellow would have to use to keep that room warm in wintertime. But my doctor was smarter than that – he had central heating installed, so that his rooms would grow warmer or colder with the twist of a knob, and he could use wood in his for-show fireplace whenever he missed the reassuring smell of smoke in his home. When I thought about our neighbor waking up in his pajamas and turning up the heat on a cold morning, I wondered why I hadn't become a well-paid doctor myself.

My doctor had the same straight-backed, sensei manner of communicating that Väino did. Every word in every sentence seemed well thought out. His hair was cut straight across the front, too, in an old-fashioned Asian manner. He buttoned his shirts up to the top. When I would visit him, he would sometimes be sitting before his for-show fireplace and reading something interesting, like Haruki Murakami.

But he was often working outside, too. His yard was immaculate. Every stray branch or leaf was identified by his laser vision and removed to a pile. Later it would be placed onto a black grill and burned. The blue and white smoke would drift across our yard for days in late autumn and early spring, when such neighborhood brush burning bonanzas occurred. Sometimes, when we met at the fence to discuss my health issues, I would catch the doctor looking beyond me, into my yard. Maybe he saw a branch that hadn't been picked up or a rotten apple. Whatever it was, there was something that was not perfect and it bothered him. In this Estonian's world, there were no broken branches, there were no rotten apples, and if there were, they were eradicated quickly and without mercy.

What probably annoyed him most was the overflowing heap of compost rubbish we had piled into one corner of our yard that just so happened to border one corner of his.

When we had moved in, we had swept up the mounds of rotting apples from our little orchard into that spot. But what had started as a small collection of rotten apples had over time grown into a fermenting trash heap of moldy bread and egg shells and banana skins and avocado pits.

One day, while I was lugging another bucket of organic slop out to the compost dump, I saw my doctor neighbor spring from his back door and follow me to the corner where our yards met.

He surveyed the pitiful mass of brown filth and said in his restrained, sensei manner:

"This pile, it grows and it grows..."

"It sure does," I said and dumped some banana peels on top of it.

He nodded a bit and squinted at me and advised, "Put it in a box."

"Hey, you know, we were thinking of getting one of those compost containers now that you mention it. We just haven't had time to do it. You know how things are..."

"Put it in a box," he repeated and nodded at me again. Then he went back into his house to sip his tea and read his Murakami and enjoy his centrally heated, big windowed castle.

Our home was less of a castle and more of a 19th century coal-powered steam ship. And I was its boiler room stoker, keeping the fires lit and hot. There were four furnaces, each of which needed tending to in order to produce enough heat to remain comfortable. And one main problem was how quickly the heat escaped.

The main furnace downstairs was large and covered with long, dark brown tiles. At night, I would leave it warm, only to find most of the first floor cold in the morning when it was many degrees below freezing outside. There was pain and dread in my appendages as I descended the steps early in the morning to light up another fire.

And the hardest thing was that sometimes the fire just would not start!

I stacked the wood exactly as others had taught me, crumpled and placed the paper like so and put in a few pieces of cardboard. But maybe the cardboard was a bit damp from being left outside, or the crumpled up newspaper burned too fast. Whatever it was, the fire just wouldn't start for me sometimes.

I had been instructed by professional Estonian fire start-ers to use the local business daily, *Äripäev*, because, as they said, it burned better than the other papers, especially the weekend editions for some reason. But I didn't always have last Saturday's *Äripäev* handy. Sometimes I just had a glossy *Kroonika* celebrity magazine, which burned poorly. Then I would have to start the process again, and again. Sometimes I got so bored doing it, day after day, that I would pause to read about Kristina Šmigun's skiing exploits or Minister Juhan Parts' new economic plan or my horoscope from two years ago or to see what Estonian celebrity's birthday it was. Then I would continue the process of starting a fire. I admit that it amused me sometimes to watch Kristina and Juhan's faces go up in smoke. I had nothing personal against either of them. We were just cold.

The furnace in the kitchen was used for especially cold days, and I enjoyed cooking on top of it. When I made meatballs at Easter, I imagined that I was like one of my Italian great grandfathers or grandmothers, cooking a savory meal on a holiday using a wood-burning stove. It helped to distract me from the weather outside. By Easter, winter should be over. But sometimes it snowed straight through Easter. And so my Italian fantasies and our four wood-heated furnaces kept on burning until May.

The furnace that the two bedrooms upstairs shared was straightforward enough, and covered in corrugated metal that had been painted over with thick, light green, goopy "furnace paint." It held heat well, and it felt good to snuggle up beside it. It was the other furnace, the fourth one, that gave us the most trouble. Something was wrong with its shape, its pull. The metal on the furnace would get too hot, the paint would give off fumes.

Most times, we didn't even bother using it. Instead, we kept the room it heated cold. We referred to this room in our house as The Cold Room. "Hey, do you know where my notebook is?" – "I think you left it in The Cold Room."

Sometimes I would go into The Cold Room to do interviews or write articles about the international biotech market. I would wear my coat and hat and sit down before the laptop and imagine what would happen if the person on the other end of that Skype call in California could see me.

How would I even go about explaining the details of my new Estonian life, how I now knew which newspapers burned better than others, or about the thermodynamics of The Cold Room?

Would they believe that there were still active chimney sweeps in Estonia? It was true. One day a young man arrived at our door. He was all dressed in black, and wore a medieval-looking hat. To me, he looked as if he could have been one of the Vatican's secret assassins. He worked his way from the top of the house to the bottom, doing something to make those furnaces burn more efficiently. Sometimes he would stop to inform Epp and me about the state of our furnaces and chimneys. She would relay the messages to me. "He says there was more tar up there than usual, which is why the fires haven't been starting well recently," she would say, and I would answer, "Well, that's good to know."

What puzzled me most was how this young guy even came into that line of work. Here was a country that prided itself on its affinity for innovation and technology, its WiFi connections and IT start-ups. Here was a country that scoffed at people who paid for parking with paper tickets or still had landline phones. And yet here was a country that was still producing cadres of chimney sweeps.

When I would ask my Estonian friends about these contradictions, I was often rebuffed. For them, burning things – leaves, tree branches, firewood – had always been and would always be a part of daily life and to suggest changing it was to insult them to the core.

For me, it was a tougher life than I was used to. I had grown up in suburbia, with thermostats and basement oil burners. Stoking the fires of four furnaces was tiring. And what would happen if one fire happened to go out? It happened. Sometimes, when we got back from a trip, and the house was cold, I would get a good fire working upstairs, only to fall asleep reading some old newspaper or tabloid beside it. When I would awake, next to a dark, cool furnace, I had two choices – to close it and pretend it never happened or to start all over again. In these instances, I imagined myself as one of those punished mythical figures, condemned to push a boulder up a hill, only to see it roll back down again.

So many things went in that fireplace, so many things disappeared: pizza boxes, broken wooden toys, even Christmas trees. We'd leave the tree in the barn over winter to dry out, and then slice it up, feeding it into the flames. It burned quickly. The needles were gone in a second. The sappy trunks took the most time. But, usually, within minutes, the whole tree had vanished. It was as if it had never existed.

But some things did escape immolation. Sometimes you would walk down the street and see a piece of burned newspaper that had floated out of somebody's chimney. One day, while I was walking down Hiie Street, I even caught a glimpse of Andrus Ansip, looking up at me from the wet leaves on the side of the road. I knelt down to examine the curiosity and picked it up and brushed away the charred edges. That's when I saw that all of the paper around the prime minister's head had burned away, and yet, by some miracle, Ansip's determined face had survived completely unscathed.

As harmless as the Estonians considered wood heating, it had its perils. Once, my daughter came home from day care with three little pink burns on her bottom. She had accidentally backed into the corrugated metal of the kindergarten's furnace. After that, they put a small barrier around the furnace, and after a lot of cream application and several months, the burns turned to light marks and then disappeared altogether.

Such tales mortified my parents, if they ever found out about them. "If that happened in our country, you would sue the day care and get a lot of money," my mother would say.

"Do you know how bad that wood smoke is for you?" my father would chime in. "It's like smoking two packs a day." Little did he know that I did know an Estonian guy who smoked two packs of cigarettes a day AND was constantly exposed to wood smoke. He needed less oxygen than me, I guessed.

But my father was right. It was a dirty, polluting form of energy. In the winters, the smoke would rise straight out of the chimneys and sail off to somewhere beside the stars, but in the damper autumns and springs, the moisture created a net that trapped the smoke, especially later in our life, in Viljandi, where it choked the old cobblestone lanes and broken dirt streets of the Old Town. On some black November days, it was so thick, that I really suspected that the freshest air was indoors. I seriously considered wearing a gas mask in our yard where the smoke of five neighborhood chimneys gathered, not to prove a point, but because I really needed it. Too many men in our family had died from lung issues. "You know our family history," my father said. "It's not good. You should think about moving back to New York..."

Sometimes the wood heating was quite pleasant though. We would start up the furnace and get so wonderfully snug and warm on the floor. My daughter would fall asleep as I read to her, the only light from a reading lamp and the crackling fire in the ancient black furnace. I could see tiny beads of sweat on the girl's forehead. I loved how the wooden floors would get warm, too. We didn't need blankets there, next to our warm furnace. We slumbered so majestically on those cold tranquil winter nights.

Other times, down in Setomaa, where we had acquired a country house, the smoke reassured you, it relieved you, it smelled of civilization. Down there on the Russian border among the rolling hills and giant-treed forests, the air was pure and perfect, but there were few neighbors, and at night the glow of a distant window or the smell of a house or sauna chimney letting off smoke was like a friend's embrace.

My relationship with wood-heated homes reached its zenith and low point in Viljandi.

Zenith in that I had finally developed some talent for starting fires, and that I knew how to stack wood. Woodsman Mats had gone from our lives, but he had been replaced by the firewood A-Team. These were four young guys who drove a van around that was loaded with wood. They would speed around the corner and drive up on your lawn, and then the van's side door would slide open and they would all jump out. Somebody would grunt and you would gesture to the correct barn, and then they would unload half of the wood in about five minutes. One man would stand in the truck and they'd hand the bags of kindling off, down the line. Then they'd collect their money, hop back in the van, and be off, zooming down the street to the next family in need of more wood.

That was a high point for me, because I knew how to communicate with these men, knew how to handle the wood, to the point that I was as good as them at stacking it fast. Maybe they didn't even think I was a foreigner, the way I handled that wood.

My skills had obviously developed.

The low point came on the first cold day of autumn, months after we had moved into our new home in Viljandi, the one we had actually bought after renting various places for years. Epp said she was cold, indicating that I should do something about it. So I went looking around for the thermostat because the owners had said something about central heating when we bought the place. After a while, Epp asked me why I hadn't brought any wood in. I yawned and scratched myself and told her that we didn't need it because we had central heating.

"You're joking, right? The wood-heated furnace IS our central heating." She came in and explained it to me. "The fire in the kitchen heats the boiler, which sends the heat to the radiators in each room."

"Oh," I said. I remembered how the previous owner had actually given me instructions about the house's heating system, and how I had nodded throughout but barely understood a word because he spoke so quickly.

"And you actually thought we had gas heating or something?" asked Epp. "What did you think, why did we need to get the barn full of wood?"

"I just thought it was for special occasions!"

Out in the barn that afternoon, I began to collect large pieces of wood from a stack that I had imagined would only be used on nights when we felt like having a fire, not when we needed to.

But somehow I grabbed the wrong piece and the whole wall-high stack came tumbling down on my feet and legs. There was wood on everything and everywhere.

And that's when I lost it, picking up the pieces of wood and chucking them at the wall and cursing just about everything and everyone, but especially wood and wood heating. The word *kurat* (devil) was used many times that day in the barn. Other words, too.

That was one of the days when I felt that Estonia secretly had it in for me.

BIRTH OF PETRONE PRINT

To get into our Karlova house, you had to come down the pebble-stone driveway, hang left, and enter a back entrance that led into a cramped vestibule enclosing two yellow doors, one of which was ours.

The ladies who came to visit all passed through this vortex perhaps not knowing what to expect, and when they arrived, it was if they had just been beamed through the passageway from the future. You could hear their steps in the hallway, the thuds of the winter boots, the rustling fabrics of their clothes as they moved, and could only wonder about what they looked like before you heard that soft knock.

Knock! Knock!

Epp got up from her new laptop and went to the door.

Then the ladies entered, took off their icy footwear, disrobed from their thick winter coats. Epp made them coffee or tea and they drank and talked about projects in whispering voices with tight bursts of laughter. Some of them ignored me, some of them eye-balled me. Most of all I amused them.

For example, it amused Daki that I wore a pink shirt and it amused her more that I didn't understand there was something wrong with wearing a pink shirt.

On the first day I met Daki, I had gone to the barn to bring in wood. For whatever reason, I returned with just one piece swinging from my hand. Maybe there were nine logs inside, and the weather-furnace metrics called for a 10-log fire. I don't know. All I can remember is that Daki was outside and she was titillated to see me.

"A man goes to the barn," she howled, "and comes back with one piece of wood!"

Daki was just getting into the writing game back then, which is how we came to know her. She is and was a passionate person, full-figured, with big, feline eyes. She had long, straight hair that draped about her shoulders, colored between straw and amber, framing her face like a great circus tent. The hair distracted you from the eyes, which is where you should have kept your attention. I wondered about the men who stared too long into those eyes and if they knew what they were getting themselves into. They were like drowned sailors. Their names should have been chiseled onto a rock somewhere. Some of those names had at one point or another even been Daki's. Married twice, she had been published under three different names: Dagmar Lamp, Dagmar Reintam, and Dagmar Lamp-Jōgi.

It was all the same: Daki. Hers was a world of whispers and rumors and love songs and heart-wrenching melancholia and then big belly laughter. It was a world where crazy decisions might make perfect sense. With Daki on your shoulder egging you on to live, who knows what you might do? I dreaded the day when Epp would announce, "We are all moving to India! Tomorrow! And Daki thinks it's a great idea, too!" Whenever

Miss Daki arrived, I would sense that danger. The hair in my ears would prick up. If I had to drive her home, or to meet someone, I would hold my breath until she was safely out of the car and ten feet away.

Epp had fallen for Daki for the same reasons that I kept a wary eye on her. They met online and then co-wrote a serial story that was published in a local tabloid. The story was called "To Eat the Apple?," the answer to which for both of them had been an emphatic YES!... at first. A bored young Estonian professional woman meets an intriguing Western European man on the Internet. He invites her to stay with him, promising to advance her career, and away she goes, only to learn that this charming man is not who he pretended to be at all.

He has a dark side.

And that's really when our book business began. The real spark was Epp's desire to publish her material from living in America as a book. Estonian publishers weren't interested though. They published memoirs of old people and travel books, they said, not travel memoirs of young people. Then Epp decided to publish the book on her own. In Estonia, it was easier than ever to start your own company. We had some money leftover from the sale of our apartment in Tallinn, and Epp knew enough people to get the project running. Soon enough, Estonia had its newest publishing house. Its founders met daily in our Karlova kitchen. The newborn was called Petrone Print.

The visits and vigils continued: Daki, Tui, Tiina, Kati, Anna, Kairit, and then Daki again and then Anna again,and then Tiina again. The phone rang like a crying babe. Something was happening in our kitchen. A simmering cauldron of business-savvy Estonian estrogen was bubbling and brewing. Notebooks were being filled with boxes and arrows. A led to B and staircased to D, then diagonal to N and then horizontal to P, over and under to Õ. Epp said she wanted to publish Daki's blog as a book, a revolutionary new "blog book," that would let Estonia's most dangerous house guest into the hearts and minds of unsuspecting readers.

To make that happen, would require the assistance of Anna Tamm.

Epp told me that Anna was a *kujundaja,* which translated in English to something tedious like "graphic designer," but Anna has remained a *kujundaja* to me ever since, no matter the language.

Sometimes the Estonian word really was the truest word for something.

Miss Anna was half Hungarian, and this translated as "half human" in my mind, as if our non-Estonianess made us similar. Even the fact that she had long brown hair, like mine. And she looked different. Anna spoke Estonian, Finnish, and Hungarian, but she looked like a freckly Catalan lady from up in the Pyrenees.

Anna was also nice to me. I will tell you more later.

Once there was a book event at Tampere Maja in downtown Tartu, down in the ancient stone cellar. It was crowded with prominent faces, all of whom had gathered to see Merca Jääger interview Kati Murutar about her new book, some special kind of memoir about being born as a woman and living as a woman, which had on its cover a black and white image of a woman's pregnant figure clutching her stomach, complete with bellybutton piercing.

Murutar. That was her name back then. Now she is known as Vatmann and for a while she was Murdmaa. At some point in her lifetime, she was also a Vasar. Go consult the tabloids. Whatever her name, Kati had big, aware eyes and a respectable nose and ruby red lips and a fondness for declarative sentences. Listening to the woman converse was like going to a one-woman show. What splendid diction! The rhythmic grace. Kati was a walking declamation contest, I tell you.

My most outstanding memory of Miss Kati Murutar Murdmaa Vatmann (nee Vasar) is of her standing in a red bikini and bathrobe cooking us seljanka in her country house kitchen way out in the very Chinesey sounding village of Liu, which is on the coast north of Pärnu. I tried to make some kind of silly joke but Murutar didn't get it. She was preoccupied, slicing sausages into the bubbling red stew. Murutar had many children, around five, and she had lots of horses, too.

My most vivid memory of Merca, the other big name of that book launch night, is the time she showed up at the Prima

Vista Festival Concert. This is an event held in Tartu each year where they let writers play music in public. So Merca showed up and serenaded the audience with rousing *chansons*, backed by a band of four or five big country guys who all looked like Hells Angels, pausing between songs to siphon some strong spirit off a flask of moonshine she kept in her long black coat. She was a real witch, Merca, with a round, pleasant country girl's face and bangs of orange-red unruly hair. Her real name was Merle Jääger, which brought to mind a certain Rolling Stone. She had an intensity to her voice, too, a restrained punk growl, and she reminded me of a pirate for some reason.

An Estonian back-country pirate singer writer with one name, yeah, that was her. Merca.

How one little country managed to create so many weirdos, I have no idea. But that night down in the Tampere Maja cellar was a meeting of the most notorious Estonian women who had ever lived. And Epp hosted it.

I kept a journal with me in those days to write down new words, and Miss Anna sat beside me as I scribbled away as Miss Merca and Miss Murutar discussed and deliberated. Two of the words Murutar used over and over and over again were *kentsakas* and *häirima*.

"*Kentsakas* means strange or funny, or odd, or creepy," Anna whispered helpfully to me when she saw me writing.

"And *häirima*?"

"*Häirima* is like, well it's something like to disturb or bother... Hey, Justin, would you like a cookie?"

Anna pulled out a pink box of chocolate-covered biscuits filled with orange marmalade. These were cookies I always noticed whenever I was in supermarket but wasn't brave enough to buy. Something seemed too decadent about snuggling up with a whole box of chocolate-covered orange marmalade cookies. And yet here was shameless Anna wandering around Tartu with a whole scrumptious box of the cookies in her bag. I shook my head, took one and ate it.

"Anna," I whispered to her.

"Yes, Justin?" she whispered back.

"Do you mind if I have another cookie?"

"Oh," she smiled. "Here you go. You can have the rest of the box if you like."

"Hmm. Maybe I'll just take two. Or three."

"*Palun, palun.*"

"Aitäh. Hey, thanks for helping me with the words. Munch munch munch. From now on, munch, whenever I hear the word *kentsakas*, I will think of Kati Murutar."

Anna snorted a bit when I said this, so that some of the chocolate-dipped orange marmalade cookies might have come flying out of her mouth if she hadn't put her wrist up to stop it. But she didn't say anything more about Miss Murutar that night.

It was rare to see Anna during the day, because she usually worked at night. In a way, you could say that the new publishing house already operated round the clock. When Epp had finished something, it would go to Anna. When Epp awoke, it was already laid out.

Anna usually wore her hair up, and so I didn't know that she had stopped cutting it a long time ago. I remember the first time I saw her wear her hair down. She and Epp had arranged a meeting at a bookshop to discuss ideas. When she walked into the shop, though, I saw her mane was flowing down below God-knows-what part of her body. It was super long, almost to the floor, and I got tangled up in it like plankton in a jellyfish's tentacles. Any man who works with a lot of women has these moments from time to time when he is reminded that deadlines, and emails, and schedules aside, he still has eyes.

Epp had eyes too. "Check out her hair," she whispered in my ear as Anna approached.

"What?"

"I said, 'Check out Anna's hair.'"

"What?"

"Never mind!"

Then the dance began. Epp and Anna strolled about the stacks and shelves "feeling" and admiring the books. There was a mutual appreciation of rough textured books, and a disdain for the glossy and flashy.

"We're thinking of something like this for the cover," Epp said, handing me a book. "What do you think?"

I touched the book. It felt like a paper bag.

"It seems nice," I said.

She handed me another volume that looked as if it had been cut from an old burlap sack. "Hey, why do you have that dumb expression on your face anyway?"

"What?"

"Hello? Are you here? On this planet?"

"What?"

"Do you like the texture?"

"Oh. It seems nice."

It *was* nice to observe the interesting women. One of them was like the sun, with wild, red-gold hair, a hot ball of fire. The other was like the moon, dark and mysterious. Just a glance into either set of eyes and I would start to have that drowning sailor feeling, so I buried my face in a book about the former Estonian President Konstantin Päts. But I couldn't help but watch them. On that day in the shop, the sun spun around the moon, and the moon orbited the sun, and earth sat alone in the corner with a very stupid look on its face.

The only lady who didn't trouble me at all was Tiina Tamme-org.

Tiina was too chummy and easygoing, too business-like to cause me any distress. When she was not talking or listening and just thinking she looked very serious, but if you said something to her she would leap after it like a hungry cat and devour it and then spit it back up at you with words of agreement and laughter and play with it some more.

Tiina. I guess she was a bit bigger than Epp and Anna and Daki, but this largeness came less from her body and more from her presence. If Daki was the one with the mischievous eyes and Anna was the elegant lady with the sweet tooth and the long, long, long hair, then Tiina was the serious-minded girl with the Microsoft Excel.

Tiina would never encourage you to move to India. Instead she would put together a spreadsheet of potential risks and tell you it was probably not a very wise idea. Tiina had the potato-peel brown hair and sea-colored eyes that are common to the indigenous people of this land, with a face that was a perfect mix of German and Finnish, so that if you had introduced her to me as the finance chief of Bremen or Oulu I would have believed you.

Tiina, or "Tinn" as she was known to those who cared most for her, was a number lover. She dreamed of spreadsheets and inventories. But I always counted the books wrong, and this would create problems. Where did the missing books go? Where did the new books come from? Yet when the recount was done and the book numbers matched previous inventories, Tiina would forget all about the first count because she was so happy. "We should have 268 books and *we have 268 books!*" Tiina lived around the corner from us on the top floor of an apartment block with a nice view of Annelinn. She was strong as an ox. She would carry baby Matilda down all five flights of stairs and put her in the carriage and roll her over to our apartment. Then, if Matilda was asleep, Tiina would wheel the carriage up by the window and come in. She would greet Epp, who was very pregnant and sitting with her legs folded beneath her for comfort, and Epp would gesture for her to remove her coat and sit down, pour her some coffee, and the two of them would have their first Petrone Print "business meetings."

It amused me that Epp had decided to call the print house Petrone Print because no one else in my Petrone family had ever been inclined toward the literary world. My father's only reading material was car magazines and my grandfather Jerry Petrone enjoyed tooling around in the garage where he kept a bottle of scotch hidden beneath his workbench. Years later, after he died and my father was cleaning out the garage, he came upon the bottle. I tried to tell Epp and Tiina the story about the scotch, but they weren't listening. These were two very industrious Estonian women. They had things to do.

In all my years spent in this land, it never ceased to mystify me. Estonia was on its face a male-dominated society. The prime minister had always been a man, as had the president. Most, if not all, of the ministers in government were men. The editors of the largest newspapers were also all men, and Estonia's richest people were all men, too. And yet, if you wanted to get something done in Estonia, desired to, for example, write, layout, publish, and distribute your own books, then you would have to deal with Estonian women, because they were the only ones who knew how to do things.

It was the so-called "Saaremaa Woman Syndrome." There was an anecdote that a Saaremaa island woman had to be ready to take care of seven children as well as an alcoholic husband. It was too easy to imagine, to see the Saaremaa wench breastfeeding two brats beneath an overhanging thatched roof and lines of fish set out to dry, to see her ordering her elder children around at the time of the harvest, to see the look of discomfort on her face when reminded of her husband, who was either playing cards in the pub or sleeping off a hangover in the barn.

It wasn't just the islanders who were like this though. The whole of Estonia was rife with the breed.

You had to watch the pretty blonde ladies whose names you could never remember at the print house rise from their desks and sashay to the back office to get the right documents. Then they would hand you the master copy of the book, the one they kept for their personal library, and you would initial it to show you approved. After that, the golden ladies would ask you to follow them downstairs, hips swinging, to the warehouse. You would back your used SUV up to the gate and they would help you load it with the books. They were usually wrapped in discarded paper from other projects, four to ten to a package, so you might pause to read the cartoons or horoscopes on the papers before one of these print house queen bees would come bearing a dozen more packages stacked up to her chin. After that, you would drive them home to be stored for future deliveries.

We had to store the books under our bed in our Karlova place. There was no other place to put them.

The print house shipped the books directly to the warehouses of the bookstores and we would maintain the rest of the edition in stock. But in the beginning, when it was hard to gauge demand, I would often have to load up the car again, removing the books from under the bed and stacking them up in the back of the SUV. Since our car was parked on the street, and you entered the house from the back, it made the most sense to do this work through the window. I would stack up all the books on one side of the window sill and then jump out of the window and load them into the car and repeat the process. I did wonder sometimes what the neighbors might think about the strange person who kept leaping in and out of that window, but I didn't speak to the neighbors much.

The warehouses in Tallinn stood at the perimeter of the city, surrounded by rusty wires and dead trees. It was hard to believe that such beautiful books spent most of their first nights in such ugly places.

It was in these warehouses that I encountered the only other males involved in the book industry. They drove forklifts or pushed carts full of actresses' memoirs. The appearance of the strange-looking man with the accent from the strangely-named publishing house would confuse these other men. They would scratch their matted hair and grizzly beards and call in their older, cleaner female supervisors, who would pepper me with questions until I finally just called up our Tiina and handed over the phone.

After many quick sentences, the *Jah! Jah!* moment would be achieved. This was the point in the conversation where Tiina and the other woman, both of whom were probably juiced up on their sixth coffee of the day, would say, "*Jah, jah,*" about fourteen times to show that they were in agreement about the numbers of the books and their destinations. Then my male counterpart would be given the go ahead to receive my delivery.

Often these guys kept a pen tucked behind one ear, so that they could brandish it when I handed them the all-important invoice. Then we would both sign and I would say "*Tehtud!*", a word I had heard during the election season that meant something like, "Done!"

Estonians liked that word, *Tehtud*. It pleased them. Each time I used that special word *Tehtud*, the other man signing would chuckle a bit and say, "Oh, it's *tehtud,* all right."

But even if I had the paper in hand, marked with both signatures, it didn't mean the transaction was *tehtud*, because I still had to give that paper back to Tiina and, for some reason, those papers had a habit of disappearing on me during the long, two-and-a-half hour trip back to Tartu, only to resurface with coffee stains on them in an underwear drawer or some other embarrassing place a month or so later.

Tiina was never harsh with me though. She never came down on me over the stained papers. Maybe she understood my flakiness because she lived with Kristofer, who was usually at home, making music on his computer. Kristofer was mild mannered and Swedish and referred to himself as a "dormant rock star" but spent most of his days working for a Swedish call center in Tartu. Old helpless Swedish ladies in Umeå would call up and request a ride to the supermarket and Kristofer would arrange it for them. With long brown hair and some fuzz on his chin, he did look like a rock star, or Jesus, or both. Tiina and Kristofer had met at a Depeche Mode concert in Stockholm. I liked Kristofer and Depeche Mode and made no secret of it. When I told Tiina this, she knocked me down again with her speed and boistrousness – "Of course, you like Kristofer! Of course! I like him too, you know!" And her cheeks grew rosier. "*Jah, jah, jah!*"

Depeche Mode to this day is a kind of emotional currency among the Northern Europeans. The band's melancholic music matches well with the stiff-lipped brooding that comes with the long darkness. It was a feeling they all shared. Even if they didn't speak the same language, if an Estonian and Swede happened to meet, all one would have to say to the other was "Depeche Mode" and touch her chest right where the heart was, and there would be a mutual understanding, a flickering acknowledgment of sameness in their sad gray eyes. In Tallinn, there is even a Depeche Mode Bar, where you can sit and drink and listen to "I Just Can't Get Enough" over and over and over again.

Tiina credited the British group with her relationship and child. "You know, if there was no Depeche Mode, there would be no Matilda," she would say. Sometimes I thought that our publishing company also owed the Depeche Men something, because in a way it was Kristofer who accidentally had brought Tiina into contact with Epp.

It went like this. Epp and I had just moved back to Estonia, and Epp had been dispatched to write another "Estonian women and foreign men" feature for the magazine *Eesti Naine*. This topic appeared at least once a year, and I often suspected it was assigned by female editors to vengefully emasculate their homegrown ex-boyfriends and ex-husbands.

Or maybe there just weren't that many things to write about in Estonia.

Whatever the reason, if you happened to be flipping through that magazine sometime that spring of our female guests in 2007, you might have seen an image of Tiina with her ponytail and Finnic cheeks holding a tiny Matilda with her own personal Swedish dormant rock star Kristofer, and the faces of Depeche Mode looking down on it all from the posters behind them, like New Wave patron saints. But what you couldn't see in that picture was a brain that put others to shame, a mind made for the numbers and spreadsheets of a busy publishing house that would fulfill Epp's fantasy of putting out a new "My"-series book every month. There would soon be "My Australia," "My Argentina," "My Thailand," "My This," and "My That."

But the very first "My"-book was called "My Ameerika", written by Epp Petrone.

I remember one day after I had dropped off the books at the warehouse how I took a walk down the main street in Tallinn's Old Town.

It was raining and chilly that day, even if they said it was June, and I had my hands in my pockets and kept my head down in the wind. But something in that window distracted me. I walked over to it and wiped the moisture off the glass and pressed my nose up against it.

There was a familiar name on a book. And on the back cover, displayed beside it, a familiar image of a familiar woman. She had red-gold hair, high cheeks, and a determined squint, with the skyline of Manhattan behind her.

Then I realized, with some surprise, that Epp's book was number one in that store.

WAKE UP, IT'S *HOMMIK*[*]

When it was still winter and we had just arrived to live in Estonia, I would take the child to the preschool on a little red plastic sled drawn by a rope.

There was enough ice on the sidewalks and crosswalks to ease the way, and she would sit there in the back as I tugged her past traffic and gas stations, as if it was all quite natural and we had always traveled to school that way. There was much to be learned though, the way to hold the line, to curl your wrist when the sled got stuck, or that quick tug that would set the sled sliding over ice that had melted down to the gravel so that it was propelled forward without damage. Marta also had to learn. How to sit. How to hold on. Sometimes the sled would suddenly feel lighter and I would look behind to see she had fallen off half a block back.

The Mesipuu or "Honey Tree" preschool was a great cream-colored house with windows cut by old-fashioned panes and a gabled, red-tiled roof that would have looked just fine in a Dutch country town. At the school I would leave the sled behind the door and accompany Marta inside, where we would remove her heavy outdoor wear, boots, woolen socks,

---

*   Morning (in Estonian).

waterproof pants, gloves and scarf, sweater and hat. The other children's clothes hung dripping in the entrance, and I would already begin to sweat because of the captured humidity, glancing at the paintings of the bees and flowers on the walls.

Once that was done, and her indoor slippers were on, I would escort our daughter to the big classroom where all the other Estonian children were seated around wooden tables eating morning snacks of porridge and jam or small pieces of toasted bread with melted cheese. Already at age 3, Marta was aware that the other children were looking at her, and she made sure to pick out a nice dress that would rise in the air if she spun around, and also made sure that her mother had worked her straw-colored hair into two tight Pippi Long-stocking braids.

There were a number of teachers in the Mesipuu pre-school, but the one who we dealt with most was called *Tädi** Kati. She was a small, firm, middle-aged woman with short hair and fine features and I thought she embodied the precision and discipline that Estonia hoped to ingrain into its tiny pupils' heads. Her shirt, always a calming, solid color like blue or green, was tucked in perfectly, and her pants were equally as snug and well fitting. But when Marta would make her entrance with her flamboyant skirt and pigtails, Tädi Kati would indulge the child and say, "Good morning, Miss Marta. It *is* nice to see you again."

"Good morning, Tädi Mati," Marta would say. Marta always called Tädi Kati "Tädi Mati" for some reason, and Tädi

---

*   Auntie (in Estonian).

Kati ignored it, even though Mati was a boy's name, and the other children always giggled.

"Marta, come over here, show us what a beautiful skirt you have on today."

Marta would feign shyness and then grin and turn so that the skirt would rise into the air just as she intended. Then she would skip over to her desk to sit beside her friend Doris who was a full-blooded Estonian with fair hair and skin so light it was almost silver. Doris was very tidy and wore a skirt and a bow in her hair. She didn't say much. Most of the other children, both boys and girls, were like that.

When Marta had made her entrance, I slipped back out in the hall and then out the door, taking the sled in hand. I would leave it in a barn behind the building that had a nice, old-fashioned door with a big iron handle. All of the other parents left their sleds in that barn, so that the children could play with them when they went outside. The children almost always went outside, even when it was snowing, so that you would arrive to pick them up in the afternoons and there would be snowmen and tiny sled jumps and even makeshift snow kitchens, where they molded the wet snow into carrots and other things.

The sight of the sleds in the barn cheered me up because they were so many different colors. You would see red, green, and blue sleds, even a yellow one. Another kaleidoscopic treat awaited back in the school house, where the plastic training toilets, all of them different colors, were arranged on shelves, with names written on them: Marta, Doris, Lauri, Tormi, Sander, Margus, Eliisabet.

On Marta's first day at preschool, Tädi Kati joined me in the little potty alcove and spoke about Marta's language development, and I tried to converse with her as best I could. Tädi Kati had a problem: Marta only spoke English with her and the other children. She delivered the message to me as if I had some control over the situation, but I told her to just be patient. On the second day at preschool, Tädi Kati was pleased, because Marta had spoken some kind of a mix that day. By the third day, she had switched completely. After that, Marta spoke no English there.

I still remember that day very well, because Marta had walked into the bedroom and rather than saying, "Wake up Daddy, it's morning," she had said, "*Issi*, wake up, it's *hommik*," instead.

It made me feel good that Marta was learning her mother tongue. My wife Epp didn't walk from Tallinn to Vilnius during the Baltic Freedom Walk in 1991 so that her child would become some amnesiac American with a faint grasp of her past. That fate had befallen us too recently, even within the past generation, and I couldn't take part in perpetuating such a feeling of loss, the loss I felt, to see Italians, to feel Italian, to know in your heart that you are still in some way an Italian forever, but not to know how to communicate with your own countrymen and so to be forever cut off from some mystery of yourself.

My grandfather had been born in New York to Italian immigrants and he couldn't speak English until he was seven and a neighborhood girl took pity and taught him. Later, as he went to work in a 1950s American world, where to be fair-haired and light-eyed with a short name was to be normal, he was stuck with dark hair and dark eyes and a last name that was 10 letters long, half of them vowels. Abbatecola! Not wishing to pass this shame on, my grandfather forbade the speaking of Italian in his home. After speaking Italian for centuries, our family became American and spoke only English. Sometimes when I was a boy, my mother would be making food in the kitchen and she would remember some childhood words and share each one of these treasures with me, as if displaying the terracotta shards of what had once been a very ancient and glorious Roman drinking vessel.

I knew it could happen to Estonians, too. I had seen the families at the Estonian House in New York where the parents spoke Estonian to each other but English with their children.

It always made me very sad, but I never said anything about it. Who was I to judge them?

As soon as the spring solstice arrived, the streets of Tartu were wet with estuaries of melting snow and ice and you could feel the heat of the sun on your neck. You would wake up in the earliest hours now and see light through the windows, and know that it was starting again, and that soon, very soon there would barely be any night at all. During the cold months, the locals shoveled sand out onto the sidewalks to make them traversable, and now that the ice was gone, there were piles all over. It felt as if one big wave had covered the city, leaving sand and gravel everywhere after it withdrew.

The winter-wearied people of Tartu kicked the sand up into the air, and the dust got into your lungs, even as the trees began to grow green and lovely once again and the birds returned to their branches, singing.

At home, the grand experiment in bilingualism continued, with ever odder results. The child who had spoken mostly English in January returned to visit her American grandparents in April speaking mostly Estonian to them. Her poor American grandmother had to explain to the nervous cashiers at the supermarkets that they shouldn't worry, and that the bizarre sound escaping from the three year old's mouth was a real language. At some point it clicked in the tot's head that there were actually two languages, and one was spoken one way and the other another. She learned to speak English with her grandmother at the store, and Estonian with her mother on the phone. When we returned to Estonia, the context was reversed, and she switched, too. At night in bed, we would train her with games. "Mommy says *pilv*, but what does Daddy say?" – "Cloud!" – "Daddy says cow but what does Mommy say?" – "*Lehm*!" And so on. But more and more, we started to speak to each other in a strange mixed language that only the three of us could understand.

First, it happened that Estonian sentences were translated directly into English, so that Marta would say, "Put the door shut" – *Pane uks kinni* – instead of "Close the door," or complain that she had an "open belly" – *kõht lahti* – if she had diarrhea. Then she started to confuse "he" and "she" because there was no gender in Estonian, it was all just *tema*, and soon I began to confuse them, too. An Estonian speaking English would start out using "she" to talk about his sister, and then the sister would magically grow a mustache and don pants mid-sentence and become a burly and masculine "he." But when you called an Estonian on it, they would dismiss you with a wave of the hand. "He, she, who cares? We don't have gender in Estonian." Later, I would also start sentences with a clumsy "he/she" blend, catching myself and blushing as my wife made fun of me. I didn't even understand how it was possible. I was speaking English as my mother tongue, but was making the same mistakes that Estonians made. Had I heard too many mistakes, or had my brain begun to function on Estonian grammar at some subliminal level?

As the last traces of ice vanished beneath the sun, and even the massive pyramids of snow that had been piled in the corners of parking lots withered to pathetic, dirty humps, Marta could no longer travel to the Mesipuu preschool on a sled. Instead, I took her on my shoulders. At first, she still wore the warm, insulated waterproofs of winter, but soon the warmth became so undeniable that even the most protective Estonian mother would let her child go to preschool in a long-sleeved shirt and pair of pants. She still would have a bandana scarf tied around her neck, and a hat on her head, just in case.

"*Issi,* when *lasteaed* is over later, can we go and get some, um, *jäätis?*" Marta would ask me.

"You mean when preschool is over, you would like to have some ice cream?"

"Mmhmm. And then after we get the *jäätis*, I mean, ice cream, can we go, uh, *mänguväljakule*?"

"You mean to the playground? Yes, we can, honey."

While I was undoing her bandana in the corridor, which was now as cool and dry in spring as it had been warm and humid in winter, I would sit and look at the names of the other Estonian children and sigh. It felt lonely to be the only one speaking English to Marta, and sometimes I even wondered why I bothered. She knew I understood what she was talking about, and I knew she knew. It was all hopeless. I was starting to understand what those New York Estonians were up against.

But one day as I went to retrieve Marta from Mesipuu, I heard a woman speaking a language that wasn't Estonian. It took a moment for my ears to focus in and identify it as British English. And when I saw the woman, I knew that she could not possibly be an Estonian. She was too casual in her dress, with blue jeans and a t-shirt, and her hair was pulled back in a careless, loose ponytail. She had red hair and freckles and glasses and she was trying to convince her little blond-haired boy to put on his shoes.

"Henri, you have to put on your own shoes. You're four years old, it's time you did it on your own."

Henri mumbled something and kicked at the shoes.

"Is he giving you a hard time?" I asked.

"Oh, no," the woman answered and then smiled. "Hey, you must be that Yank! The teachers told me that there was an American girl in the other class here. My name is Liz, by the way." She waved to me.

"I'm Justin," I said. "I guess we are the only two foreign parents here."

"No, I don't think so," Liz said and shook her head. "At least some of them have Russian parents."

"Do they count as foreigners?"

Liz shrugged. "They don't speak Estonian at home."

"Oh," I said. "Do you speak any Estonian?"

"Not really. Just a little," Liz said. "You know, I hadn't even heard of Estonia before. But then one day a few years ago Henri's dad Toomas came to work on my father's farm in Somerset and, well," she looked away and pushed her glasses up her nose, "well, a little bit after that, we found out Henri was coming."

"But why did you move here? The West Country is nice."

"My husband is a builder and most of his work is here. Henri, will you please put on your shoes?"

The child kicked at them again and mumbled something I couldn't understand. It sounded a bit different from Estonian, but as many times as I replayed it in my head, it remained indecipherable.

"Oh," I said as my heart sank a little. "I guess your son speaks Estonian to you, too."

"Who? Henri?" Liz looked at me, blinking through her glasses. "Oh, no. We have the opposite problem here. Henri refuses to speak Estonian. The teachers say Henri's teaching the other children English."

"Maybe he should be in the same class with Marta. Then they could speak English together."

"Now that would be splendid wouldn't it? And you're a proper little British boy, aren't you. Henri?"

Henri stared down at his shoes.

"But how can that be? It took Marta three days to switch over. Now she speaks to *me* in Estonian."

"I don't know," Liz said. "Hey – maybe it has to do with the mother. I think the children bond with the mother's language first because the attachment is so close. That's probably why Henri is the way he is."

"You really think so? Does he speak to his father in English?"

"He does actually," she laughed a bit. "It makes sense though, right? I mean, nobody calls it a father tongue, it's a mother tongue. And English is your mother tongue, right Henri?" The boy said nothing.

"*Emakeel*," I said.

"What?"

"It's in Estonian, too. *Emakeel* – mother tongue. But they call their country of birth *Isamaa*, fatherland."

"Well, you certainly have learned more Estonian than me," said Liz. "Okay, this one last time," Liz said and crouched down to put Henri's shoes on. "This is the very last time, do you understand me?"

Henri nodded and slid off the bench. "Thank you very much, Mummy," he said.

A moment later they were out the door. Through the window, I watched as Liz hoisted Henri into a bicycle seat and the two of them cycled away, as free and European as if they were on one of Somerset's country lanes.

I only saw Liz a few times after that, but I always felt good to see her. I didn't know her last name, but she still felt like a friend. And it was good to know there was an English woman in Tartu who was living the same kind of life that I was, even if her son was born to be a proper little British boy and my daughter was evidently destined to become a proper little Estonian girl.

A REAL OPPORTUNITY

Almost immediately upon our return to Estonia, opportunities began to pop up. There was a strange sort of magic at work in the land. In New York, I had to seek out opportunities because nobody knew me or wanted to have anything to do with me, but in Estonia, somebody wanted me to do something for them.

They would even pay.

One of these first somebodies was named Kadri Liik, an old acquaintance of Epp's who called to her one afternoon. It was the dull end of winter and the yard was flushed with icy runoff and last year's wet leaves. Epp came out in her rubber boots to where I was stacking firewood to tell me that something called ICDS – the International Centre for Defence Studies – was looking for a transcriber for the first Lennart Meri Conference.

It would be a gathering of statesmen, analysts and press in Tallinn, Kadri explained to Epp, and the cream of global thought-leaders would spend days talking about foreign policy in the spirit of the brainy, swashbuckling polyglot Meri, the late and former Estonian president, who was still loved by all and would have enjoyed nothing more than to be there himself, had he not succumbed to illness the prior year.

Of course, I said yes. It was something new. Interesting. Different. A real opportunity.

It was an opportunity to discover a new world. What I now recall best about the Lennart Meri Conferences I attended my first years back in Estonia is not the bigwig attendees or the incisive foreign policy debates, but the well-catered lunches and the impressive drinking that went on.

Now, when I look back, it's not hard to understand why. I had already been living in Tartu for two months, during one of the frostier winters in recent memory, really pushed to the edge by the ice and the snow, kept warm by wood-heated furnaces and nourished by cutlets and potatoes. I may have worn my best jacket and tie to the event, shaved and tried to look presentable, but inside, I was already an Estonian country boy in the big city.

I was so lucky to be there.

Oh, those platters of potatoes and carrots smothered in Mediterranean cheeses that melted in your mouth like cotton candy. Oh, those cuts of long-roasted savory lamb so heavenly tender, seasoned with rosemary. Jugs of delicious coffee, brewed dark and strong, to keep the exciting discussions going. They served up this luxury on the second floor of the Radisson hotel to *The Economist* editors, to the traveling Davos jet set, to the think tank fellows, the analysts, the NATO and EU emissaries...

As I ladled a helping of poached salmon in orange cream sauce onto my plate, the thought did cross my mind.

I really should work for *The Economist*.

Or become an Estonian politician. Or a diplomat. Somebody. Nobody else in that country ate so well.

When an old Estonian died and the relatives gathered around in the countryside, they served up pork and potatoes and, to top it off, a chocolate-covered raisin strudel. There were a few bottles of vodka, too, and one man would be charged with refilling the glasses. For the introductory shot, there would be a solemn toast, and after three or so mouthfuls of the hard stuff had gone down, and the guests loosened up, there would be some light conversation. Then they would drink coffee and go home.

This was how average Estonians celebrated a person's whole life. But at the Lennart Meri Conference in Tallinn, they celebrated the end of the session "Nordic-Baltic Security Co-operation: Supplementing or Supplanting NATO?" with much more fanfare.

It was inspiring. Here I was, 27 years old, out of college five years, married for four, a husband, a father, and a guy in Tartu who spent much of his time lighting fires in furnaces and not getting anywhere. And yet here I was, the same exact person except in a shirt and tie, elbowing General Wesley Clark out of the way to get another helping of tiramisu in Tallinn...

There were moments when I could not believe it was happening. Was it really Wes Clark, the man who led NATO during the Kosovo War, sitting up there during the opening session beside President Toomas Hendrik Ilves, former Danish Foreign Minister Uffe Ellemann-Jensen, and Ivan Krastev, a spirited Bulgarian analyst, who uttered one of the more memorable lines from the conference, "Corruption is like Nokia. It connects people"?

According to Clark, it had actually been Lennart Meri who urged him to take action in Kosovo.

"And I talked to President Meri and he told me, 'NATO has just about lost its credibility in dealing with this issue,'" Clark told the attendees. "It was a devastating comment. It just cut me right to the quick. That comment, coming from Meri, caused me to fly back to Washington and confront the secretary of defense and ask him to please make the threat real before it was too late for NATO and the Kosovars."

Listening to Clark and others talk about Meri's influence at the conference I began to understand that what I had suspected for many years was true.

Estonia actually was the center of the world, masquerading as the middle of nowhere.

Sometimes people would look down to my name tag and be puzzled because it only said my name there and no affiliation. There was no sign identifying me as "Senior Fellow, The Jamestown Foundation" or "Middle East Bureau Chief, *The Economist*." I was just who I was, Justin Petrone, and that's all I was and that was a pity.

"Who exactly are you?" Kadri had asked me before the conference. "What should we put on your name tag?"

A terrifying question. Who was I? A genetics journalist? The author of that widely read blog about Estonia called *Itching for Eestimaa*? A blogger? Was that who I was? Maybe.

But to people like Wes Clark or Edward Lucas or Toomas Hendrik Ilves, I was no-one. Especially to Ilves.

Ilves. Here was a man who name-dropped Roman historians as if he had known them personally. "Tacitus!" he might exclaim while raising one of his very wise eyebrows as if he expected everyone to know what he was talking about, just by using that name. I imagined many diplomats would nod whenever he did this, pretending that they knew what he was referring to. Maybe a few did. The adventurer and writer Tom Bissell, who would later hole up in the Old Town of Tallinn, binging on video games and writing novellas, had called Ilves "owlishly appealing" in *The New Republic*, and after that, every time I caught a glimpse of Ilves' gray blue eyes and Finnic jowls, the slope of his knowledgeable cranium with its short-cut, brown-gray hair, I imagined a wise owl strutting about in a bow tie. "Owlishly appealing."

Ilves. Of all the attendees at the conference, he was the one I feared most. I dreaded any collision with his intellect. What if we bumped into each other while sampling the mango sorbet, and he happened to mention some military theorist I had never even read?

"Well, er, we both know what Clausewitz had to say about that." Or even worse – what if he glared down at my name tag with his owlish eyes, asking, "And you? Who are you?"

"I-I'm a blogger, M-Mr. Ilves, sir," I m-might s-stutter back. "*I-itching f-for E-eestimaa?*"

It would take a few more years before I understood that being yourself could be your calling.

So I hovered in the corners, cast aside, feeling like nobody. I imagined that a lot of Estonians there might have felt the same way deep down. Wait a second, weren't Ansip, Lang and Aaviksoo also from the same world as me? Didn't most of them have parents or grandparents in the countryside who still had dry toilets, alcohol problems and a barn full of stray cats? Yet here they were, right beside me and EU Commissioner Olli Rehn ande President Putin's former economic advisor Andrei Illarionov, trying to get another dish of crème brûlée. Ansip, Lang and Aaviksoo probably felt inspired, too, seeing their country put on a first-class show for the foreign policy elite, an event so lavish and thought-provoking that they would keep coming back for years. And the reason for this event?

Their own homegrown Lennart Meri.

As I came to know Kadri Liik, the director of the International Centre for Defence Studies, I discovered she also was an Estonian through and through. She was like Lennart Meri, advising ambassadors and generals, but in her soul she enjoyed the simple country life. In our brief asides, Kadri mentioned that she liked to chase away the stress of Tallinn life with summer retreats on Muhu, where she would go swimming with the swans at dusk. At the conference, when she stood up, reminded me of a swan herself, with her long and graceful countenance, dressed in black at the podium and asking questions about Putinism.

Raven dark hair, soft features, a trim and tall figure. She had a soft, feminine voice, and yet there was a coldness to it too, an icy crystal hardness. People were in awe of her. An older female ambassador with gray hair and kind eyes even whispered a joke into my ear. "I want to be like *her* when I grow up." And Kadri wasn't even 40 years old yet. I felt an affinity for Kadri as well. Not an affection but affinity.

She belonged to that great gallery of fearless northern women. She was somebody important, and she had made Tallinn important.

Even the Finns were dumbstruck.

"This conference could never take place in Helsinki," grumbled an analyst at brunch. "Helsinki is provincial. But Tallinn?" he grimaced. "Tallinn has become cosmopolitan."

So much for the middle of nowhere.

Other than Ilves, the other man I feared at the Lennart Meri Conference was Edward Lucas, the legendary correspondent, and I feared Lucas mostly because he was British.

Not that I had anything against Englishmen. I had long since abandoned my fear of drunk hooligan football fans and embraced my inner John Cleese. Wasn't my grandmother Margaret mostly English? But Edward Lucas was a different sort of scion of Albion. His father was an Oxford philosopher. He was a graduate of the London School of Economics. A former Moscow Bureau Chief for the supremely important and widely read weekly magazine *The Economist* and at the time its Central and Eastern European correspondent.

His good friends were Anne Applebaum and Radek Sikorski, the admired American writer and the future Polish foreign minister, respectively. My good friends were a Filipino-American hip hop artist in Los Angeles who called himself Cookie Jar, and a game designer who had moved to San Francisco where the dope was plentiful and who referred to himself as "Jocko." There was Eamon, too, now teaching English in Czech Republic with his girlfriend Anja, whom he called *kočka*, which meant "kitten" in Czech. Can't leave him out.

Basically, we were from very different worlds, Edward Lucas and me, and I would never feel comfortable in his world of palace dinners and barroom eavesdropping.

Yet despite this impressive curriculum vitae, the resume of a real somebody, an important man, Edward Lucas had once been nobody special. An editor at a little newspaper called *The Baltic Independent* in the early 1990s, *The Baltic Times* of its day, staying up late nights to bang out articles from some cramped office while scarfing down some of the thin, alien pizzas that still abounded in Tallinn's periphery. It was eerily familiar how Lucas had once lived my life. I also had worked for *The Baltic Times*. And his first son had even been born at Tallinn Central Hospital, a mere decade before Marta. As his fondness for the little land continues to prove (Lucas became Estonia's first e-resident in 2014) he had also been brainwashed by the Estonians – perhaps by Mart Laar himself – so that it felt as if he *was* part Estonian inside.

Lucas was also a fixture of the Estonian media. His word was gold. Should he even mention the country in his articles, it would result in front page headlines: "Edward Lucas says...."

As we reached for the asparagus, Lucas looked down and squinted at my name tag.

"Ah, you must be Giustino," he said, "the author of *Itching for Eestimaa*. I read your blog all the time."

"You do?" I stepped back and looked at Lucas. He was as British as they come, wiry build, a thin nose, thin lips, wisps of graying dark hair, smart glasses, dark eyes, a Monty Python character in a brown suit, except earnest and serious and smart.

"Certainly I do," said Lucas with his British accent, ladling the steamed greens onto his plate. "It's just splendid. Fantastic. Finely written."

I tilted my head as if I didn't hear him right.

"So," he cleared his throat. "Are you enjoying the conference, Giustino?"

"Well, I'm the official transcriber."

Lucas forked a stalk of asparagus into his mouth, chewed it and swallowed. Then he dabbed at the corners of his mouth with a napkin and cleared his throat.

"Now there's a job. So, you really have to write down everything we say?"

"Everything except the Chatham House Rule sessions."

"Mmm. Yes. Quite right. You do know what the Chatham House Rule is, right Justin?" Lucas raised an eyebrow.

"It allows for an open, anonymous debate. People can say whatever they want without being held to it later on."

I hadn't known what it was before Kadri told me, but that conference had a bluff of a learning curve.

"I can tell you've done this before."

"Right, Ed."

"You can call me Edward or Mr. Lucas. But never Ed."

"I'm sorry, Edward."

"It's quite all right. Just so you know."

"I read somewhere that your son was born at Tallinn Central Hospital. Is that true?"

"Ah, yes! That was my first son, Johnny, way back in 1993. It was a completely different country back then, you know. I mean, Russian troops were still here."

He looked around as if there still might be a Russian soldier lurking somewhere, perhaps refilling that NATO representative's gin and tonic by the corner table over there. As he looked, the memories of our daughter Marta's birth smoked in my memory a bit. The pulse of the vintage 1980s monitor. That fear of not knowing what the doctors were saying in that weird language that I tried to follow but could not always understand. My daughter was born in a foreign country. Except it wasn't foreign.

It was hers.

"How did you feel about that?"

"About what?" Lucas forked another stalk of asparagus into his mouth and chewed.

"Weren't you a bit intimidated?"

He chewed and swallowed again. "What do you mean?"

"You know?" I leaned in and whispered. "Having him here? In an old Soviet hospital?"

Lucas relaxed his shoulders a bit and chuckled to himself. "Well, yes. It certainly was a leap of faith..." He looked like he might say something else, but then he saw somebody more important coming and swiveled away to talk to him.

Even though I lunched with Lucas, Ilves, Laar, Wes Clark, and the rest of the important people at the Lennart Meri Conference, I was still not permitted to join them for the grand dinners at Kadriorg, that little wedding cake of a palace that had once been Peter the Great's summer residence before the Estonian kitchen help rebelled two centuries later, remaking it as their presidential quarters.

I imagined the real discussions of the conference cadre went on there, under sparkling chandeliers with string quartets playing while Ilves, who was the closest thing Estonia had ever produced to a real emperor, reigned over discussions about the OECD and the CIS and the UN and NATO's MAP.

I did find my way into a tour of the Old Town given by Mart Laar, though, as well as a private Arvo Pärt concert at *Niguliste Kirik*, Saint Nicholas Church, where the Estonian and Georgian prime ministers sat together in the pews, as well as the mysterious, bearded composer himself, who looked like a peaceful monk. This was the kind of company I now kept.

But Mart Laar. If there was one person at that conference who did not intimidate me, it was him. He was just too disarming and kid-like. A round head garnished by sandy reddish hair and a fuzzy beard on an oval body, with two slits enclosing light blue eyes, he was well deserving of his nickname *Mõmmibeebi*, which translated as "teddy bear." Laar sat through the sessions with his laptop open, as if he was surfing the net or chatting with fellow party members while half-listening to questions about EU Neighborhood Policy.

And then, just when you thought he wasn't listening at all, he would join the conversation and ask something that woke everyone up. Later on, at home, sitting with headphones during the countless hours I spent transcribing it all, I was always waiting for Mart Laar to say something.

[Mart Laar: The Georgian attitude is like this wonderful TV series *Sex and the City*. Georgia is not really interested in promises, Georgia is interested in having real sex. But Europe at this moment is acting like an old man who is looking, maybe touching, and talking, but [some dramatic hand gestures] there is no sex available.

[Laughter]

Moderator Sir Garry Johnson (Chairman, International Security Advisory Board, UK): I am not sure that Georgia isn't getting any sex. But, please, let's raise the tone of the event. Yes, sir.

Artis Pabriks [former Minister of Foreign Affairs, Republic of Latvia]: Just to ask a question before we wrap up, I think we have a Neighborhood Policy, but not a single, not a coherent ..."]*

What a true Estonian! There was Laar, talking about *Sex and the City* and the EU Neighborhood Policy at the same time and still unable to get away from the Internet. Part of me wanted to send him an email during that session, too, just to see if he would answer me while he was talking.

---

* All of the Lennart Meri Conference transcripts are accessible online at http://lmc.icds.ee/.

Laar's tour of the Old Town was just as much fun. Whenever he mentioned the Danish invasion in the 13th century he would skip over to Uffe Ellemann-Jensen, who had been foreign minister of Denmark for most of the Eighties and Nineties, and grab him by the hands.

"It was your people, Uffe, we were fighting here," Laar would grin. "*Your* people."

Uffe, an older chap with a white mustache who had been in politics since the Sixties, held hands with Laar and bobbed up and down a little bit and laughed.

I could see how Laar won so many people over to Estonia's side when he was prime minister from 1992 to 1994, and then from 1999 to 2002, pivotal years for the country when its NATO and EU membership was essentially decided by this same gang of very important old men. With his bear-like frame, off-kilter character, and choppy but endearing accent, Laar did seem out of step with Andrus Ansip's clean cut, dark suited Reform Party politicians that now ruled Estonia. He was charismatic and interesting. No matter your politics, one could not help but love Mart Laar and believe everything that he said.

That was a fine day. Late March, but it felt like May. A pleasant light breeze was coming in off the shimmering midnight blue of the Gulf of Finland. The sun shone on the red tiled roofs of the Old Town, and reflected off the white spires of Saint Olaf and Saint Nicholas. Smell of springtime in the air, newly returned birds singing from the ancient stone towers. I thought of Epp, I thought of our first walk around this same perfect place during my very first day in Tallinn, and was grateful for the memory. And there I was, in a suit, a step away from *the* Mart Laar, standing beside *the* Uffe Ellemann-Jensen, dodging the glares of *the* think tank analysts, who kept peering over to see if they could tell my affiliation from my name tag.

"Is he from the Heritage Foundation? Or the Brookings Institution?" I heard one whisper to another.

"I saw him talking to Kadri before. He's with ICDS.'"

"Ah."

Whenever they did this, I would turn myself toward Mart Laar who didn't care who I was or where I was from. I would not let anyone else read my mysterious name tag, not even the drunk Estonian Russian punk rock kids who were gathered at a viewing point on Toompea. They were sitting up there, surrounded by empty cans, chattering away in Tolstoy and Pushkin's tongue, when our entourage of ex-foreign ministers and thoughtful analysts showed up, and one of the ICDS representatives walked over to shoo them away before they could embarrass *Eesti* in front of such important people.

"I told you to leave," she said to them in Estonian. "Please leave right now. This instant!"

"Don't worry, lady," one of the punks, who had a purple mohawk, told the ICDS representative in her red skirt and high heels. "We're just having a good time, you know. None of us wants to kill Mart Laar."

---

*   In 2007, ICDS was known as the International Centre for Defence Studies. Nowadays, it is called the International Centre for Defence and Security. ICDS is based in Tallinn, Estonia. http://www.icds.ee/

So far I have told you about the gourmet food and big personalities at the Lennart Meri Conference. I haven't told you about the drinking.

The drinking started in the evening during the Chatham House Rule sessions, where the various fellows and ambassadors would swill gin and tonics and scotch on the rocks. But the real drinking took place much later, at a bar on the top floor of the hotel that had a view of the city.

To get there, you had to take the elevator up, squeezing in among some of the more influential thinkers in Estonia, Russia, or anywhere else. I stood between Marko Mihkelson and Boris Nemtsov, each of whom was taller than me, which amazed me, because I was almost always the tallest in any group. Marko chaired the foreign affairs committee in parliament, and looked a bit like Laar, should Laar have been stretched out a foot, padded with muscles, shaved, and made to look tough. Nemtsov was just as huge, a giant from Southern Russia with thick dark hair and the handsome face of a singer or an actor. Yet he was a smart politician and activist, too, a Russian liberal. Nemtsov was not the only dissident there. Th e former economic advisor Andrei Illarionov, the analyst Andrei Piontkovsky, as well as Kremlinologist Lilia Shevtsova, all of them critics of Putin. They seemed to be the only Russian contingent at the conference, although there were rumors that the embassy was secretly listening.

But where were they?

At the top floor, Mihkelson and Nemtsov got out and continued their discussion at the bar, where Lucas was sitting at the end, observing and listening. The room was full of Estonian politicians and public intellectuals from around the world, reclining, standing, trading drinks and regaling each other with stories. The smell of cigar smoke was in the air. Whether it was legal or not didn't seem to matter. In public, this was a dour crowd. Should you meet any one of these Estonians on the street, they would be straightforward and businesslike with you. But up on top of the Radisson, lit up by steins of beer or shots of vodka, they came alive, with bursts of big laughter. It was fun to drink and talk. But the more I watched the scene, the more I kept thinking about the Estonian politicians of the interwar period, the dandy clothes, the excess, the parties that must have gone on. Was this how it was? I could almost see former President Konstantin Päts sitting in the corner with his cane and top hat. Maybe it was because I was talking to the head of an organization that was commissioned to document Stalinist crimes, but Päts' ghost was there. I could just see him floating. He tipped his hat to me.

When they dimmed the lights to show the bar would close, there were groans. But then a figure appeared at the elevator. Who it was, I still do not know. It could have been Ilves himself. But I do recall that I heard the strange figure cry out. "Hey everybody! There's an open bar downstairs. Ten bottles of whiskey! Ten bottles of vodka!"

"*HURRAH!*"

You should have seen that crowd of politicians run toward the elevator. Lift-full by lift-full they went down to get their hands on the strong stuff. I imbibed down there, too, and the room felt a bit warmer and took on that special booze-blurred crimson glow. Nemtsov was there. Mihkelson. I saw Kadri standing in the middle, but this was not the same stiff-backed, restrained moderator we had seen. This Kadri was sipping wine and loving it.

The vodka bottle came around. Illarionov took a swig from it and passed it to me. Then I drank from it. The vodka burned on the way down and its aura stung my sinuses.

Hannes Rumm, a Social Democrat, was there, too. Tall with fine blond hair and fancy glasses, he looked more like the head of a Swiss chocolate factory than a Tallinn city politician. He was concerned for his friend Kadri who had adopted the air of a hobnobbing socialite, spinning like a weather vane, managing to carry on five conversations at one time.

"Kadri, shouldn't you be getting home?"

"I'm fine, Hannes, honest. Oh, my dear Mart! How are you? So good to see you." She kissed Mart Nutt, another Estonian politician, on the cheeks.

"Kadri, please," Hannes placed a hand at her elbow. "Let's go. You should get some sleep."

"Hannes, what are you talking about? I'm having a good time. Yes, Pierre, mmm, yes, it's so good to see you again, too. Yes, you are always welcome here in Tallinn, yes." She kissed someone else on the cheek.

"Kadri! Please!"

In the frenetic melee I noticed Kasekamp looking across at me. Andres Kasekamp, the historian! He was a so-called "foreign Estonian," a *väliseestlane* from Ontario who had returned to the land of his blood after 1991. Soft spoken with light blue eyes, a boyish face, and short-trimmed beard, Kasekamp had the perpetually amused expression of a university professor, with an equal dash of Old Western sensibility with his sports jacket and blue jeans, as if you might run into him at some saloon in the Rocky Mountains.

We had met earlier that same day in the first floor lounge to talk about my possible admission to the Baltic Studies program at the University of Tartu in the fall, and he assured me I would be accepted. He had read my blog and said it would be no trouble to get in. The process was mostly there to weed out all of those bogus applications from Nigeria and Cambodia from people who just wanted an excuse to get into Europe, Kasekamp said. Now at 1 a.m., he was grinning through the crowd with a drink in hand, as if to say, "Isn't this the greatest party on Earth? Or in Tallinn at least?"

And maybe it was, because that's the last thing I remember about that night.

I think what happened next was that I took a cab out to Vello Vikerkaar's house in Nõmme in the wee hours and crashed on his couch, kept warm by his fluffy Siberian husky. Just a few hours after that, I was back on my feet at the Radisson for the morning session, dry-mouthed and hungover, unable to say anything intelligent, dreading a run in with Ilves, who might start speaking to me about Tacitus or Clausewitz.

The strange thing was that everybody who had been at the party the night before was already seated in the conference room waiting for the first session. Nemtsov was there, his clothes neatly ironed, sitting with his hands in his lap. Mihkelson was there beside him, fiddling with his smartphone. And Kadri Liik was there too, serious and calm, dressed elegantly in sober black with a white collar that made her look more swan-like than ever before. Her voice retained that elegant, diamond quality. It was as if the night's booze-fueled revelries had never happened. Or maybe it had all been a dream?

Had it?

Kasekamp was in the front thumbing through a book when I came and sat beside him.

"I can't believe it," I said.

"What is it that you cannot believe?" he responded in his deep professor's voice.

"It's just..."

"Just?"

"Everybody looks so sober."

"Sober?" Kasekamp shot me a curious look, then returned his gaze to the book.

"Oh, well," I said and yawned and stretched a bit. "I guess these people do this often. They get used to it."

"Uh huh."

Those were the earlier, more idealistic and merry days of the Lennart Meri Conference. In those days, people spoke of Georgian and Ukrainian NATO membership as if they were inevitable. I imagined that in a few years, Kiev and Tbilisi would already be members of the alliance, and the discussions would be about Membership Action Plans for Tashkent or Dushanbe.

But it wasn't to be. What I had witnessed there in Tallinn in 2007, was the high water mark before the global economic crisis, before the collapse of the post-1991 order. A year later, in August 2008, Russian tanks would be occupying Georgian cities. I met with Kadri Liik once more around that time, at a cafe near Radisson hotel. She looked the same, but not totally: she looked down as she spoke and tinkered with her hands.

"Are you okay?" I asked.

"I'm sorry," she said in her crystalline voice, staring at her soup. "I've just been on the phone all weekend with everybody. I keep cracking nuts in my apartment and pretending they are Russian tanks."

I said nothing. I had sensed that something was about to burst in the Caucasus for weeks before it did, and yet there was nothing I could do except follow the news like anybody else. But Kadri – she had internalized the world's chaos, brought it within herself. I had learned to shut the world out, like turning a faucet. You had to shut it off sometimes just to stay sane.

"Did you like this year's conference?" she asked. "We are going to keep doing them."

"It was very good. Especially the food." I attempted a chuckle. "And the wine."

Kadri sighed. "Well, I think the conference is very important for Estonian security."

"Sure it is, Kadri. Isn't that kind of obvious though?"

Kadri's eyes widened a bit. "Not at all," she shook her head from side to side. "Some people are quite critical of it. They think it's just another wasteful extravagance for the... for the cynical elite so that they can feel full of themselves and brown nose. They probably think it's just one big party where everybody is eating and drinking. I hope you haven't told people that's all it's about, have you?"

"No," I recoiled. "Not at all. I've said it's a very intellectually stimulating, important event where..."

"For us it is so important," Kadri cut me off. "It's so very important that these important officials, journalists, and others have been to Estonia and seen with their own eyes what it is really like here..."

This was true. Although I did wonder if they ever left the Radisson or the lanes of the Old Town.

"...So that one day, when Russian propaganda is informing everyone that Estonia is a fascist country, these people will know that it is wrong."

"But of course it's not a fascist country. Who would be stupid enough to believe that?"

"Some people will believe anything if they hear it often enough," whispered Kadri. "And if they come to Estonia, then they make contacts here whom they can call and ask what's really going on."

"Look, I really didn't mean to say it was only about food and drinking. It was just a nice conference..."

"Yes, yes, of course it's a nice conference in that way that you mentioned. Yes, people eat and drink. Normal. But it's also very different from other conferences, you know. In most countries in Europe, the president will come out and give some long, boring speech in the local language and then disappear. Here, the president takes part in the panel discussions. He hangs around and talks. One time he was even sitting on the floor, because there weren't enough chairs. Can you imagine another president..."

"No, no, that's all true, Kadri. I remember how Ilves was sitting on the floor. I'm sorry I mentioned the food."

"We are so lucky to have someone like him," she said.

Meanwhile, my relationship with President Ilves had moved on too. He had actually sent me a few emails about things I had written on my blog. Some of these emails were informative, a few slightly critical, and more than a handful corrected some grammatical errors. They arrived late at night or sometimes very early in the morning. Sometimes he wrote them, I assumed, from his farm house at Ärma in Viljandi County, and other times on the road. For the most part, he seemed to enjoy what I was doing on my blog.

"I keep reading your posts and find them a riot and a welcome respite from the grasping self-importance I yawn over in the Estonian opinion pages," the owlishly appealing president wrote. "It's great to have someone with an almost New Jerseyan sensibility writing about E-land. But do you do more serious English-language stuff on Estonia? Not panegyrics but analytical pieces?"

Did I? Not really. I checked the time on the email. It had arrived at 1 a.m., Local Time. Did that Ilves guy ever sleep? Or was he just worrying about Estonia round the clock?

From those emails I got the sense that it could get really hard being the president of Estonia. It was a lonely job, because though Estonia was on the Western side of the dividing line, it was still on the dividing line, and so Ilves could see too clearly what was going on in Georgia and, much later, in Ukraine. And yet there was very little he or anybody else could do about it.

As for me, I decided to take President Ilves' encouragement to heart, and keep on writing about Estonia.

FIRST TRUE WRITER

It amuses me now when I think of it, but Vello Vikerkaar was the first true writer I met.

Not that Epp wasn't a writer. She spent every spare second writing. Even in our tiny room in South London many years earlier, she had told me of her dream to be a writer. But even as the books began to appear, first under our bed and then later on the shelves of the new Petrone Print office, she continued to think of herself as if she hadn't written a thing. Epp hurt herself to write. She lost sleep over those texts and did not finish them. And so she continued to think of the craft of writing as something she had not yet achieved, that she had not yet written that great novel that would stun all Estonians in perpetuity. I don't know if she was waiting for Peeter Sauter or Jaan Kaplinski or some other Estonian writer to call her one day and tell her, "Congratulations, you're now a writer" or what.

Vello on the other hand was already a writer and he knew it since he was born. It was in the way the Canadian Estonian ran his hands through his mop of gray hair, the way he stood with a cup of spicy tea, pondering something big, or the way he studied you as you spoke, as if he was taking notes for a story. Vello was so writerly that he didn't even need to write a page. You just had to look at the magazines stacked on his desk and that beautiful old typewriter of his to know he was for real.

"Here, read this," he might say, thrusting a fresh copy of *The New Yorker* into your hands.

You would read a paragraph. "Looks like an excerpt from a novel about an Indian prostitute."

"It sucks. My husky writes better than that. Can you believe that arrogant prick won an award? Some idiots think that's some fine writing. I think it's all a bunch of bullshit."

"But it's the top story in *The New Yorker*."

"Bullshit." He pronounced every sound in the word. "But, eh, you know what they say. Garbage in, garbage out."

"Garbage in, garbage out?"

"If all you read is bullshit then all you write is bullshit."

It was my first writing lesson.

I usually went to Vello late at night or early morning, to crash on his couch. We first met at the restaurant of a casino in the center of the city to discuss ideas for a now defunct Nordic literary magazine that also dabbled in non-fiction. He wanted me to go out and interview ice fishermen on Lake Peipus in midwinter. Somehow I never got around to doing it.

When the last sessions of the Lennart Meri conferences were over, or the early morning parties ran out of drink, I would hire a cab outside the hotel and ride it all the way out into the woods of Nõmme, in the south of the city.

Nõmme. It was one of those districts of Tallinn where people like Vello lived. Kadriorg and Kalamaja were too central and Pirita, with its yacht club, too posh. Nõmme promised pines, picket fences, grand homes set back from its curiously named streets. Hiiu-Maleva. Hämariku. Aate. The names had the chime and percussion of Japanese poetry.

Vello lived on a street that had a name that sounded like another street in Nõmme, so that every time I took a cab out to sleep on the couch in his straw house beside his white husky Karl Vaino, the driver would either correct me, thinking I had the street's name wrong, or get lost trying to find it. But that was all fine with Vello Vikerkaar. He had no desire to be found.

The house was different. Unusual. Strange. A free standing, wobbly legged drunken sailor of a home. On a street lined with wooden structures painted sky blue or canary yellow with old-fashioned gingerbread trim about the eaves, Vello Vikerkaar lived in an odd dwelling that was made of bales of straw sealed with clay. It was a straw-clay pueblo painted Mediterranean white, half Santa Fe, half Beirut. His office was way in the back on the second floor, big windows, plenty of light, Oriental carpet, and wall-to-wall books, some new, some antique. There was an old swivel chair and a great desk where he said he did all of his writing. The heirloom typewriter was the centerpiece – he claimed the great William S. Burroughs had gifted it to him – and I would sometimes marvel at its golden keys. There was an Estonian flag on the wall and a ukulele in the corner that Vello would tinker with sometimes when he wasn't complaining about Savisaar and the malaise he felt toward his fellow Estonians.

"The thing you should know about Estonians," he announced, "is that they fight like peasants."

"Peasants?" I looked over at him while he stroked the husky Karl Vaino behind the ears. Vello said that his wife Liina's aunt had named the animal. "It's a good name for a dog," she had said. Liina had not yet come home that night. We sat in his living room, watching the yellow flames curl behind the glass of his black iron furnace, drinking strong Indian tea from ceramic mugs.

"Peasants!" Vello tossed an arm in the air. "I mean shit goes on in this country that would never happen in Finland. And that's what Estonia wants to be like, right? Finland Junior. That's the idea of Estonia. To be as rich as the Finns. But the difference is that the Finns fought for their independence like men. The Estonians fought like peasants. Now they have to catch up."

"I still don't get it. Fight like peasants? What? With rakes and torches?"

"No, no," Vello shifted in his seat. "The Estonians' idea of fighting is like, 'Let's get the master drunk and stab him in the back.' Or, 'Let's wait until the master falls asleep and then we'll slit his throat.' That's how peasants fight. Here, look at this," he pulled a book off a shelf and flipped through the pages. "This will help you to understand." He handed the book to me.

I looked up. "You want me to read *A History of Finland's Literature*?"

"Page 108. Underlined."

I flipped to the page and found the quotation and began to read aloud. "The first was a political assassination, rare in Finland: a junior official of the Senate, Eugene Schauman..."

"Schauman."

"That's what I said."

"Never mind. Go on."

"A junior official of the Senate, Eugene Schauman shot Governor-General Bobrikov on 16 June 1904 and then immediately turned the pistol on himself. Hmm." Beside the underlined words was a note that Vello had written in magic marker: "Would never happen in Estonia."

I looked back at him. "You think the Estonians would never do a thing like that?"

"Isn't that obvious! Nobody shot Andrei Zhdanov when he came here to organize the Soviet takeover. Nobody shot Johannes Käbin or Karl Vaino." The dog yelped a bit and Vello kissed his head. "Not you, Karl Vaino. The other Karl Vaino. Nobody's tried to kill Edgar Savisaar."

"Why would they want to kill the Mayor of Tallinn?"

Vello squinted at me as if he doubted severely in my intelligence. "Well it's *his* party that has a special agreement with Putin's party, isn't it? It is *he* who is the greatest agent of Russian power in Estonia, right?" Vello folded his legs and leaned in. "Ask yourself this, Justin, if there is a Governor-General Nikolai Ivanovich Bobrikov in Estonia today, then what is *his* name?"

"Edgar Savisaar?"

Vello nodded many times. "Can you imagine what might have happened if someone had put a bullet in Andrei Zhdanov in 1940? He's up there welcoming the so-called peoples' revolution and then – bang – Zhdanov drops dead. I wonder what Stalin might have thought of that."

"He wouldn't have been very happy."

"It would have sent a message. Don't fuck with Estonia."

"But that didn't happen."

"Because Estonians fight like peasants. I'm telling you. Have you ever heard of Simo Häyhä?"

"Häy who?"

"Häyhä. Oh, you should see this." Vello stood up and plucked a thick volume from the top of a bookcase. Then he sat down beside me and opened the big glossy pages of the book. There were gray images of a Finn with a grin on his face, dressed in white army fatigues and holding a rifle in a forest. In another photo, you could see that half of his face was drooping. His mouth curved downward to the left, and his cheek was lumpy and sagging. And yet the man was still smiling. It was the most enthusiastic grin I had seen on any face, let alone a disfigured one.

"Simo Häyhä was a marksman in the Finnish army during the Winter War." Vello said. "He had 505 confirmed kills as a sniper before he was wounded in the face. Do you know what his nickname was?" He stared at me.

"No."

"*Valkoinen kuolema.* The White Death."

"You're crazy."

"He died a few years ago, you know," Vello said, standing up and walking back to his armchair. "Ninety-seven years old. Lived a good long life breeding dogs. Maybe even owned some Nokia stock. Could you imagine what might have happened to him in Estonia?"

"He probably would have been shot when they took over the country."

"Or sent to Siberia. Or forced to die for Germany."

We were both silent for a moment.

"Why are you so down on the Estonians anyway? Aren't you an Estonian?"

Vello leered at me over his bowl of tea. That smart author's squint. "You don't know this?"

"Know what?"

"Didn't Val tell you this?"

"What the hell are you talking about? Of course not. I only met Val one time."

"Oh," he ran a finger along his nose. "Well, my grandfather's name was not actually Vello Vikerkaar."

"Okay."

"He was a bank clerk in Vyborg in the Twenties. Then he met my grandmother Aino and moved to Tallinn. His real name was Ville Vikkenkoski, but the Estonians couldn't say that. Idiots. They called him Vello Vikerkaar. During the name campaigns of the 1930s, he had it changed to make his life easier. I think it was a mistake though. Vikkenkoski is a bad ass name."

"You're full of shit."

Vello recoiled and blinked. "What do you mean?"

"You're making that up, it's a bullshit story."

"Oh, well," he clicked his tongue. Then he stood up and walked into the kitchen. "He doesn't believe me," I heard him mutter aloud. "Hey, want some more tea?" He called out. "Or some *tapas*? I've got some hot *chorizo*. Just bought it in Madrid."

I'm not sure if Vello was being his true writer self that night or just a highly skilled bullshit artist. Maybe both. Later, as I began to follow him down into the rabbit hole of the literary world, I would wonder from time to time if there was any difference.

I had first heard of Vello through Val Koso, an Eskimo who used to work at the Estonian Foreign Ministry in the Nineties and early Noughties. It happened when Epp and I lived in New York. I had been thinking of ways to get back to the promised land and one was as a Fulbright Scholar. It was a moon shot, and it didn't happen in the end, but I tried anyway. That was an interesting time, when I was busy filling out application forms and collecting recommendation letters. Val, who was a reader of *Itching for Eestimaa*, had read about my activities and agreed to write a letter on my behalf, to further my nascent academic career.

But first, Val wanted to meet me in person. He asked me to buy him a copy of *The New Republic* magazine, which had a new article about Estonia authored by Tom Bissell in it, and to come to the Estonian House on 34th Street in Manhattan. I stopped by three kiosks on the way uptown before I finally grasped the sacred issue of *The New Republic* in hand, and laid it before the very brown man with the weathered face, squinty eyes, crop of jet black hair, pencil-thin mustache, and the smell of grill smoke about him. He was sitting patiently behind the old wooden bar sipping a drink.

"Here it is, Estonia in *The New Republic*!" he held the magazine aloft. "We've finally made it. Forgive my exuberance," he set the magazine down beside his beer. "I just get excited."

It's been a while, but I can sort of sketch out what I remember about that brief meeting with Val Koso. First, I still have no idea why Val Koso came to be connected with Estonia. He said he was an Aleut, and that his father ran a gallery in San Francisco that specialized in indigenous people's art. "It was just a part of the world that always intrigued me," Val said and grinned, revealing a row of very square, very ivory teeth. "I mean, coming from California ..."

That was the end of his explanation.

This intrigue had brought him into contact with some of the more influential politicians in the region, including Toomas Hendrik Ilves, Mart Laar, Lennart Meri, and Lithuanian President Valdas Adamkus.

"And I'll never forget what Valdas said to me after I had been working in Tallinn for a while and returned to Vilnius and he heard me talking. He said, 'Oh, no. Mart has brainwashed you, too.'" A light chuckle. "But Lennart, he never liked me. I don't know why. They sent me to meet him at the airport and he wouldn't even look me in the eye. Maybe it's because of the way I look," every line on his Eskimo face curled up into a delighted grin. "But Tom, the new president, and Mart; they liked me. Even though they locked me in the basement of the embassy in Washington one time."

"Locked you in the basement?"

"This was just how the embassy was," Val sighed. "They thought, 'We're Estonia, nobody knows us, so we always have to throw the wildest parties.' And I mean everybody in Washington came to those parties when Tom was there. Even the Russians came and partied. This was the Yeltsin era. So one night, everybody was really lit up and I was down in the basement and they shut the door on me. I thought they were joking. I'll never forget how Mart said, 'Explain this to the police when the alarms go off,' and waved a hand in front of his face, you know, because what the hell is an Eskimo like me doing in the Estonian embassy?"

There were other good stories that night. How Val was living in an old house in Kalamaja once when the roof blew off in a storm. Or how he was still in touch with Mart and how Mart was hoping to become foreign minister after the coming elections. "I think it's a position he would enjoy," Val said.

As for "Tom," Val still couldn't believe that he had become president. "But I know he is a great president. This is a position he has really coveted." But Val Koso was no longer working for the Estonians. He said he had just opened an Alaskan restaurant on the Lower East Side that specialized in seal and salmon burgers.

"We also have a vegetarian burger that tastes like seal," he said with a twinkle in his eye. "But I still do foreign relations. In fact, I have to go down to Washington in a week to train some new diplomats."

"Train them about what?"

"Estonia," he shrugged.

"What, do you teach them the proper way to eat blood sausage?"

Val just gave me another one of his titillated grins. He swallowed the rest of his beer, shook my hand, paid his bill, put on his winter parka, and walked with me to the door. Before we parted ways on the New York City sidewalks, he said one last thing to me.

"When you get to Estonia, either with the scholarship, or on your own, make sure to look up Vello Vikerkaar."

"Vello Vikerkaar," I repeated.

"Yeah, Vello Vikerkaar. He's an old friend of mine."

"What's your take on Val Koso?" Vello asked me at breakfast. "Do you think he's CIA?"

"Maybe," I said. "Not the best cover though. I mean an Eskimo? In Tallinn? Did Val ever tell you the story about how he got locked in the basement of the embassy in Washington?"

"He did," said Vello, ruffling a fresh copy of *Postimees*, the daily newspaper. "But did he tell you how he got out?"

"No."

"Yeah. He never told me how he got out either. I believe that Ilves did it to him though," he said. "That arrogant prick."

"I think he said Laar did it. Who knows though? Maybe he doesn't remember it right. Sounds like they were all drunk."

"They're all arrogant pricks. Politicians. But the absolute worst of them is still Edgar Savisaar."

We sat around a long wooden table talking, while Vello's wife Liina made us some herbal teas. There was a pitcher of tap water on the table, the base of which was filled with different colored rocks and crystals. "Liina says it has some kind of healing properties," Vello said, with a roll of the eyes.

Liina Vikerkaar was about as close to an Iroquois woman as an Estonian could get, with very dark eyes, and a very fine pretty features, and very fine, charcoal-colored hair, pulled up in a bun. She had a very fine speaking voice, too, clear, soft, precise, undulating in its femininity. Liina wore a light blue blouse and a pair of flowing Indian pajama pants, the kind the dancers wear in Bollywood movies. Liina had hitchhiked to India when she was younger.

"I really did, I went out here to the Tallinn-Tartu highway and held a sign that said 'India.'"

"What did your parents say?"

"I don't remember," she said. "I don't think they said anything."

Eventually, traveling via Greece to Turkey, through Iran and Pakistan, she made it, although she almost got caught up in a drug smuggling operation. "The Pakistani guard said, 'Just give me the bag. Don't ask what's in it. These people who gave you the bag are criminals.' She had recited this story once at a dinner party where all of the guests believed her. All but one.

"And I said, 'You didn't hitchhike to India! That story is just a load of bullshit.'"

That was the night she met Vello. They were married soon after.

The more I watched Liina in her Indian pants, and drank that special, crystal water, the more I came to understand that Vello and I had married the same woman. They had all met once already, just briefly, on that night when Vello and I had

had our first encounter at a casino restaurant to discuss ideas for his magazine. Vello, Liina, and me were in the car waiting for Epp to show up from an interview, and down the street she came in a red coat, with her locks of golden-red hair swinging about her shoulders, looking straight ahead as if lost in some fantasy of a story she had just made up. She was coming back from an interview, and I remember how proud I felt at that moment to see this big golden sun of a person, and realizing that we would go home together.

Vello was also impressed by Epp. "I don't care much for the writing on your blog," he said over breakfast. "But your wife's book about America had some truly fine writing. The way she raged against American materialism. She was like Carrie Nation, one of these firebrand temperance activists who went out before Prohibition, smashing up saloons with a hatchet."

"Yeah. It was a good book. What I could understand of it."

"You mean you didn't read it all?"

"Oh, come on. I'm not fluent in Estonian. "

"You're getting better though, Justin," Liina said softly. "You are already speaking quite well. Compared to that first night we met."

"You won't notice yourself improving, either," Vello said. "It will just happen over time. Anyway, Epp's book was great. Much better than this bullshit they serve up in *Postimees*."

He folded the paper and cast it away, where it landed beside a bowl of tropical fruit.

"Bitch, bitch, bitch," Liina muttered behind him, "bitch, bitch, bitch. That's all you do."

"This *Postimees* is like some pathetic local newspaper from Ontario," Vello said. "Half of it is full of stories about some Estonian who came in fourth in a pie-eating contest somewhere, you know, 'Local boy done good.' Any time an Estonian does anything of slight interest abroad they slap it on the front page. 'Estonian goes to Antarctica!' The other half is by guys like Priit Pullerits."

"The godfather of Estonian journalism?"

"Yeah, Pullerits. God, I'd love to punch him in the face. Him and all of them. These so-called 'media stars' with their opinion columns. 'How I see it.' As if anybody else gives a shit."

"Bitch, bitch, bitch," Liina said aloud again and walked out of the room.

"What? I'm just talking to Justin here. He's a young writer. He gets it. As I was saying, there are only a few Estonian journalists worth reading, and most of them write for *Eesti Ekspress*. It's still not as good as what you would get in most European cities but it's better than anything else. I am in touch with most of these reporters, I've taken them under my wing, to advise them on their craft. Which reminds me," he pushed a stack of books toward me across the table, "have a look at these."

I took Vello's books up and examined them one by one. The first was a biography of Chairman Mao, the Chinese Communist. The second was *Blink* by Malcolm Gladwell. And the third was *Chasing the Sea: Lost Among the Ghosts of Central Asia* by Tom Bissell.

"Now there's some fine writing," Vello nodded toward the last book. "It's about Uzbekistan. Bissell gave it to me when he visited. He's a talented young writer. Not much older than you, but he's written books, been published in most of the finest newspapers and magazines."

"Oh, cool."

There was a bit of jealousy in my throat as I said this, and I thought about my empty name tag at the conference. "And you, who are you?" A sad feeling weighted itself on my shoulders as I stared at the orange cover of the book, at the black and white image at its center, a camel, a rusted ship on a sandy prairie, and a solitary figure treading through the foreground.

Not much older than you… been published in most of the finest newspapers and magazines.

I looked back at Vello. "Why are you showing me this?"

"Oh, I've got too many books lying around," he chuffed. "I need to give them to another writer."

THE SPRING DISTURBANCES

*It wasn't long after that when Estonia was beset by the
spring disturbances.*

These were the events that followed the Andrus Ansip
government's decision to relocate the Bronze Soldier, a Soviet
World War II monument, from Tõnismägi in the center of
Tallinn, to a military cemetery.

To be honest, the statue did look out of place in that
triangular park situated between Saint Charles Church, the
Estonian National Library, and the stretch of avenue that led
to the Old Town. Tall and dark, with a morose but tough face,
a Red Army uniform on, complete with cape, backed by a
stone structure, he stood there. I walked by the bronze man
many times, only pausing sometimes to take note of him. The
statue made me uneasy, even back then, but I couldn't say
why. It was just troubling.

They called the soldier Alyosha, a nickname for Aleksei, a
common Russian name. Every year on May 9, Soviet Victory
Day, Tallinn's large Russian community would gather around
Alyosha and honor the sacrifice of the few white-headed
veterans who stood nearby with bouquets of red flowers in

their hands and decorations on their chests. This was one of the few times when you would see the old red and gold Soviet flag in public in Tallinn. It was like a scene from another century, a wrinkle in time.

The stone-faced Estonians would watch the curious festivities from the windows of the Tallinn trolleys. For them, May 9 was just another working day.

I had no idea that there were a dozen Soviet soldiers and military personnel buried beneath the statue, or that there had been a wooden memorial there before that had been blown up by two teenage dissidents, Aili Jurgenson and Ageeda Paavel, in 1946. Both girls were sent to the Gulag labor camp. Supposedly it was revenge for all the memorials to the Estonian War of Independence that had been crushed by the demolition-happy Soviets.

Six decades later, when the controversy broke out, Aili was interviewed in *Postimees*. She looked like a cute old grandmother with light pretty eyes, spectacles, curly white hair, and rosy red cheeks with dimples. You would never have thought her capable of blowing up anything.

It was bad, that's all I can say about the Bronze Soldier. Bad, bad, and more bad. It looked innocent. It looked like a simple war monument. But beneath that monument was blood and tragedy. When the Soviets took Estonia in 1940 and again in 1944, they purged its leadership, its social organizations, and waged total war. There were nightmare tales of pillage, rape, and murder. The Estonians' greatest fear was that it could happen again: to their daughters, sons, parents, themselves. To many Estonians, the image of a Soviet soldier represented this old wound and the 50-year-long period of submission to Moscow that followed.

The Russians, though, had suffered similar terrors on the other side of the border at the hands of the Germans and their accomplices. For them, the soldier represented their heroic sacrifice against the invading army. For them, it was good and holy.

So the monument was divisive. There was a geyser of septic blood contained beneath it. The Russian government knew this, the Estonian government knew this, and so when brawls began to break out there, and then the mass rioting, looting, and hysteria that coincided with its removal, it shouldn't have surprised anyone. My university professor Heiko Pääbo would later say that it happened because the older generation, the one that had experienced the war as adults, was dying out.

Lennart Meri was gone, and his cousin Arnold, who had been charged recently with genocide by the Estonian government for taking part in the 1949 deportations, would soon be gone, too. There would be one final battle between Communism and Fascism on the streets of Tallinn. Even I would come to hear the words Fascism and Communism as if they were still relevant, to understand the zero-sum mentality of authoritarian thinking. Because to some Russians under the spell of Stalin, the deportation and murder of Estonian civilians was *necessary* to prevent their collaboration with the Germans.

To some Estonians, the collaboration with the Germans was *necessary* to prevent the Soviet Army of Darkness from returning and revisiting hell upon the land. There were no more people, there was only right and wrong, good and evil and if you happened to be on the other side, then you were evil and not human. All of that killing was *necessary* in the eyes of the Fascists and the Communists. So violence in the streets of Estonia was *necessary*, to defend the men who had exerted so much energy killing each other.

But that violence was in Tallinn.

Tartu was different. In Tartu, those were but heavenly spring days. Sun on the Town Hall Square, a light breeze to chase away the winter blues and give a lift to the ladies' hair and skirts as they cycled by fountains. Living in Tartu, I thought that the spring disturbances would never touch me personally.

Yet the morning after the first night of unrest, I went outside to find that someone had torn the windshield wipers off my car, perhaps to demonstrate displeasure with Ansip's decision to move the monument.

For me, that meant one thing. I would have to visit the Scotsman and his partner Tähendab in Ülejõe.

The garage was hard to find, nestled in all of the construction and sprawl of the district, and the only real sign of the place was an old tire that had been mounted on the second story of the building.

To bring your car in, you had to drive around the back of the house and navigate a dirt courtyard. Inside, there were usually four guys, all of them albinos in jumpsuits who said little. It didn't matter what they said though because whatever they replied, it came out like the sound of someone trying to tell you something underwater, or an old record played backwards at the wrong speed in order to hear a secret message.

"*Möh möh. Möh möh. Möh möh möh.*"

Once I told my friend Andrei the blogger about the guys in the garage and my difficulty understanding them. Andrei told me not to worry, and that "nobody else can understand them, not even me, because they all come from Võru and speak the South Estonian dialect, which is like Finnish but stranger."

I always liked going into the garage though because of the posters of women on the walls. There were creative juxtapositions of leggy blondes and brunettes with motorcycles and quads and sports cars, so it looked like tanned brown arms morphed naturally into sets of metallic handle bars. These were Estonian posters, not imports, and there were calendars, too, for 2005 and 2006. That was one good thing about those calendars. Even when the year was over, there was no need to replace them. You could just mount the 2007 calendar girls next to the '05s and '06s. Though the nudity was a bit gratuitous, you had to admit that the calendars kept the peace in the garage, and the men worked in silence, covered in grease, with sparks shooting out and machines whirring.

I never learned the names of the two men I dealt with in the front office, but I referred to one as the Scotsman and the other as Tähendab. The Scotsman wore a tartan sweater. He would squint at me from behind his silver-rimmed glasses and tell me what was wrong with my car, and I would watch his mouth and imagine he was speaking Highland English instead. "*Süüteküünal*" would become "Haggis and cock-a-leekie soup." Then I would rush home and consult my illustrated Estonian-English dictionary to find out what the word *süüteküünal* meant.

It was a spark plug.

Tähendab also wore a sweater, but his was a more drab color like brown or maroon. Tähendab was a tall man with curly hair, a long face and big arms that ended with a shiny watch and hairy knuckles. He would fold those arms whenever he discussed a situation with me, frowning all the way through with the drawn-out restraint of an emergency room doctor. He started each sentence with the word, "*Tähendab*," which translates as "It means." Some Estonians begin sentences like this by habit, but for me it felt as if the man was translating some Sanskrit text as he knuckled through an auto parts catalog. "It means that it's time to order new tires," or, "It means that you need to change your oil."

It was Tähendab that I dealt with on the morning after the spring disturbances in Tallinn. Someone had torn my windshield wipers off in the middle of the night, taking one with him and leaving the other in a puddle in the street. Or so I thought. Because later I found out that our landlord Väino had seen a second windshield wiper lying further down the street and just left it there. "I thought it looked like one of yours," he said. I didn't bother to ask why he hadn't considered picking it up or returning it to us, because I knew that it wasn't Väino's problem.

So we had one windshield wiper. I was able to reattach this one, but I needed a replacement for the other. It wouldn't be that easy though because the SUV was what Estonians referred to as an "American car," which made it impossible to order a quick replacement.

"It means that you have an American car," Tähendab said. "It means that we could order it through Finland."

"How long do you think it could take?"

"It means that it could take a month."

"What? Come on. Finland isn't so far away, man. A whole month? It takes a whole month to get it? You mean that I have to drive with one windshield wiper around Estonia for a whole damn month?"

Tähendab folded his arms and frowned, as if he was about to tell me I had some terminal disease.

"It means that this is how things are. It means that, if you had a German car, I could fix it right away."

Epp's father Andres had warned me about this. When we were searching for a vehicle, the old man had made it very clear that we should buy a "German car," implying a Volks- wagen, although for the Estonians the brands of automobiles paled in importance when compared with the nation of ori- gin. Whether it was a Mercedes-Benz, Audi, a Volkswagen or Opel, it didn't matter. What mattered was that it was German, and even if VW's car manufacturing hub was outside of Lis- bon, that didn't enter into it, because there was likely a fussy manager named Fritz overseeing the operation.

Americans tended to ridicule what they saw as the Ger- mans' anal retentiveness, yet the Estonians respected it because they valued that same order and precision. They adored the fact that there were Volkswagen service points all over Estonia and that spare parts were plentiful. That meant that their cars could be fixed within hours, or even minutes, and that they wouldn't waste time, and could get back to work.

The odd thing was that the Estonians' main issues with Russia, including all of the problems that led up to the spring disturbances, derived from that special fondness for Germany. No one would admit it, but what the Russians hated about the Estonians, really hated about them, was their Germanic way of doing things. Their transparency, their punctuality, their love for every letter of the law. The way they adored new technology, with their online banking and pay-by-phone parking. It was all too nice and neat.

Around that time, I heard a story. Once, a Russian guy was speeding on the highways of Estonia and was pulled over by the police. He tried to pay the officer to get out of trouble, as is the custom in his country, and was promptly arrested for trying to bribe a public official. There could be no more egregious sin in Estonia than breaking the rules.

If the Germans as an occupying power during the Second World War were ever regarded positively by some Estonians, it wasn't because of their sterling human rights record, but because they were a source of high quality modern goods. For the Estonian who whispered to another in his cramped Khrushchevka kitchen in the darkest Brezhnev years that, "It might have been better had the Germans won," did not say so out of his belief in the superiority of the master race, but because had the Germans won the war, they might have built sturdier apartments with roomier kitchens. Even the Estonian Russians agreed on this. We had seen apartments during our real estate search that had been advertised by local Russians as being built by German prisoners after the war as a sign of craftsmanship! Had the Germans won there might have been Volkswagen service points all over the land, replenished by weekly shipments of spark plugs and windshield wipers. Efficiency! Reliability! This is what the Estonians treasured more than any gold.

It was this deeply-held belief in the superiority of the Germans and their Northern Germanic cousins in Scandinavia, this feeling of soul mate kinship, that led the Estonians to look West as the Soviet Union fell apart and induced them to join the European Union and then the common currency. Soon it looked as if the Germans *had* won the war, as Volkswagen service centers opened everywhere and Angela Merkel descended the steps of the Estonian Parlament to the applause of all lawmakers. Nothing could have annoyed the Russians more, to see the peasants of a former imperial province turn their backs on their ballet and literature in favor of Germany and its cars. What the Russians didn't understand was that the Estonians were practical people, and while Bulgakov and Tchaikovsky were nice, getting a replacement part for that broken down Volkswagen Sharan was just more important. And as for Russian cars? Those were a joke.

I returned home from the garage with one windshield wiper. Epp was in the kitchen leaning over her computer and I informed her of the news. She didn't seem to pay it much notice. Who could care about a windshield wiper when a teenager named Dmitri Ganin lay dead in a Tallinn hospital from stab wounds, Tallinn was littered with broken glass, stolen goods and burned cars, and foreign media had already begin to refer to events as the worst civil disturbances to hit the country since the 1940s.

A hundred people were arrested that first night, and up to a thousand would be detained in coming days. The Estonian embassy in Moscow would be besieged by Nashi activists, members of the pro-Kremlin youth group. Licenses for strong liquor were suspended by the Tallinn City Government. Soon after, Estonian authorities announced a ban on all liquor sales across the country until May 9. This meant that every Tartu student was in the supermarket before prohibition went into effect, loading up shopping carts with as many bottles of vodka, beer, cider, and anything remotely alcoholic as would fit. After that, the rows of wines and stacks of beer were covered in tarps and the local youth had to drive south to Latvia to replenish their stockpiles. No Tartu student could go to bed sober on Walpurgis Night.

"It's just terrible," Epp told me that day in the kitchen, with a distressed look in her eyes. "A young man has been stabbed to death, hundreds have been arrested."

"They should have been arrested," I said. "That's what happens when you fight with the police."

"But can't you see? Now they will all go to prison together. This is how terrorist cells are formed!"

She had a point.

"You have to understand how holy the war is for the Russians," Epp continued. "When I was a girl there were only war movies on at this time of year. It's a major part of their identity. Oh, why did Ansip have to move that soldier?"

"But they deported both of your mother's grandfathers. They deported your aunt. Your father's uncle died in one of their camps. Aren't you angry about that? Doesn't the monument remind you of that?"

Epp shook her head. "Nobody talked about that when I was a child. That came later. But the movies, they were like the first layer. And the other layers came later. It's just, I can see with that first layer how badly this hurts Russians. It could have been handled a different way. They knew they were going to move the monument. They could have just waited until May 9, given them one last ceremony there, and then done it when it was over. Not like this, with fences and tents, with the soldier whisked away in the middle of the night."

She wasn't alone. Edward Lucas had said more or less the same thing on his blog about how it had all been handled poorly. It was only later, after a delegation from Moscow suggested the Ansip government should resign, and the Swedish ambassador's car was attacked on its way to the Estonian Embassy in Moscow, and cyber attacks on the country captured the international imagination, that arguments over whether or not it was wise to move the monument were drowned out by other concerns.

"It's just a war monument," I said in the kitchen.

"But that's not how Russians see it. For them, it's a holy monument. Holy Alyosha."

Just then, Epp's phone rang. Through the line, I could hear the husky, exuberant voice of an older man. Epp listened to the older man speak and speak. For some reason, older men always liked to talk to her a lot, and carry on such one-sided conversations, and she only managed to get in a few affirmative declarations before the conversation was over. "That was one of my blog readers," she sighed.

"What did he say?"

"Oh, he's very happy that Ansip decided to move the monument. He said that for his generation, this was one of the most hated symbols of Soviet power in Tallinn. He says Ansip has some real balls. He said that the Red Army behaved the same way when they came into Tallinn in 1944."

At that moment, Aili Jurgenson, one of those teenage Estonian girls who had blown up the first monument on Tõnismägi in 1946, was probably listening to the radio and sipping tea at home, smiling to herself.

Ansip actually spent some of those restless nights in Tartu, or so I heard. It was said that he was being kept in a safe house somewhere nearby that was heavily guarded by *Kaitseliit*, the National Guard, as were all of the houses in the vicinity. They had received threats against Ansip's life. I imagined our prime minister quivering in bed in his pajamas. And, to think all of this had happened because he wanted to move a war memorial.

In retrospect, I think Ansip had a much more metaphysical grasp on what was at stake on Tõnismägi. An avid cross country skier with the face of a fox, he sensed Estonia was a magical country. All over the land, one encountered *energiasambad*, energy columns, specific places pinpointed by psychics where the energy was so strong it could heal various maladies. The strongest energy column was near the Tuhala Witch's Well in Kose Parish, but one nearly as strong stood in Otepää, the winter capital and home to Olympic gold medal skier Kristina Šmigun.

What Ansip perhaps grasped was that the Bronze Soldier was a massive Soviet energy column built to collect and discharge the energy of Stalin's regime. It had stood peacefully through the tumult of the 1990s and early 2000s, but with Putin's regime again transmitting, it was imperative that the Bronze transponder be switched off, removed, and reassigned an Estonian context – in a military cemetery – before the rejuvenated satanic Stalinist energy became too powerful for even NATO to resist.

Ansip had surgery in mind, as I now see it. He would at last pluck the splinter from Estonia's wound. It would be painful and messy, but it had to be done.

Epp didn't see it that way. Hers was an open, caring soul. All through that day, the unease of what was going on in Tallinn seemed to engulf Tartu. I tried to log on for online banking only to see the website was down. Nobody had spread the news about the cyber attacks, but you could see something was going on. In the afternoon, I saw a young girl with yellow locks skipping down the street, crying out "*Kuradi venelased*"

(Fucking Russians). It was then I understood the anguish that lingered in the souls of these people. I also understood that Epp was in the minority when it came to having empathy for those on Alyosha's side. Mostly there were only two options: the Estonian viewpoint and the Russian viewpoint.

That was that.

There were two things that calmed the passion of the rioters. One was the ban on alcohol, and the other was the weather. Most people don't recall this now, but the days on April 26 and April 27, when most of the spring disturbances took place, were warm. The iconic image of Jevgeni Kazakov, better known as Kokk Ženja, the young cook who was photographed by *Postimees* shoplifting a bottle of Sprite, candy bars, and a package of feminine hygienic pads from a shop on the first night of looting, shows a young, sandy-haired, blue-eyed man, dressed in a light jacket with a thrill-loving grin on his face.

But when I went out in Tartu on Walpurgis Night, April 30th, with Andrei the blogger and Jens, another blogger friend who had come up to visit us from Germany, it became so cold that it began to sleet. It snowed on May 1 in Estonia. It would snow on May 2 as well. And with the snow, all of the unrest withered. Estonia was not Israel. It was just too cold for endless domestic conflicts.

On Walpurgis Night, even as the students paraded around in their caps and uniforms, from party to party, the three of us had witnessed a young angry man wearing a Russian flag as a cape get an earful from a policeman down on Rüütli Street, one of the main streets in Tartu city center. The young man, a muscular sort who had shaved all the hair from his head and was dressed all in black, had been screaming about fascists, or so Andrei, who was a native Russian speaker, had translated. The two argued until the bad weather forced both of them to go home. But Jens and I were baffled by how well the police officer knew Russian. He seemed to speak it fluently. When we said this to Andrei, he dismissed us as idiots.

"But don't you know?" said Andrei. "Most of the police force in Estonia *is* Russian."

What kind of quicksand had I stepped into in Estonia? From the outside, the country looked so cute and quaint. It was only once you were deep inside it that you realized just how difficult it would be to sort any of this out. It was just absurd, as absurd as Estonian Russian kids throwing Molotov cocktails at Estonian Russian policemen. Some students even had live grenades with them, it was rumored. Were they about to throw those towards their fathers and uncles in the police force?

You can imagine the great relief I felt when we packed up our car in the first days of May and headed up to the north coast, through miles of gorgeous countryside and forests, to visit our new friends David and Triin. We needed a bit of a holiday, some peace, a chance to let go of our long-held breath.

Everybody did.

TINY PEARLS

We were the exceptions, the "tiny pearls" as Triin called us, the foreign men who were willing to blend in.

We were the Yankees who refused to Americanize their families, or to live as tourists in Tallinn in perpetuity. We were Justin and David and we were very weird.

"Most American guys aren't like you two," said Triin, rinsing out rhubarb stalks in the kitchen of her north coast country house. "Most of them stay in and around Tallinn for 10 or 20 years, only know how to say 'Tere,' and that's about it. Actually most of them come for a few years and then have to move back to America, you know. *Marjamaa.*"

"*Marjamaa*?

"It's an expression," she said. "It means the 'Land of Berries.' The hills there are made of cake and the rivers flow with milk."

"Oh, the Land of Milk and Honey."

"I am just not one of these Estonians, who goes to America and looks at all of the shopping centers and thinks 'Wow, everything is better.' It is possible to live well here, too."

"Are you some kind of nationalist?"

"Oh, I don't know. It's just possible to live different ways. Not everybody has to live the same way."

That was Triin. She was a feisty, effervescent little woman. Blue dress with spiraling pink and white flower patterns, golden hair, Gulf-of-Finland-green eyes, and a face that brought to mind a lion or a tiger. Some kind of impressive jungle beast. Triin had a very elegant, clipped manner of speaking, too, with influences from American and British English, so that when she spoke, if you closed your eyes, you might think you were on a yacht off Hyannis. She pronounced her husband's name lovingly. David was never just David.

For Triin, he was always "Dayyy-vid."

How did this Dayyy-vid look? He looked like a man. Every bit of him was mannish, from his toes to the short gray hairs on the crown of his head. It was only his face that retained a boyish, mischievous quality. It was the face of a 1960s cartoon character boy. His eyes, his nose, his mouth, it was like they had been drawn in ink. David had the facial expressions of a cartoon character, too. When David was really happy, you knew David was really happy. When David was thirsty, you knew David was thirsty.

You also knew that David was thirsty because he would stride over to his liquor cabinet and pull out a bottle of amber-colored Japanese Hibiki Whiskey that he kept mostly for private consumption.

"Gentlemen," he would announce. "I am starting to feel a certain ... *itch* in the back of my throat. I do believe it is about that time."

Then me and Laur, who was Triin's younger brother, would rise solemnly from the kitchen table, and David would distribute the shot glasses to all of us as if they would be our last victuals before heading into battle. He would raise his glass and look each of us in the eye through the liquid, and then he would tip his glass back and we would tip ours back and the whiskey would rush down hot.

I was never a hard liquor lover, and I tried to keep my face straight while the jet fuel napalmed the lining of my stomach and sent a plume of atomic gas up my esophagus and out through my ear canals. My eyes watered, my tongue burned, and there was a restrained cough. David had a happy face through the whole ceremony. It was such great fun to watch the two little brothers choke and gargle on big brother's hooch. "You know, boys, I was up until three o'clock this morning on a conference call with Japan sipping whiskey," he said with a wink.

David usually drank hard liquor, seldom wine, and never beer. I brought him two cases of ale on our first visit to his summer house. That was eight years ago. As far as I know, those two cases of beer are still sitting where I left them.

David was unusual in many ways.

For one, he ran a rare metals factory out in Sillamäe, a coastal town not too far from Narva, the real border metropolis, so close to Russia and full of Russians that it almost *was* Russia. But Sillamäe was even more unusual than Narva. Its factory was originally started as a Swedish shale oil extraction plant in 1926, and by the look of it, some of those brick buildings might have dated to that time. It was nationalized by the Soviets in 1941, who used the plant to produce uranium for the remainder of their rule. Uranium, enriched and unenriched. It was used to power nuclear applications, power plants, and submarines. A closed town of about 15,000 Russophone workers and their families was one of these legacies. A radioactive pond was another.

"The Russians took a lot of the equipment back with them when they left," David told me when we drove out to visit his factory in Sillamäe. "But they took no responsibility for the radioactive pond. They blamed that one on the 'Soviets.' 'It wasn't us.'" It took a decade for Estonia, working together with the other Nordic countries, to treat the site and make it environmentally safe.

The city of Sillamäe was like a big pink, yellow, and white wedding cake of Stalinist architecture. Everything about the city, which had been closed to outsiders during most of Soviet rule, was planned, from Pavlov Avenue to Gagarin Boulevard. To me, this orderliness gave it the peaceful air of a giant outdoor mental institution. The old men and women in its perfectly symmetrical parks were not mere residents of this City of Sillamäe. They were lifelong patients.

The rare metals plant itself was something out of a James Bond movie. All of those levers and cranes and shafts. The metallic ramps leading out one window and into another. The lasers for metal cutting. It was just built for good fight scenes. David was not in as great shape as Daniel Craig, and yet he had that same sensei-like countenance to him, perhaps acquired from working with Estonian men. I believed that if there had been a brawl across the territory of the factory, he would have easily won. The two main products at the factory were called niobium and tantalum. When David spoke about either of these metals, he would become strangely excited.

"The thing about tantalum," he would say, in a higher pitched, full-throttle-thrilled voice, "is that it is highly non-corrosive. That's why it's used in DVD players, mobile phones, video game systems, and computers. Niobium, on the other hand, can be added to strengthen steel or so-called superalloys. That's why it's used in jet engine components, gas turbines, rocket sub-assemblies, turbocharger systems, and heat resisting and combustion equipment."

Then he gave you a look as if to say, "Isn't that so cool?"

He really was a Bond villain. Except that he was on our side.

Niobium and tantalum were what David talked about at 3 a.m. on the phone with Japan while sipping whiskey. This was what hundreds of people in Sillamäe produced day in and day out at the plant. To get in and out, you had to go through a metal detector, not only because they were afraid you might bring in a rifle and start shooting, but because some of the more devious Silmet employees would hide the rare metals in their pockets and sell them on the black market.

"The black market metals trade was huge in Estonia in the Nineties," David said.

"But do you really lose so much when a guy pockets a piece of metal?"

"If he walks out of here with his pockets full every day, we have a big problem."

The company was starting to experience unusual problems since the spring disturbances. It imported much of its raw materials from Russia. But suddenly, the tracks into Estonia were shut down for maintenance – indefinitely. David had to route everything through Latvia instead. Russia and Estonia were no longer trading. One influential Russian politician, Sergei Ivanov, suggested that Russians should show their displeasure by boycotting Estonian sprats.

"Somebody somewhere better figure out a solution to this," David said. "Soon."

Little did he know, but the sudden "renovations" on the Estonian-Russian railroad lines would last for years...

The company's headquarters was a creamy palatial white building in the Stalinist style that had been built by orphans after the war. "We tried to get those darn hammers and sickles off the columns, but they told us that the columns would crumble if we did," David said inside the building. Then we went to his office where he spoke British English to a colleague on speaker phone.

Perfect British English. Yet David was just some kid from Ohio. At least, that's what he said.

David's story was that he had left Ohio as a teenager to go surfing in Australia. "That's where I learned to take care of myself. Live by my own wits." He can still speak Australian as good as any other surfer. But back in the US, he became restless and got a sponsorship to Estonia.

That's where he met his host sister Triin. They managed to stay uninvolved for two weeks.

David was famous for speaking pure Estonian and purer English. These were distilled, unaccented versions of the languages, so that anybody in a conference room in São Paulo or Kohtla-Järve would be able to understand. The joke was that someone had complimented Lembit, his father-in-law, on David's English-speaking abilities.

"He sounds almost like a real American!"

David and Triin lived in Ohio for a few years, but moved back to Estonia when their first daughter was born in 1998. Then David went to work at an industrial firm in Kohtla-Järve. From the beginning, his working language was Estonian.

"I remember coming home and not wanting to talk to anyone because my head hurt so bad," David said. "I was like, 'Don't speak Estonian to me. Don't speak English to me.' It was tough."

Though his English was flawless, when David brought out the whiskey, his voice acquired a bit of a southern hillbilly twang, and you remembered that he was from the country. It was like David was gone and we were drinking with Huckleberry Finn. Huckleberry Dave looked skeptically at me as I recounted my wood heating stories, about Väino's Magic Trick, about Woodsman Mats, about how sad I felt burning Kristina Šmigun's picture, even while he paused to toss logs on his own great fire. The blue-yellow flames flickered behind the wall of glass.

"That's right," he said. "I forgot you was city folk. I guess you New Yorkers don't have those furnaces anymore. I learned this stuff when I was a kid! Hey, want some peanut butter and crackers?"

"Sure." I took some off a plate. Peanut butter never tasted better than after a shot of whiskey.

"Hang on, just a sec." David pointed a remote at the stereo system and music came on.

It was the Beastie Boys. "Brass Monkey." An old school rap song I used to listen to with my friends when I was about eight years old. I guess David was about seventeen then. But we both knew it. *"Put your left leg down your right leg up/ Tilt your head back let's finish the cup."*

"That's better," he said. "Gentlemen. Could I interest you in another round of moonshine?"

In these moments with David and his whiskey, peanut butter, and "Brass Monkey," it was easy to forget that you weren't in America. We could be in a cabin somewhere in the hills of Ohio. You had to look out the window, to all of those pines, to remind yourself that you were still in Estonia.

One other thing I can tell you about David and Triin's place is that it always felt like home, homier than any of our homes, though we tried to make all of them homey. They were just more settled people than we were, I guess, and it came out in the calm air of that brightly lit kitchen, of wooden floor boards sanded so smooth it was soothing just to walk barefoot across them.

That sense of eternal peace was something I always missed when I was in America. The things I missed in Estonia about America were distinct. I missed the sand dunes on the coast, or the harbors with all of the masts from the sailing ships. I missed the clam chowder, the salty sea. But when I was in America, I missed the comfort of wooden Estonian homes like Triin and David's, houses that breathed tranquility, houses that had always been alive.

Epp and I both felt content in such a setting and started to scheme about getting our own summer place. I can't remember many of our conversations, but I do know that Epp nestled into a nook on the deck and started writing, while Marta played with Teele and Toomas, who weren't much older than our little three year old, beneath giant trees, in treehouses, on enormous boulders covered in moss.

It was so ideal that the original plan of us staying in Estonia only for a few years started to feel false. Wrong. Off. I couldn't say why. I had told so many people in the US we would come back. It just felt like we were *supposed* to be there in Estonia. It felt like we were *supposed* to stay forever.

Big decisions were made on those nights, made without even speaking.

On the wall in David and Triin's home there was a framed black and white image from a century past. The same house was there, though covered in planks of dark wood and looking a bit more ramshackle. Pictured was an old woman beside it, dressed in a black dress, smoking a pipe.

"I have always wondered who that woman was," David said.

To get to their retreat, you came down a winding driveway under tall pine trees until you reached the cozy rectangle of a home with its fine glassed-in porch. Inside the house, there was the kitchen and the living room with its couches, the porch with its lounges and tables, and then upstairs, three bedrooms, one for David and Triin, one for their daughter Teele, and the last for their son Toomas. The stairs were little more than a built-out ladder, which gave the place that added feeling of wildness and remoteness. Beyond the house stood the log guest cabins and the outhouse, with its rough wooden seat. There was also a cellar built into the side of a hill, so that one could descend through its porthole-like aged wooden door to the dark underground space, where David kept jams and some of the pump paraphernalia associated with the well.

At the very edge of this small estate stood the sauna, a hot temple of thick dark logs and tiny windows that glowed yellow at night. The smoke puffed from the chimney, filling the air with the sweet aroma of civilization. You heard owls and strange unknown creatures in the forests, and accommodated the heaviness of the sea, which made no sound but could be sensed and felt.

"You know, if we had stayed in the US, there's just no way I could have had a life like this," David said.

The sauna had a way of pulling the truth out of people, the same way it made them sweat. David sweat and I sweat beside him. On the otherside of David, Laur was perspiring too, and way down on the other side of the sauna, Lembit, David's father-in-law lay stretched out in silence, barely aware of our conversation.

"What were you doing in America? Before you came here and your business career took off?"

"Working for Victoria's Secret."

"The women's lingerie store?"

"Yep. We worked like hell. And before that, I worked for the postal service. Unloading all of those boxes. We started working at 5 a.m." He wiped the sweat from his eyes like he was wiping away bad dream.

"Don't you think it's a little weird?"

"What?"

"In America, you were moving boxes. Here, you are the head of a rare metals company. You have a beautiful family, you have a house right on the Gulf of Finland."

"Sure, I'm lucky."

"It's not luck, I'm talking to you about, David. How the heck does that happen?"

David raised an eyebrow. "What are you trying to say?"

"There's a weird sort of energy in this country. It pulls some people in and it spits others out."

"Well, I don't know about weird energy," David said and chuckled. "I think it's just that you and me took the risk. Most people, they do what they think they are expected to do. But I think that in life, you have to take risks. Sometimes they work out, sometimes they don't. I've taken plenty of risks in my life that didn't turn out well. But some of them turned out great."

Most of our conversations took this big-brother-little-brother trajectory. When David spoke, I listened, but I listened so carefully because I agreed with a lot of what he said. I envied him because he was so certain in his opinions. Mine were all wishy-washy, and even if I tried to feign confidence, there was still that quiver or waver in the voice that projected deep uncertainty.

When it has been made to clear to you by family members and friends that most of the risks you have taken in life were tragic mistakes that robbed you of some brighter, better future, you come to doubt yourself, even if to any other person your life might seem ideal.

"How does your family feel about you living here?" were the next words out of my mouth.

David just shook his head, as if he didn't understand the question. "My parents gave up on me when I was a teenager," he said. "Of course, they wish I was there in Ohio. But if I let them know that I am happy, and these are the people I want to be with, then they have to respect that."

It sounded so simple.

How would my brother feel if he were here in a sauna between me, David, his brother-in-law Laur, and his father-in-law Lembit? Had my brother ever been in a sauna? What about my dad? Would he even try it, or would it seem too weird to run naked down to the beach and dive in? I had gone to the sauna before with some friends in college. But we were offbeat, adventurous types. If they saw me now, relatives and friends might call me a freak. Too few people at home knew what I now knew in Estonia. Too few of them had come to know that delicious smell of hot wood.

"One more *leili**?" David asked. Lembit and Laur grunted.
"Leili?" I said. "Who's Leili?"

There was no time to hear David's answer. He tossed more water onto the rocks, maybe too much, because when the steam came off it stung my ears and I reached to cover them. Then my fingernails and toenails began to ache down to their roots. A real throbbing pain. All of my body hurt like that, and with that kind of hot sauna steam it was hard to breathe, and so you did it slowly, letting the hot air into your lungs little by little, even though your lungs ached. I pressed my back up against the hot wall of the sauna and that stung too. It was a pain trap. Everywhere I turned, there was only more pain. I longed for something cool to take it off, something really, really cold, but I didn't want to move until the others made the first move. But nobody stirred. They just sat there in the heat, David all sweaty and pink, Laur, a big blotchy mess, Lembit still stretched out on a lower bench, nearly invisible because of all the sauna steam.

At last David said, "I'm done," and sprang for the door. We all followed. Down the mossy path to the rocky beach and then into the cool, black waters of the gulf that ease every ache.

"I'm so glad you decided to get out of the sauna," I said. "I was going to die in there."

"Then why didn't you leave?" asked Laur.

"I didn't want you guys to think I was a coward."

"Why would you be a coward?" David asked, floating nearby.

---

*   The Estonian word «Leili» translates as «vapor» or «steam.» And Leili also is a woman's name in Estonia.

"Because I couldn't stand the heat."

"So what?" said Laur. "Do you want to win a competition for who can stay in the sauna longest?"

"Nobody will notice if you stay the longest," David said. "They'll start talking about you if you pass out in the sauna because you stayed too long. Then you will look stupid."

"Oh, yeah, people will talk about you," said Laur. "They'll be like, everybody, look. There goes the guy who passed out in David's sauna last week."

We were silent for a while.

"Hey – when is your wife due?" David said to me. "I could see she's got a big beautiful belly under her dress."

"You could see that, huh?"

"That's right. I could see all of it."

"That's funny. I noticed your wife had a nice dress on."

"Oh, that? I bought it for Triin in Brazil on a business trip. You liked it, huh?"

"Will you guys stop talking about my sister," said Laur. "When's the baby coming?"

"A little girl due for late July. Maybe Epp will even give birth on her birthday."

"Wouldn't that be something. A baby for a birthday gift," said David.

And so it went, on the edge of a dark wood, where one could imagine the giants of folk tales stomping about the ferns and the boulders. After the steam and clash of the sauna, we stayed there, with arms stretched out beneath the stars, in the cool waters of the gulf, where we floated like angels.

ANNA, LIKE ANNA HAAVA

The phone tinkled from its place on the window sill and I went to fetch it.

It was about eight o'clock at night, but still sunny out. Warm, a fine breeze coming in over the rooftops of the pretty city with a fresh, clean smell. I loved Tartu, I could snuggle endlessly in its embrace. Yet I felt it was too different from my childhood home to become my real home.

Sometimes, when I was out there driving around its outskirts, among all those yellow fields, sweat on my head, I felt as if I had been transplanted there by a spaceship, with memory erased. I wasn't from here. I had not known its ancient cobblestone streets as a child, the same way I knew the fine grainy texture of the Atlantic's sand dune beaches. But Tartu would soon enough be somebody's home. It would even be her birthplace.

I remember that soft summer light, the rectangle of shine it cast on the floor of the hospital room, and the way it glinted off the green and golden leaves on the thick old trees that guarded the perimeter of the cream-colored building on Toomemägi. You could see the reflections of the leaves and the sky on the face of a Nokia telephone.

"Hello?"

"Justin, it's Triin and David." I could hear the sound of a car in the background. I imagined them both driving around in a convertible, somewhere on the coast. I wasn't sure if they had a convertible, but that's how I saw it. I could see them, how wonderful they were. David was wearing a flat cap and Triin's golden hair was blowing in the wind.

"Hello!"

"We just called to wish Epp a happy birthday and see how she is doing today. *Kas ta on veel ühes tükis või?*"

This was a question that Estonian women asked on a certain occasion. It meant, "Is she still in one piece?"

"She is," I answered them and looked at the woman in the bed. "But won't be for long."

"What? Really?" I heard my American friend David say in Estonian. "Right now?"

The headline on one website the following day read, "Epp Petrone Gave Birth on Her 33rd Birthday." I wasn't sure how newsworthy it was, and I did think about Vello Vikerkaar's bitching about the self-centeredness of the Estonian media, but I saved the story anyway for posterity. Miss Anna Petrone, born at Tartu University Hospital, in a big old house surrounded by big old trees.

That hospital was closed shortly after, and the maternity ward was moved to the new clinic, a more modern, Scandinavian-feeling jumble of geometry, metal and glass outside of the city center. Today, the previous hospital houses the journalism department of the university. The delivery rooms have been converted into classrooms. But the splendid interior remains. The creamy peach color of the walls, the black and white checkered tile floors, the dark wooden handrails that lead up the staircases, the great chandelier that hangs above the desk at the front, but the old nurse seated behind it is gone.

We didn't come through the front that day. We came in through the side, checked in at a desk downstairs, where there was a nurse who looked exactly like Brunhilde, that fat Viking goddess, and took an elevator up. At least, I think we did, and I think that nurse looked exactly like Brunhilde. All of my children's births have this blurry, dream-like quality.

But this much is true – Anna was born there on her mother's birthday. Not only do I remember it, but there was even an Internet news article written about it. It must be true.

A lot of important people were born in that hospital, such as the politicians Andrus Ansip, Rein Lang, Jaak Aaviksoo, and Jürgen Ligi. Even the Olympic gold medalist skier Kristina Šmigun had been born there. It was a place where great people were born, and our littlest greatest person, too, perhaps in the same room where Ansip and Šmigun first saw light.

To get there by car, you drove straight up the cobblestones of Lossi Street, passing between the columns that supported the ancient *Inglisild*, or Angel's Bridge, which connected two of Toomemägi Park's steep hills and was traversable only by foot. Or you could opt for the path that led straight up from behind the University's main building, at an almost perfect 45 degree angle. This way was notorious among women for its back-breaking incline, especially in winter, when the icy path was treacherous. Yet generations of pregnant women had ascended that hill on foot, in any weather, most of them already in labor, perhaps a few in heels. Estonian ladies. They were a tough breed.

I climbed the same path that evening, with Marta on my shoulders, and a phone at my ear, so that I could call my mother and father, from whom the word of the new arrival would spread across the Atlantic. Marta was only three and a half then, with her light brown hair cut in bangs across the front, and sat alert as we trudged up the slope of that path that had tortured so many pregnant ladies. I did break a sweat by the time we reached the top. We slumbered together that night in one of the rooms they had for families. All four of us in a row. The room didn't cost much, and we lived there peacefully for a few days, as Anna adjusted to her new life. I would leave and go clean our new Tähtvere house and when I returned, Epp would be sitting by the window, reading a newspaper, with the gorgeous baby sleeping across her lap.

Summer is a great time to be born. In the weeks that followed, the angel child slept in a little cradle in our new backyard, surrounded by buzzing insects that, for some reason, didn't even notice she was there. She was a round and

154

pleasant chubby baby, with light peach fuzz for hair, peaceful and curious about the world when she was awake, mesmerized by the movement of a bird, or of her own hand. Maybe I was mowing the lawn or picking some plums from the trees, but I don't even really remember where I was at this time. I lived by deadlines, churning out transcripts and papers and articles and it seemed like some deadening machine was running me around, like I was empty within. I plucked Anna up into my arms and brought her around the yard to show her some of the flowers. I loved to hold her, but it was one of the few things I truly loved at that time. I didn't love work, and I didn't love feeling guilty for living so far away from my parents. But I did love to kiss my baby's head, or to stroke the soft bit of her chest, right below the neck as she dozed while we took her with us to the post office or the market.

We bought the berries that were in season, and bags full of pickles, some more fermented than others. We bought yellow potatoes, fresh dill, and butter, and ate them with gusto at the table I had made from old wood and a metal frame in the backyard. Epp had recommended I try to make one. In Estonia, you just made tables like that, you see. You measured it and cut it and screwed it together. Done.

Just do it yourself. Like a real Estonian man.

But I wasn't a real Estonian man. I felt like an alien within myself. Maybe it was all of the moves that had created this oblivion space empty feeling within me. In half a year I had

155

moved from New York to Estonia, into an apartment in Karlova, only to dump it within a few months for a house with a yard in Tähtvere.

How did this latter move happen? Even this is blurry in my memory. I was on a business trip in Oxford, staring at a PowerPoint presentation about population genetics, when Epp called me to say that she wanted to move out of Väino's luxury apartment. I excused myself and went to speak to her in the hall.

"Wait. You want to do what?"

"Move. I've already found a few places online. They are all in Tähtvere."

"Again?" I slapped a hand over my eyes. "But – but we just moved in! This is crazy."

That Epp. She was full of crazy ideas. And yet sometimes they were pretty good.

One of Epp's finds was a house on Anna Haava Street, a two-story construction from the 1930s, with a walk-up staircase, old wooden windows with vintage undulating glass panes, and a run-down but charming tiled roof.

The street was named after a famous poetess who was active in the late 19th and early 20th centuries. An old black-and-white photo showed a pleasant enough country woman's face, with a hint of empathy around the eyes, and even a little sadness. I knew her name because I had it in the back of my head that our children should all be named after Estonian writers. This was because I had discovered a line of verse by a lesser-known poetess named Marta Lepp and was so pleased that we had named our first child Marta. In her photo, Marta Lepp looked like a stout, more childish-looking wench with thick lips and a thick plaited braid on one side of her head. I thought she was pretty. I liked those Estonian artist girls.

And Marta Lepp had written the greatest poem I ever read, in Estonian, English or any tongue

It began, "*Vurr, vurr... vurr, vurr... Udu, muda... muda, udu... Voki vurrab. Igav on mu vaikne kodu. Südant murrab.*"

It meant something like this: "Whirl, whirl... whirl, whirl... fog, mud... mud, fog... The spinning wheel whirls. Boring is my quiet home. It breaks my heart."

At that time I had only a vague idea what it meant, but I loved it, loved the sounds, the repetition, the music. In my mind our Marta and Anna had some translucent ghost line connecting them to Marta Lepp and Anna Haava. These two Estonian woman had created beautiful things that gave comfort to others, which, to me, was the most significant thing a person could do.

That's why they named streets after them.

The interior of the house on Anna Haava Street had not been changed in seven decades. Glossy dark wood furniture, camel hump sofas, an antique radio, stacks of moldy-smelling books, an ancient toilet complete with chain, a furnace for the bath water, an archaic kitchenette with aged pipes hanging everywhere and vibrant patterns on the walls that reminded me of the lickable wallpaper from Willie Wonka's factory. The door to the toilet had a moveable disc, encased in metal and hand operated by a switch, so that if it was occupied, it would show *Kinni*, and if it was unoccupied, it showed *Lahti*.

The real estate agent said that the house had belonged to a deceased relative, and that he may or may not leave the furniture, if we decided to buy it. He also said that some of the more important Estonian politicians had visited there in the 1930s, including Jaan Tõnisson himself.

Jaan Tõnisson?

Born near Viljandi in 1868, Tõnisson was a tall, lanky lawyer, with a bushy mustache, a long, angular face that recalled some kind of Arctic bird, and black top hat that made him even more imposing. Tõnisson was one of the architects of the Estonian state and its outlook. He had served as its state elder, its prime minister, and its foreign minister. He was also head of the last fully democratic government, before Konstantin Päts and Johan Laidoner took power in 1934. From then on, Tõnisson was estranged from any powerful position, yet was always lurking to reemerge. One can only imagine that had Estonian democracy been reestablished at the end of the war, he might have served as an elder statesman for the remainder of his life, comparable to West Germany's Konrad Adenauer, or Finland's Juha Paasikivi – someone from the Old Europe that had been blasted away during the world wars, somebody with a long memory, somebody wise.

But that was not to be. The Soviets arrested Tõnisson in 1940 and tried him for resisting their rule. What happened to Tõnisson after the trial is a mystery, though most believe he was shot by the NKVD, precursor to the KGB and modern-day FSB, in July 1941.

Whatever his awful fate, the fact that he had visited the house, perhaps even used its nifty *Kinni/Lahti* switch while he was occupying its WC, was a major selling point for me. I imagined that should I sit on the same toilet as Tõnisson, his arch greatness might pass to me. I was ready to buy it, and Epp was in love with it, too. Until she was informed that the floors would have to be sanded several times, all of the plumbing would have to be redone, the walls would have to be inspected for mold, the windows did not retain warmth, and so on. Plus she was trying to start a publishing company at the same time. And was pregnant, with a rambunctious three-year-old daughter. Also, we didn't have enough money and did not feel like taking a bank loan. So we just had to forget about our beautiful Anna Haava dream.

Someone else bought that house, a girl who read about it in Epp's blog. She was also bewitched by its history and vintage furniture, which the agent said might or might not be part of the deal. In the end, it wasn't. When they moved in, all of the gems from that place were gone. Only the *Kinni/Lahti* switch and the vintage toilet pot were still there.

So we moved to the rental house in Tähtvere instead, the one with the four furnaces, the one with the cold room, although I only learned about that later.

Most of the burning that went on in those early summer days was in the backyard, where we used brush as kindling for the grill, over which were roasted hundreds of sausages. It was the Era of Renovation. The deal with the owners was that we would renovate it in return for a break on the rent.

Epp's father Andres, her brothers Aap and Priit, and several other young Estonian guys – Tauno, Indrek, Kusti – came along to help out. This might have seemed like a great chance to get to know my in-laws, but they remained as remote and monosyllabic as ever. It wasn't that they were unfriendly. They were just busy doing their own things, absorbed by the work before them.

My Estonian wasn't that good either and so the silence suited me just fine.

Aap, who was now as tall as me, and who had a very bushy head of hair, would say something that to me sounded like "Blurp." My father-in-law Andres would only approach me when he was looking for something like a measuring tape. They would work until evening then jump into a car and head over to the supermarket to load up on buns and beer. Then at morning light it was back to work.

They plastered and painted the facade twice, and they built a bathroom. Since it was built in the 1950s, the house had actually never had a real bathroom. The Estonians just took a sauna every Saturday and washed there, that's it. We were more modern people, and so a pantry in the downstairs hallway was turned into a bathroom, with a big tub. The rooms were wallpapered and the windows painted. Then there were all the floors inside that needed to be painted too, which is where I came in. I would come to our new house in the weeks before Anna came to us at night. You could see a strip of light on the horizon, just below the stars, I remember that, and it was an incredibly peaceful feeling to work through the evening rolling out the floor paints, once, twice, three times and listening to good music. Then I would sleep at home before the coffee was made and it was time to resume work. Even though all my muscles ached, there was love in the coffee and in the work. Painting became an expression of my affection. Very Estonian.

You just can't imagine the power source that propelled this project forward. It was Epp's mystical nesting instinct, the same force that years ago had assembled the apartment in Kalamaja in a few weeks. She worked furiously on that project, consulting with any number of workmen and women. Once, a lady showed up and put wallpaper up overnight, just as I painted floors in the other rooms. I remember how strong that girl was, the muscles in her arms and legs. I watched her feet arch as she tossed up the paper. Her only sustenance was instant coffee and a little cream. This was how she worked. During the day painting, during the night tossing up wallpaper. In the morning, a car came and picked her up and she sped off to another job.

It seemed like everybody around me was working, and if they weren't working, they were drinking coffee so they could work more or discuss more work. Even the neighbor was out sawing wood at midnight. It was the only sound in the neighborhood.

The reality was that some Estonians didn't know how to do anything else *but* work. They were workaholics, which may still be a foreign term to them. If this word was said among the Estonians, then it was in jest. Because how was it possible that a person could work *too* much? The more work you could do, the better person you were.

Normaalne.

I felt guilty, like a lazy Italian, and while being a lazy Italian is something celebrated among other Italians, who dream of an old age where they idle away the days telling jokes on the piazza, I imagined that an Estonian's ideal end was probably more like heading up a hand-made ladder with a saw in hand, only to drop dead of a stroke.

At least that's what a friend of mine would tell me years later in Viljandi.

"An Estonian's dream is that he works so hard that he dies," he said matter-of-factly. They really were a bunch of industrious masochists. But I had married into the tribe. What else was there to do but pick up your own hammer and build your own ladder?

Epp's work energy was awesome. Sometimes I had that same feeling I had as a boy standing at the beach, watching an ocean wave crash over me. One white summer evening, as Epp was walking around in the back yard, I noticed the breeze pick up behind her and ruffle her shirt and saw just how big she had become. She walked more slowly, and even seemed tired, which was so unusual for this powerhouse. At that moment, I understood it would be soon.

And so she came, a new daughter. I held her in my sling and walked around the supermarket, collecting containers of cereal, bags of milk, and other easy foods for a family with a barely functioning kitchen. An older woman with curly gray hair came up to me to gaze at the tiny beauty as she slept across her father's chest.

"And what is the child's name?" I heard her ask.

"Anna," I said.

"Anne?" she glared at me with two little blue eyes.

"No. Anna."

The woman blinked at me, annoyed. Maybe it was because Anna was thought of as being a more Russian name, and Anne, pronounced Ann-eh, was the purer, more Estonian version? How could this Estonian baby have the same name as *Anna Karenina*? Personally, I thought the Estonians had gone a bit overboard with their Estonianness. Anna was the top name in Sweden and Norway and Iceland. They were genuine Scandinavian countries. Somehow that was all too far away for some of the locals. What mattered was whether your child had an Estonian or a Russian name.

Would the child be an Anna or an Anne? A Mihkel or a Mikhail?

"Anne?" she tried once more.

"No, it's Anna. Like Anna Haava, the famous poet," I said the name proudly.

"Who? What Anna Haava?"

How could it be? How could an older Estonian not know the name of this famous poet?

I scratched my head. "Um, like the tennis player, Anna Kournikova?"

There at last was some recognition in those eyes. "Oh. Like Anna Kournikova."

She looked once more at our tiny snoozing Anna Haava Kournikova Petrone. Then she walked away.

Later, when I recounted the story to Epp, she was also very confused.

"But how could an Estonian not know who Anna Haava was?" she said.

"I don't know," I said. "Maybe she was an Estonianized Russian," I suggested. "She refused to readily use the name Anna because it would have given away her real identity."

"Maybe," Epp said, while nursing the tiny tot. "Or maybe she was just an idiot."

BACK TO SCHOOL

They said that if you joined EÜS, you could get a good job, even one at the foreign ministry.

Ilves was EÜS. Laar was EÜS. All three Tarands – Indrek, Kaarel, and Andres – were EÜS. Indrek was an diplomat, Kaarel an editor-in-chief, and Andres, their esteemed papa, had been prime minister. The writer Jaan Kross had been EÜS and his son, the politician Eerik-Niiles Kross, was also. It was a mark of good breeding.

EÜS stood for *Eesti Üliõpilaste Selts*, or the Estonian Students' Society. Tartu didn't have fraternities and sororities, like you saw in the US. There were *seltsid*, societies, or there were *korporatsioonid*, corporations, or *korpid* for short. These were Tartu organizations with histories, their own uniforms, colorful caps, special codes, secret handshakes and customs. On April 30th, Walpurgis Night, they assembled in public and marched alongside each other like a university band. Yet instead of tubas and trumpets they had flags and flagons of beer.

Their names were interesting, too. Rotalia, Sakala, Estica, Indla, Amicitia, Lembela, Liivika.

There were male organizations and female ones. There were a few mixed groups like Põhjala but Epp told me not to bother with them. "Just join EÜS, if you want to join. That's the real one. My grandfather was in it, too. They say that most of the Estonian foreign ministry belongs to EÜS."

Many other great men were EÜS, too. Even Jaan Tõnisson, the political figure from the interwar years, known for his intellect, wisdom, top hat, and commitment to democracy, had been EÜS. As Kasekamp the historian was later to inform me, most of the political rivalries in the interwar period were between student societies. Tõnisson was EÜS and his nemesis Konstantin Päts was Estica. EÜS seemed to be more closely aligned with the state. It was the society's blue, black, and white tricolor that had been adopted as the national flag in 1918, when all of its members joined the army to fight for independence.

Thirteen EÜS members died in the War of Independence, but their victory lived on and was maintained from the society's headquarters close to the Tartu Railroad Station on Jaan Tõnisson Street, a brick, vaguely Asian-looking building with a pagoda-like sloping roof. My friend Ott the economist once showed me around, and told me about how the Soviets had taken over the building during the war and turned its grand meeting hall into a basketball court. After independence was restored the house was returned to its former owners and repaired. The fencing swords were placed again on the wall and the important society members – Ilves, Laar, the Tarands, Kross, and others – met in the building's cellar to speak privately.

"You wouldn't believe what I have seen down here," Ott told me. "And you wouldn't believe the things that have gone on down here."

I imagined a burlesque show, but they probably just decided who would be the next president.

Later, Ott announced that if I wanted to join EÜS, I was more than welcome to try. "I'm sure everybody in EÜS knows your blog," he affirmed. But joining wasn't so easy. You didn't just sign up and get your hat and flag and sinecure on Iceland Square. Oh, no. You had to work for it. That meant reporting for duty several times a month to clean up all the bottles emptied by the great men from the great society who had met secretly to do great things. I imagined myself stacking crates of empties, entranced by how close I had come to such greatness.

Of course, I said no, or rather, I said nothing. I would sooner have had Laar and Ilves clean up *my* empty bottles, especially after hearing about how they had locked that poor Eskimo Val Koso in the basement of the Washington embassy. But that trip to the EÜS house was my first introduction to Tartu University life, a new existence, where wearing silly hats, drinking beer, and attending secret basement meetings might set you on a path to a new and exciting future. It was time for me to go back to school.

My teacher Loone Ots was a voluptuous woman with fine reddish locks, and dramatic movements who spoke faster than a Mexican high on cocaine. She seemed to turn at the waist like a plastic action figure and then she would jaunt over to the windows to throw the curtains open and let in the sunshine. There was sunshine now, as it was spring, and I was very grateful for it. The sun would fight its way through the dirt on the windows and onto the handouts on our desks. Even if there was so much dust in the air, and there was the stink of sweat from students still wearing their winter clothing in warm weather, there was Loone Ots and her declarations.

Such as, "No, no. Kristjan Jaak Peterson was absolutely not gay!"

Kristjan Jaak, that rediscovered 19th century Estonian poet. There was a long and towering angular statue of the man atop Toomemägi, where he stood looking out with his shoulder-length hair, dandy scarf, long coat, and walking staff like some kind of hybrid of Moses, Nick Cave, and Oscar Wilde. The walking staff was significant, because, as I later learned, Kristjan Jaak was famous not only for his wardrobe, but his long-haul sojourns between the University of Tartu and Riga, where his family lived and where he was raised. According to Loone, it was these hard treks that had exposed him to the bad weather and had worsened the young man's tuberculosis.

I would often pass the statue of Kristjan Jaak on long walks to clear my mind.

You would enter from the stairs near Kassitoome, the bowl-shaped depression at the back of the hill that was a favorite sledding spot, and then climb up past the ruins of the ancient Tartu Cathedral, and then turn left around the path toward the statue, which stood among mossed-over boulders and cairns. The walk would calm you, because it was so quiet, and even in summer you might only pass a jogger or a young mother pushing a carriage.

Whether you passed Kristjan Jaak amidst the slick red and orange fallen foliage of autumn or the white deserts of winter snow, it was always pleasant to look up and see him, and know that at least one monument in this world had been done right. He looked wild, with his hair long and unruly, his coat rough around the edges, and that tall walking stick, like he had just ascended the Matterhorn*.

At the base of the statue on the hill were the numbers 1801–1822. Twenty-one years. That's all he got. If you saw the numbers you would wonder how this wunderkind could become the founder of modern Estonian poetry with such a short life span. But the knowledgeable Estonian Literature professor Loone told us that his poems were in fact not published until ninety years after his death.

As she spoke of Kristjan Jaak, she recited his most beloved lines before us:

"Cannot the tongue of this land
In the wind of incantation
Rising up to the heavens
Seek for eternity?"

She would raise one hand while she recited the lines, as if she was holding a tray, and move her fingers about. Her

---

* A mountain of the Alps, 4,478 meters high.

voice was steady, and there was strength in it, but also a touch of neurotic titillation, a quiver, as if she was sharing with us her most valuable treasures. Yes, Loone was a true woman of literature. When she recounted the romantic affairs of the country's legendary artists, Loone's voice seemed to tremble a bit, as if she herself had got love letters from Friedebert Tuglas, one of the country's best known poets in the 20th Century, known by his mop of curly dark hair, playboy mustache, and *pince-nez* glasses.

"Kristjan Jaak was absolutely astounding, because this was at the very darkest, most frozen part of the Tsarist Era, and yet there was an Estonian who was writing patriotic words about the Estonian language," Loone said, standing very still, as if giving a political address. "The most curious thing about Kristjan Jaak was that he often wrote lovingly in his poems and diaries about someone called Alo."

A hand went up. "Who was Alo?"

"I wish I could say. Nobody has been able to determine that. Alo, taken literally, is a nickname for Alexander. But why would Kristjan Jaak have dedicated all of his poems, and some of these are really quite beautiful and romantic love poems, to someone named Alexander?"

There was silence. I cast another eye on the drawing of Kristjan Jaak projected on the wall. That flashy scarf, that flamboyant pose. Maybe he was in love with some guy named Alo.

A student beside me, a fair-headed, good-humored woman, whom I had learned was a lesbian activist from the Netherlands, stirred uncomfortably a bit, and someone whispered something to her and patted her on the back, as if to restrain her, and then Loone Ots seemed to sense the conclusion we had all arrived at based on the "Alo" evidence.

Her eyes lit up, almost in terror. "No, no, Kristjan Jaak Peterson was absolutely not gay!"

"How can you be so sure?" asked the Dutch activist.

"Because homosexuality was absolutely not tolerated during that period of time," Loone said. "If anyone had found out about it, even from reading his journals...."

But just because it was not tolerated doesn't mean it didn't exist. Just look at that scarf that his statue has.

Loone looked around and then down at her white, high-heeled sandals. Then she looked up.

"My darling girl, my sweet
I would like to have you
As a blossom in my bed
For the day upon my heart
Your little white breasts
Like snowy hills of winter," Loone recited the lines. "That is from one of his poems, 'Jaak's Song.' And I can go on if you like?"

She glanced at me and I nodded profusely yes. She continued:

"The sun shines upon them
Your tender little hand
Soft as a flower's petal
But what you have beneath
Could be prettier still.'"

When Loone was done reciting the words, even I was blushing. After class, I approached her.

"Did you have something you wanted to say?" she asked while sorting through papers.

"I just wanted to say that I feel bad about what happened before."

"That what happened, exactly?"

"That you had to get into defending Kristjan Jaak's sexuality. As if you didn't want to admit that he was gay. It's so complicated. If you say someone isn't gay, it's as if you are lying."

"It's quite common, actually," said Loone, tilting her head toward me. "Many others, even some Estonian academics, have reached a similar conclusion without consulting the body of his work, which is really quite erotic in its description of women, I must admit," said Loone, looking up at me through her glasses and making me blush even more. "I believe that Alo was just a nickname for a girl he was in love with. Alo was not at all a popular man's name at that time. He probably just chose it because it sounded pretty. I am going to write a new research article about this very issue!"

She zipped up her bag and slung it over her shoulder. A moment later she was out the door.

Loone's picture hung amongst a temporary display of other female poets and writers in the stairwell of the Lutsu Library in downtown Tartu. Sometimes I would linger a bit there and look at it. It was a typical Estonian face, but a bit more Finnish feeling, with those disarming eastern eyes.

She terrified me a bit, I'll admit, not just because of those strange eyes, but because she was so deep in that literary world. It was a world full of tormented people. Some of them committed suicide, while others had settled for alcoholism. Yet writing remained their sole salvation. I had still not connected my own inner torment with such a path even though I was killing myself with work. Articles, blog posts, more articles, more blog posts, and now class assignments and term papers. I lived on coffee and deadlines and beer, often writing with a sleeping baby in my arms.

I spoke a lot about Loone with Epp as our children played in the big room downstairs that had wooden boxes of toys and a rocking horse.

"Do you know what Loone Ots told us about Tuglas and Marie Under?"

Epp laughed at me and teased me. She called me "Loone Ots' biggest fan."

She still liked hearing the stories though, about Estonian author Friedebert Tuglas and the poet Marie Under's secret affair, how they were remodeling the old Tuglas home and found their correspondence hidden behind the old wallpaper. I could see why Friedebert had that affair – because Marie Under was one of the best-looking dead people Estonia had to offer. Loone had shown us one particular image, where the young poetess Marie wore a striped dress with black collar, red-brown tresses pulled up girlishly, sloppily, messily, wildly, and yet so seductively, the heart-reckoning face of a stitched cloth doll, the soft light eyes, with the appropriate pinch of visible literary torment. Damn it, *I* was in love with her.

Tormented beautiful women, yeah. It got to be a bit much. So you can imagine what a relief it was for me to sit in Mertelsmann's class and listen to his stories of war crimes.

As for our teacher Mertelesmann, I thought he was an Estonian too. I even spoke to him in Estonian the first few times we met, because I was sure he was just another local with a German name. The first few times, he answered me in English, but then he spoke to me in Estonian. Olaf Mertelsmann. An Estonian name, for sure. But if he was Estonian how come he seemed so relaxed? How come he smiled at times to himself, for no reason? And why was his English so smooth?

The girl behind me in class whispered to me, "I heard he's not an Estonian. He's from Hamburg, Germany."

His head was different, too. Square. His body was equally as sturdy, and his hair was thick and curly, with only a hint of gray at the temples. Judging by the way he spoke about *perestroika* and his teenage years in Hamburg, right on the frontier of the West at the end of the Cold War, I guessed him to be about a decade older than me. Once in a while, his wardrobe – a white jacket, a red pair of trousers – would seem plucked straight out of an old music video. All he needed was a headband and one of those key-tars, keyboards in the shape of a guitar. There was the ghost of the Eighties about

Mertelsmann, the same ghost that haunted me still. For the other students, younger than me, Gorbachev was just a name, but for us, his name meant more. Gorby was like an old uncle who I could remember. "He was like a celebrity," I told the class. "Everybody in America loved his birth mark."

Mertelsmann smiled. He thrust his hands into the pockets of his white jacket and went on.

His story was not unusual. An adventurous mind, he had come to Estonia to study at some point, and then settled down with a local girl, whom he no doubt seduced with wild tales of SS Einsatzgruppen and NKVD troikas. In the 1990s, he had studied in Novosibirsk, Russia, where speaking Estonian came in handy as NATO planes bombed Serbia. "Nobody knew who we were. But if we spoke English or German, it could have aroused the antipathy of the local Russians."

I imagined a younger Mertelsmann in his white jacket walking down the main street in Novosibirsk, whispering in Estonian. That's when his brainwashing occurred. That's how he became part of the tribe. When you married a woman, you joined her tribe, or so I had heard.

Which meant that Mertesmann and I were part of the same tribe!

Mertelsmann had three sons. "It's quite lively at our home," he said with a hint of weariness.

His was a believable British accent. The Estonians had that choppiness to their cadence that continued to remind me of the Japanese. Not that they were all that stoic, sensei type. The economics professor Viktor Trasberg smiled so often that he seemed to be suppressing some insatiable laugh. A blond shock of hair, slits of wily eyes, and balloons for cheeks, Viktor Trasberg reminded me of those old sketches of Chinese poets who wandered the hills writing verse and drinking wine, except that he liked to complain about Reform Party tax policies instead.

"I told him at a party this summer. Ansip, you are making a mistake. He didn't listen to me!"

So, Trasberg was frustrated with current taxation policies but he smiled through it all.

All of my other Estonian professors retained this vaguely Asiatic tinge. I could never quite place its source, nor could I say, "You are Japanese." But there was something there that felt really foreign, as if they had been gifted with the secrets to life, ancient wisdom from beyond the Ural Mountains that no Indo-European would ever grasp. Even Marju Lauristin, that gray lady fireball of the journalism department, who seemed to dance into class the first day nearly breaking a sweat, and could not sit down for even a few minutes during a lecture because she was so excited by poll statistics, had the same wild energy as those Sami women I had seen up in Lapland beating skin drums and singing. This fire was matched by the iciness of her bearded partner and colleague Peeter Vihalemm, who deeply pondered every question before one syllable presented itself on his lips. They were an intriguing group, the University of Tartu professors. I often felt that they were guarding some hidden knowledge, some special secrets known only to them, the Estonians, and to them alone.

I learned from all of them and liked all of them. Yet it was Mertelsmann whose tales of Second World War mass murder and mass horror stayed with me. Not only did he make you feel as if you were there, but that it could have been you who did it.

"The thing you have to remember about the SS as an organization is that it was all voluntary," Mertelsmann said and stopped. He looked around the room, into the eyes of every student. "All of that was voluntary. So can anybody tell me why would a German opt to join the SS?"

There was silence. Then the hands went up. "Yes?" he nodded toward a German student.

"A better salary?"

A steady nod. "Many of them were policemen looking to advance their careers." He began to pace. "They saw it as dirty work, but thought a prosperous future awaited them after the war."

There was some more silence. You could hear the chatter of students talking out in the street.

Mertelsmann looked up. "And it wasn't so bad to be in the SS, you know."

You could feel the discomfort in the classroom air. "What do you mean?" asked the student.

The professor shrugged. "They lived well, much better than common German soldiers. Pay was higher. They had little rows of houses where their families could stay with them, and there was always plenty for them to eat and drink. Maybe even a little meat leftover for the family dog."

There was a nervous chuckle.

"Well, you have to think about what motivates people to commit such crimes. The promise of power, wealth, career, even sex. These are the kinds of incentives that authoritarian states use. The local Estonians who allied themselves with the Soviets did it for the same reasons. What really motivated the Estonians who served in the Soviet puppet government in 1940?"

Nobody answered.

"Well, they all ate quite well. Go look at the photos of all those military parades. Look at the local Estonian Communists sitting in the reviewing stands. They are fat. They are dressed in nice clothes. Then look at the thin people standing on the sides of the streets wearing ragged clothing. The higher-ranking party members got nice cars, second homes. When they were purged from leadership, do you think they tried to fight the system? No. They begged to be let back into the party. 'Oh, please, let me back into the party. Let me back into the party!'"

He took another sip of coffee.

"Now, imagine you are an occupying power. You take over. What is the first thing you do?"

My hand went up and Mertelsmann nodded toward me. "Yes, Justin."

"Secure the records," I said.

Mertelsmann took a swig from his coffee cup and started speaking before he had swallowed the gulp. "Absolutely. Any proper occupying power needs to have records on its subjects, and will be constantly refining these records and adding to them to monitor state enemies. How did you know that by the way?" he raised his eyebrows a bit. "I usually don't get that answer."

"Oh, I just read a book about the British occupation of New Amsterdam in the 17th Century. The first thing the British did when they seized power from the Dutch was seize the records."

"Mmm. We can see that some things do not change. What is very important here is the idea of the state as a gardener. The state tends to its gardens. It removes the bad weeds."

No history professor of mine had ever discussed things in such a manner. For all of the others, Nazi Germany was a well-known evil, and there was no reason to ask why you would join an organization like the SS. You just knew that it was evil and that it had done evil things. But Mertelsmann liked to delve into the psychological aspects of history. To call something evil was useless, essentially. He wanted to know what motivated them to do those things.

"Why would an Estonian join the German Army?" He looked around the classroom.

A hand went up. "To fight for Estonian independence?"

A curious look. "How exactly would fighting for Germany lead to Estonian independence?"

No answers.

"Yes, I know that some soldiers thought they were fighting for this. In fact, many of the recruitment posters in the German-occupied countries advertised joining the army as an act of patriotism. The Danish, Dutch, and Norwegian legions were no different. If you ask them about it, then that is what they will tell you. 'We were fighting against Bolshevism.' But you should also understand that a lot of young men join any army for other reasons. Why?"

An Italian student's hand went up. "To see the world. To get into adventures?"

Mertelsmann stopped his pacing. He peered out the window into the spring sunshine for a moment, and then he turned back to face the class, his arms folded across his white jacket.

"An Estonian friend of mine had a grandfather who served in the German Army," he said. "He gave me his journal. It's full of terrific stories about meeting lovely women and drinking with his mates. He had a great time. There is not one mention of Hitler or the goals of the regime."

He shrugged his shoulders and shook his head, and then there was the faintest, eeriest, most mischievous smile, because Mertelsmann was very good at teaching history, and he knew it.

Sometimes when I stepped outside of Mertelsmann's whirlwind lectures, I would run into Kasekamp as he came striding down the hall in his jeans and jacket, with his bearded face and his amused look. Or sometimes we would have those awkward back-and-forths that occur when you encounter a friend in the door of the restroom. Once in a while, there would be a third man at the third urinal in the restroom, an older English gentleman in a gray suit who would speak to

Andres in accented Estonian and then head across the hall into an office and close the door. The sign on the door said, *Krahv* Carlisle. After a few of these peculiar run-ins, I asked the historian Kasekamp who the puzzling old Britisher was, and what the word *Krahv* meant.

"*Krahv*," he said in his deep professor's voice, "is the Estonian word for earl. That man there is George William Beaumont Howard, the 13th Earl of Carlisle and noted Estophile. He's been involved in honoring the British sailors who lost their lives in the War of Independence."

"How did he become an Estophile?"

"He just has that interest. You know how the British aristocracy is."

"No."

"They can be slightly eccentric."

"But what's he doing here?"

"Earl of Carlisle was given a position at the university after Tony Blair reformed the House of Lords in 1999 and he lost his seat. So, whatever you do, don't mention Tony Blair to him."

"I won't."

"Good. No Blair." Kasekamp looked at his watch. "Anyway, I have to get going."

"Oh really? To where?"

Kasekamp shrugged as if it was the most obvious thing. "To a student society meeting, of course."

"Oh. Are you in EÜS?"

"No," Kasekamp answered. "Rotalia."

JULIUS KUPERJANOV'S GRAVE

Sometimes, when I was unable to cope with what Estonia threw at me, I would go to visit Julius Kuperjanov's grave in Raadi Cemetery.

Raadi was on the other side of the Emajõgi River, that awkward, backward half of Tartu that was known as "Ülejõe," or "Over River." Ülejõe. The word had a certain dystopian ring to it. In Ülejõe, one could encounter Estonia in all of its half-developed, half-devolved misery. You would see an older man with a 19th-century-style cap and a cane lugging kindling into a leaning wooden shack and watch the black and brown smoke fume and twirl from the dwelling's low chimney. But beside this tsarist-era sloppiness rose the tall, proud glass and metal towers of student dormitories and plastic-looking, two-story shopping centers that had been assembled in haste in the 1990s.

The rest of the district was dotted with ethnic restaurants, automotive shops, thrift stores, and, on its edges, newer housing developments. Just on the riverfront, there was a 1960s-era building with big windows, neon lights and futuristic geometries. Looking at it from the Town Hall side of the river, the good side, one wouldn't be surprised to meet Frank

Sinatra and Marilyn Monroe, or their Estonian equivalents, at the end of its bar. This fantastic place was known to all as "Atlantis."

You could take several bridges to get over the river into Ülejõe. The one I preferred was located just downwind from Tartu's great Town Hall. It was called the *Kaarsild*, or arch bridge, because of its arched shape. Students, imbued with the bravery that only alcohol can provide, would sometimes walk over this arch and other students would photograph it and upload it to Facebook and other social networking websites. Once somebody photographed a fully clothed couple that appeared to be engaged in sexual intercourse at dawn on top of the Kaarsild. I don't know if the young Estonian man and woman were taking precautions, but the image of them went viral soon after. It provided people with the joy and jolliness that comes with the wild side of university life.

Sometimes I would meet a friend on the Kaarsild as I crossed it on its lower dimension. If I met Ott, the economist, we would talk about economics. Ott was an academic, and so all of his statements came with conditional clauses. "I would say that it is probably too early to say if that is the case, but it certainly warrants further study," Ott would squint and say.

If I met Andrei, the blogger, we would talk about unsavory pieces authored by Western Kremlin stooges that had appeared in the British press, and our duties as bloggers to deconstruct them and to be merciless and ruthless in our humiliation of the men behind them.

Andrei and I always talked about politics. We never spoke about our personal lives. I never told him of my jaunts to

Raadi Cemetery to pour out my heart to the long-dead man, or of our "conversations."

Andrei's main problem was that his family came from Petserimaa, a territory that had been Estonian between the world wars, but was partly transferred to Russia by some sweep of Stalin's pen in 1944. So Andrei was an Estonian citizen by blood. When the state was restored, his Estonian passport was restored with it. Andrei didn't have to take any tests. So he voted reliably for the conservative party and called himself a "birthright Estonian citizen," and yet when you introduced dark-haired Andrei to conservative Estonians, they would stiffen up, because his Russian first name rendered him suspect.

"Oh, no, you must understand," I would tell these conservative Estonian friends and relatives who became aware of my friendship with Andrei. "He's a birthright Estonian. His family is from Petseri."

That only seemed to confuse them more. For them he was not a real Estonian.

"People in the UK and France ask me all the time, 'How can you be from Estonia and an Estonian citizen and speak fluent Estonian... and you are not a real Estonian?'" Andrei would say.

"Well what do you call yourself?"

"I say I am an Estlander – *Eestimaalane*. A person from the land of Estonia, but not an ethnic Estonian. If you think about it, a lot of the most famous Estonians have been *Eestimaalased* like me, with the wrong name."

"Like who?"

"Like Julius Kuperjanov. The greatest war hero in Estonian history was born in Pskov and had a Russian name. Think about that. "

"Yeah, but I heard he was an ethnic Estonian. He just had a Russian name for some reason."

"The sad thing," said Andrei, "is that even if you are an ethnic Estonian, if you have a Russian-sounding name like Kuperjanov, some people still won't take you as one of them."

I hadn't heard about Kuperjanov from Andrei. I had heard about him and his legend from someone else. An older foreign Estonian named Jüri who would return to Tartu from time to time would meet with Andrei and I and tell us stories he had heard from actual veterans of the Estonian War of Independence, who were not yet old men when Jüri met with them at exile parties in Toronto in the 1960s.

One had told Jüri that he thought he had seen the dark-haired, sparkly-eyed, mustachioed Kuperjanov, then just 22 years old, through the window of his school house, recruiting for the Tartu Partisan Battalion even *before* independence had been declared in February 1918. Kuperjanov was only 25 when he died from the wounds he suffered after the Battle of Paju, when the Estonian Army defeated the Red Army as part of the larger liberation of southern Estonia. After that, the battalion – that had as its symbol a fearsome white-on-black skull and cross bones – was renamed in his honor.

Kuperjanov was interred in a monument in leafy and mossy Raadi Cemetery, a proud sarcophagus mounted on columns with his years of birth and death and a bronze relief of his tough, heroic face. It was one of the few monuments that the Soviets did not destroy when they retook Estonia in 1944, for the obvious reason that even they feared the supernatural wrath of Lieutenant Julius Kuperjanov. They were less intimidated by his widow. The Soviets deported Alice Kuperjanov in 1941. She was killed the following year, probably by some idiot Russian teenager who had no idea who she was.

It wasn't exactly the most uplifting tale. Yet despite the death and skulls and cross bones and murdered widow, Kuperjanov's name still held a cheery, good old, 'those were the days' vintage. Just saying it in the company of Estonians would perk them up, get them feeling patriotic and fine. In the 1980s, especially around Christmas time, bad boy Tartu University students would dare each other to leave candles at his grave, which apparently was under round-the-clock surveillance by the KGB at that most wonderful time of year. One of them, an enterprising, self-promoting lad named Indrek Tarand, was even expelled for his late-night vigil at Kuperjanov's grave. Twenty-something years later, a middle-aged, widely grinning, shades-wearing Indrek Tarand launched an off-kilter, anti-establishment, independent campaign for the European parliament. He won.

I have no idea what Tarand used to say to Kuperjanov in the Eighties, but when I went to visit Kuperjanov's grave, it was always because I had woman troubles. You'd leave the house in a wretched rage and walk down into town and over the arch bridge, keeping your head down so that nobody would see you cursing and ask if you were okay, and you'd walk through the big, orderly park on the other side that used to be the foundation for many nice old buildings before the Germans and Soviets and Estonian partisans blew them all up. Most of the parks in Tartu had started out as the ruins of some war. Then it was up the hills of the Wild West-feeling Ülejõe until you reached the gates of Raadi Cemetery where some little old lady was selling candles and flowers. You wouldn't bother to buy any though because you were still angry with her for being so rigid, and angry with yourself for being such a disappointment to every damn woman in the world, and cursing your mother for sending you another letter where she blamed you for keeping her from her grandchildren and living far away and also for the Downfall of Western Civilization.

The cemetery was dark, no matter the weather, no matter the time of year or day, because it was a forest. What else could you call a stretch of earth covered with trees? Under the trees were the stones and the iron fences. Little black signs with arrows directed you to the resting places of poets and writers. There, farther back, was Kuperjanov.

When I got to Kuperjanov's grave, I usually took some time to stand there and study the moss on the sarcophagus, and ask myself that ageless question that people ask themselves in ancient cemeteries, "My God, is he really in there?" Then I would crouch down, stare at Kuperjanov's face, close my eyes.

"Kuperjanov?"

No answer.

"Lieutenant Julius Kuperjanov?"

No answer.

A deep breath. "I'm here today – again – because I'm under a lot of stress."

Somewhere behind me, a squirrel dropped an acorn on a stone.

"My wife is disappointed in me. She asks me to do a lot of things, but I always forget."

Some rustling of leaves. The moisture of light autumn drizzle. That natural smell.

I rubbed my face. "When I get upset because she's upset, she gets even madder at me, because, you know, Estonian men never get angry or upset. They are always working, always fine."

Kuperjanov said nothing.

"Don't even get me started on my mother. She hates me."

A contemplative pause.

"Huh. Even my daughter thinks I'm a joke."

The drizzle turned to rain, and you could hear it pound on the leaves. A few drops fell on my face.

"I'm going to school here, but I don't like it much. Working as a reporter, but I don't like it much. I'm 28 and I haven't accomplished shit. I mean, look at you, you were only 25 and they named a battalion after you. There's a street named after you. You mention your name, and everyone gets happier. 'Good old Kuperjanov!'"

Kuperjanov was very still and very silent.

He had nothing to say, but what could you really expect a stoic Estonian soldier to say to you when you complained about your mother and your wife?

Then I remembered how Epp and I had taken the children to Kuperjanov's grave on Christmas Eve. I had never seen more candles and it looked so much more beautiful covered in icicles and snow. There were no leaves on the trees at that time of year, and the stars and light from the snow and candles gave you hope. My children had lit candles for Kuperjanov, placed them at his altar, perhaps even breathed in a tiny particle of his holy corpse that happened to float free into their lungs from a crack on the tomb. I enjoyed the memory of my family standing in the snow and lighting the candles.

"Oh well, Kuperjanov," I said, standing up and feeling the strain in my legs from having crouched too long. "It's been nice chatting with you. You be good, okay?"

Kuperjanov said nothing. The rain was falling ever harder, and more orange and red leaves fell with it.

THE SPIRIT OF TARTU

All this time I was walking a lot, and whenever I went somewhere in Tartu, I would feel an itch in the muscles of my legs, an impatient twitch that carried me out and along great distances.

I walked to think, I walked to heal. I walked to breathe in the spirit of the city, the so-called *Tartu vaim*. The spirit could show you the right way forward if you could only catch it in your fingers, like a butterfly at the Botanical Gardens. You had to be patient and wait and it would come and flutter for your amusement.

I walked and I jotted down notes in my journal, and often wrote about my wife and how I envied her. Epp was full of bonfire energy. She even approached our neighbors to let us gather their leaves. Bruno, that old cheerful Latvian who rode a bike around and wore a beret and tan jacket, welcomed us into his yard, and introduced us to the love of his life, Aino, a gray-eyed, gray-haired lady in a blue headscarf and rain boots.

Bruno had given up his birthtown Riga for her and her *Tartu vaim*. As a bonus, Tartu gave him a fine yard with maple trees, and he let us gather the firm, colorful leaves they provided. Later at our house, Epp listened to the radio and sang along as she ironed the maple leaves. Each carefully prepared leaf was glued into the front page of a book about her environmental awakening, "Growing Green." Every bit of this operation came from somewhere in her spirit.

Her spirit, her *vaim*.

My own *vaim* was blistered, bruised, disoriented. I drank a lot of coffee and stayed up another hour to finish off my term papers. The ones I wrote for Mertelsmann's class were the most inspired. The others not so much. My main gig with the biotech media company based in New York had a quota of three articles per week. Besides that, I had done the Lennart Meri Conference transcripts and summaries for a second year, but by the third I was too exhausted. When Kadri Liik suggested, casually, that I might find a job at the foreign ministry, which had at one time had been my dream, I said no. Anchored in Tartu, a new Tallinn career seemed out of the question.

I had started to realize I was too bohemian for the life of catered dinners anyway. Even if it was basic cosmopolitan hospitality, something bothered me about being served by men in vests. I felt guilty about having Estonian Russian ladies clean up my hotel room. Something knocked at my sense of equality. I could never snap my fingers at a waiter and ask for another drink during the Chatham House Rule sessions, as I had seen one military intelligence officer do. He was a bolder, finger-snapping type, who was excoriating German Chancellor Angela Merkel for her resistance to offering Ukraine a NATO Membership Action Plan.

"There are three reasons for Angela Merkel's position," he said. "Moral cowardice, moral cowardice, and moral cowardice."

No, I just couldn't be that person. Or that one. Or that man over there.

But who could I be?

Whoever I was, I was on the verge of burnout and restless as hell. And my wife? She always had a publishing meeting, or a deadline. Or she had an idea for a trip to Spain, to Russia, to Malaysia, to India...

The only trips I suggested were back to the US. My family were happy to see us, but I felt guilty, as if I had not seen them long enough, or not given enough of myself, even though I was trying to please them as best I could. I knew that no matter how hard I tried, they would never forgive me for leaving America behind and becoming a European. They just couldn't understand it.

This situation troubled my heart, dispirited my *vaim*.

I had become a European, no matter what my passport said, no matter what the other Europeans thought. It had happened at some moment when I was younger and I hadn't even noticed it. Maybe the seed was planted when I watched them roast the pig in Zurich's streets when I was 14, or maybe later, at the Reykjavik swimming pools when I was 21. It could have been that day in the Finnish Foreign Ministry when that Estonian journalist Epp whispered her secret in my ear. Whenever it happened, whatever it was, it had happened, and it was all over and done with, and there was nothing else left to say.

Maybe I wasn't comfortable with myself, or had some psychological or identity issues and latched on to a great passing train in the form of that Estonian journalist. I don't know. But it seemed that I had entered onto a route that I knew would be more magical, more nourishing to the soul. Rather than choose self-denial, I had said "Yes" to some truth. I had hopped a freight train to another, more liberating land. And in that land, I could breathe, I could dream, I could sing.

I could walk.

In America, you would see commercials for European cereals and cough drops with images of braided beauties and their men yodeling in the Alps who, after a good night's bonk in a haystack, settled down to a nutritious bowl of muesli or a herbal candy if their throat felt a bit sore after all of that chill mountain air.

Even if the chimneys of Tartu left the air not as fresh as up on the Matterhorn, and even if the path to the local shopping center cut through one of the more industrial and depressing slices of the city, I still had Tartu and its legendary *vaim* to carry me through those days when I felt most tormented.

The back of Tähtvere faced the railroad tracks, and nestled beside them were white brick garages in several stages of decay, with rusty metal doors and roofs, small windows of broken glass shards, and rude graffiti in diverse languages. Supposedly people kept their tractors and other prized possessions there, but I rarely saw anyone near the garages during those days and even if I walked alongside the ruined garages, I leaned away from them, toward the road, averted my gaze and thought of braided Alpine beauties milking goats.

In the spring and summer, the garages were not so hard to look at, as the bank that ran up to the train tracks was thick with grass and little yellow and white flowers. But as the hours of daylight fell and the leaves with them, until the ground began to freeze and the white of winter came, the area took on a more nocturnal, somber air.

Spring was still best, those deliciously long May days when the trees blossomed.

Not too far from there stood a house that leaned to one side, had half its roof burned, and smelled of cat urine all around. In my restless walks, I would pass it and wonder how it was still standing. Perhaps two families lived in there: two men, three women, and countless numbers of children, who would celebrate the few warm days of the year by sitting outside with their shirts off, listening to old disco music on the radio, drinking beers or sodas, and playing made up games like "throw the rubber boot over the clothes line."

"Rasmus! Indrek! Come quick!" You would hear the boys yell. "Let's toss the boot!"

I would hear the music playing and see the boot flying and feel incredibly blessed. How could I explain that blessed feeling to anybody? You couldn't write an academic paper about it ("Tartu Boot Tossing in *Postimees*: A Discourse Analysis") or a genetics article ("Estonian Scientists Pinpoint Boot Tossing Gene"). For society's purposes, such a splendid scene had no relevance. It was just there and then it was gone.

For me it was real-life cinema on the streets. You didn't get that *vaim* anywhere else. Not in a classroom or at a genetics conference. I'm so glad I stopped to watch, because one day when I passed the Tartu shanty, there was nothing there at all, no boot-tossing children, no topless adults, no music, and no house. The whole structure had been demolished and each of its pieces removed, so that all that was left was a quiet, sandy, windblown lot.

I wonder what had happened to those people though. Where did they move?

I loved walking around Tartu but sometimes I felt lonely. The loneliness ate me up at all times of the year but winter was worst – not the front, darker half, where you were just amazed by how much a ray of orange sunlight on a December day could move you to tears, but the back half, those longer, whiter February and March days where the ice had melted overnight and then hardened again into something ugly, purple, and treacherous.

The days grew longer and my anticipation with them, so that I wished each morning that it would truly be the last vile day of winter, and that spring would come and the green trees with it, and I could once again look into my wife's eyes as she rode her bike under the boughs of the planted elms and street lanterns with our blonde angel child nestled anxiously in the back seat.

There was so much majesty in those moments, and they continued to sparkle in my eyes long after they had burst apart into the nothingness of night, like virgin stars. They kept me from starving of vagabond lonesomeness so that even when I walked down that boulevard in the frozen-over hell of Estonia in March, if I shut my eyes, I could still see her and the trees and the lights.

I walked down the boulevard and mulled it over again and again, Epp's words echoing inside me.

"Justin, you spend so much time writing. Articles, papers, transcripts, blogs. Why don't you try to write a book?"

Why don't you try? Well, I had tried, a long time ago. A trunk in a closet at my parents' house was full of half-finished manuscripts. A girlfriend had once given me a Jack Kerouac book, *Big Sur*, when I left with my mother and father for a trip to the West Coast. I loved it, and secretly began to think of myself as the main character in my own book. Kerouac had lived for a time in the same village as my grandmother, a little fishing village on the East Coast of the US, and had known all of its bartenders.

Once, Kerouac gave the bartender a copy of *The Dharma Bums* in lieu of payment.

"Of course, I couldn't make sense of that junk," the gruff old bartender had told me.

Then how come that junk had made so much sense to me?

I had started writing the manuscript for what would become my first book and Tiina and the other busy ladies in the publishing house had liked it and given it the green light. But to finish it meant that I would have to resuscitate that remaining bit of my *vaim* that hadn't been rubbed out by years of parental duties, school, and work. That little Kerouac within. I remembered a scene from *The Dharma Bums* where Kerouac was walking through a neighborhood in

1950s America, the glare from the many new TV sets dancing through the windows of the houses and into his eyes. That ache of alienation. Walking through Tartu, peeking through the windows at the Estonian families who had gathered to watch *Who Wants to be a Millionaire?* Or *Dancing with the Stars*, I felt the same beat Kerouac way.

I wrote all day and then went to fetch our firstborn, Marta Petrone. She wasn't the only child with a strange last name in the Catholic School kindergarten. There were also two little Italian children who had been born to missionaries, and one of them, the older one, was named Giacomo. It made me so happy that there were other Italians in Marta's class, and I would dream of the day Marta grew up and married the fine young Italian Giacomo. I would often wake her in the mornings with the quick lines, "Come on, Marta. Time to get up. Giacomo is waiting for you."

Marta would roll over and say, "Giacomo? Yuck! He's a boy and he's mean to girls."

On this afternoon, Giacomo and his sister Teresa were gone and Marta already had her coat on. She was the last one left. "*Issi!*" she said and ran and leaped into my arms.

"I'm so sorry I'm late again," I told the teacher, a young woman with auburn hair and glasses. She wore a long beige coat and thick-rimmed glasses, and she looked at me coldly.

"I close the kindergarten at 5:30," she said. "That means parents have to be here at 5:25 at the latest."

"What time is it now?" I asked and glimpsed the clock behind her back.

"5.35."

But she didn't say it that way. She said it in the roundabout, mathematical, Estonian way. "After ten minutes it will be three quarters of six o'clock. *Kümme minuti pärast kolmveerand kuus.* She waited while I did the backward calculations.

"Oh, I'm really terribly so so *so* sorry. I've just been working really hard on a book."

The teacher blinked at me a few times from behind her glasses but was unmoved. I had vaguely hoped that she might express some interest in my book, marvel at this modern day Kerouac standing before her, but she seemed as disinterested as that rough bartender back in Northport Village whom Kerouac had paid with copies of *The Dharma Bums.*

Estonians were often in a hurry anyway, even just to go home and watch television.

Oh well. I hoisted Marta onto my shoulders and we headed toward Kassitoome to bask a bit more in the *Tartu vaim.*

The *Tartu vaim* was different from the *Tallinna vaim.* In Tartu, if I wore an old leather jacket my father had given me that had Navajo designs on the interior and a beat up pair of old cotton pants and some artless boots, I was a bohemian, a rugged individualist, a poet, a beatnik, a professor – respectable.

In Tallinn, with the same clothes, I felt like a slacker. Each time I ventured into the nation's capital I felt like some poor hick farmer. There you needed to dress for success, to look like you worked at a bank in London. Even in August in Tallinn you would encounter hygienic men wearing colorful scarves.

I didn't remember Tallinn being so stylish when we had lived there years ago. In those days, it had felt gritty and a bit worn, but still like home. Many of its younger people had since lived abroad, though, in London, Paris, and Tokyo, and had brought back with them a heightened level of self awareness. Maybe that's where that Tallinn spirit came from?

Kassitoome was my favorite Tartu park. Its name meant, "The Cat's Dome," which to my ears meant nothing because I couldn't see how a hollow in the middle of a city had anything to do with cats. But I still liked the name, and because Kassitoome was the domain of the Tartu children and its more childlike residents, which meant that, except on rare occasions, drunks did not venture there.

It was also right beside the Catholic School and the Catholic Church. I guess I was nostalgic for Italy, even though I had never lived there. Whatever it was, I was nostalgic for something, yearning for something comforting. When I saw Pope Benedict's wrinkled face on the wall of the kindergarten, some inner part of me melted and I thought of my own Catholic kindergarten in the US in Northport Village, that same village where my soul buddy Jack Kerouac once used to drink and write.

I thought of my childhood time, how I would get lost on the school grounds, only to be rescued by a well-meaning nun. Twenty five years later, Marta would cry "*Tsau!*" to the nuns and run down the sidewalks before the big brick Catholic church with its silvery roof and be scooped up into the arms of one of the young and cheerful Czech nuns, who blessed her. The nuns lived around the corner from Kassitoome, and our paths often crossed in the park.

My mother had told me terrible stories about the German nuns who ran the Catholic school she attended as a child, in 1950s New York City. The German nuns believed in corporal punishment and would strike children with a ruler, or toss erasers across the room at them, should they get out of line. It was hard to imagine these nuns on Kassitoome acting in such a way, maybe because they were Tartu nuns, which meant that they had been possessed by the kind spirit of the place, the Tartu *vaim*.

When we left Kassitoome, the sky was still clear though the light was fading away. Marta sat on my shoulders and waved at the clouds.

"Marta, what are you doing?" I asked.

"I am waving to an angel."

"Where did you learn about angels?"

"I don't know," she said and toyed with my hair. "I just know about them."

"So, did you have fun playing with Giacomo today?"

"Ugh. How many times do I have to tell you? Giacomo is a boy."

"He seems like a nice Italian boy."

"No, he's not. He's mean to girls. Even to his sister Teresa."

"I'm sure he'll grow out of it."

"What did you do today, Daddy?"

"I worked on my book some more."

"You and Mommy are always writing. Will you ever stop?"

"We will play tonight. Okay?"

That night I kept my word and played and then read Marta to sleep. Then I set the alarm for 5 a.m. so that I could continue to write the book.

LESSONS FROM THE MASTERS

"You constantly portray yourself as this helpless guy in the hands of her. It's not believable, and I find it tough to stay with you in those scenes."

Vello's tirade went on. "Your style sometimes becomes too cute, which can be too much to take. There's a dangerous fine line between happy-go-lucky and cute. I think you should make your character smarter than you do. If you do that, you'll force more interesting dialogue."

He looked up at me from the swivel chair in his office, not even bothering to rise, too engrossed by his latest issue of *The New Yorker*.

"And another thing. What kind of crappy font are you using?"

"Arial."

"That lame, girly, journalisty font has got to go."

"What do you suggest?"

Vello shrugged and his hair flopped around a bit. Charcoal head, boyish face, faded grandpa jacket. He looked like a 1960s TV host bundled through time. "Courier New," he said. "Times New Roman."

"Okay. I think I'll use Courier New."

Vello turned his chair to face me and looked up. "As it stands now, I'm sitting on your shoulder, seeing what you see. But there's no conflict. There's nothing you want but can't have. In Epp's *My America* there was conflict, it was Epp Versus the Wasteful American Way of Life. Sometimes she was Don Quixote, sometimes Carrie Nation, sometimes she crawled into herself and gave up. The reader sees her resist, be overcome by some of it, triumph, come to terms with it all. But you..."

Why did I feel like I was at the doctor's office? Does this hurt? How about here? How about I tell you that your writing sucks, Vello?

But I did need help if I was going to attempt this great prison break. That's what this was. I was trying to break out of mainstream life. A lifetime of paycheck-to-paycheck living and TV wasn't going to do it for me. I needed to channel something greater than myself, something as eternal as the stars. Because writing didn't really come from you. It came *through* you, from somewhere else. Once you let it trickle its way through your fingers, there was no way back.

"I guess I'll have to do another rewrite then," I said. "You know I worked on that story for a long..."

"I hope you don't think I'm too negative," Vello cut me off and gestured with his hands as if yielding an invisible pipe. "But what are you up against in that book? You might say I'll find out, but I don't think a reader will stick with you. By chapter four, the reader needs to know: what is the conflict? What are you reading, by the way? It better not be Hunter S. Thompson's *Fear and Loathing in Las Vegas*. If you want to rip off new journalism, ape Gay Talese. Ever read his great story 'Frank Sinatra Has a Cold'?"

"Not yet. I've been reading Hemingway recently, different novels. Haruki Murakami's *Norwegian Wood*." And "Ivan Orav's Memoirs."

"*Ivan Orav*?" Vello squinted at me. "But that's Andrus Kivi-rähk. You can read Estonian?"

I rubbed my face. This writing business was a bit harder than I had thought. "I can now. Reading is much easier than writing."

I got all of those books at the Lutsu Library in downtown Tartu. It was a big, fine building, Stalinist maybe, but elusive in the political ideology of its architects. From the top floor window, if you rode the elevator up or walked the stairs, you had the best view of Tartu there was to be had in that area. All of those angled, tiled roofs squeezed into one window frame, one leading down to another, with a third rising between. Sometimes you would see it in winter, with the confectionery dusting of snow, or otherwise with that wild feeling of white summer nights, when the cars would roll up to the liquor store, the *alkopood*, down on the street below, and you could feel the stress of life coming off in each breath. Oh, those wild white nights of Tartu. When the library shut its doors in winter, it was always midnight black out, but during white nights in June they would close up the building and it would feel like it was still afternoon. Then you would take your books under arm and walk home. People barely slept in June and didn't feel the need to sleep. There was more time for everything. Men sawed wood in their yards at midnight, a friend might call you at the same time. "Summer etiquette," they called it.

And with all of that time, there were more opportunities to read.

From the shelf in the foreign-language section, I pulled the volumes. Ernest Hemingway's *The Sun Also Rises*. Henry Miller's *Tropic of Cancer*. Scott Fitzgerald's *Tender is the Night*. All of them wrote their books in Europe, I noticed. But why was it so? How could it be that the best American writers had all lived abroad?

The foreign-language fiction was a floor above the Estonian-language fiction. I often looked through the downstairs door and pondered venturing inside, but something about Estonian literature seemed too daunting. Even a one-word title, like Fred Jüssi's *Jäälõhkuja* (Icebreaker) could stop you dead in your tracks. Plus, there were so many English-language books I wanted to read.

But I had heard so much about Kivirähk, that I decided to give him a try. Almost every Estonian I knew had his own Kivirähk collection. They considered him the new national writer, a modern day A.H. Tammsaare. It was said that when his book, *Mees, kes teadis ussisõnu* (The Man Who Knew Snake Words) appeared, there were so many Estonians reading it while on vacation at the Red Sea resorts that the Egyptians began to wonder if the blue book with the silver snake emblem on its cover was some kind of holy testament.

One day I worked up the courage to go into the Estonian-language fiction section at the library and take out a Kivirähk book to attempt to read it. I settled on *Ivan Orava mälestused* (The Memoirs of Ivan Orav) because it was slimmer than the others and because I found its illustrations amusing. It also carried with it that cool literature feel, the feel of something necessary and seditious. Kivirähk was still thought of as a young man back then: he had a boyish face with brushy hair, so that he reminded one of a porcupine. His older brother Juhan, a political analyst, also had that special hedgehog face, except Juhan, who I had seen at the Meri Conferences, was quite serious and Andrus was the author of a children's book called *Kaka ja Kevad* (Caca and Spring).

It became an instant bestseller.

Kivirähk's best known work was probably *Rehepapp* (Old Barny), which begins with a sick peasant being surrounded by superstitious villagers, all of whom thought him to be possessed. But, it turns out, he had just swallowed some of the master's soap. Some Estonians really loved this scene in *Rehepapp*. What I think they liked about it, was how foolish everybody looked, both the peasant for eating the soap, and the other villagers for thinking he was possessed. They thought it was so funny. (Although, some of them said it was a very sad book.)

The Estonians, as I saw it, relished the stupidity of others. The premise of their comedies was to push the boundaries of idiotic behavior.

The dumber, the better.

What Kivirähk excelled at was feeding this aching national hunger for stupidity. He was like a peddler of stupidity, with a little cart of funny gags, pushing it along down the street. The people would rush to him. "Kivirähk, Oh, Kivirähk. Please, tell us something funny!" Kivirähk looked around with his porcupine face and blushed a bit. "Aww, shucks. Well... If you really want it..."

Kivirähk later complained in an interview that he hated when people asked him to say something funny. Once, I saw him out walking a dog in central Tallinn and I was so tempted to ask it too, just to see what would he answer. I literally held my breath as I passed Kivirähk, restraining myself. "Don't ask him. Don't!" I think he knew that I recognized him, but he looked away.

The writer had good reason to remain aloof in public. He made stupid jokes about everybody, so he was despised with equal passion. The conservatives, Tallinn Mayor Edgar Savisaar, the devout: everybody had a great reason to hate Kivirähk.

Even Val Koso, the Foreign Ministry's resident Eskimo, hated Kivirähk and he wasn't even Estonian.

"Oh, no. Andrus Kivirähk? I hate that guy," Koso had told me during our meeting at the Estonian House. He didn't say why, but I later understood that it had something to do with his book *Ivan Orav*.

"Ivan Orav Chronology" by Andrus Kivirähk, translated for Loone Ots' Estonian Literature class.

1908   Ivan Orav is born.

1909   Ivan Orav's first word: "*Eesti Vabaliik*" (Estonian Le-public)

1915   Orav goes to school and draws a picture of Lydia Koidula on the wall, for which he spends the whole day in the corner.

1918   Orav builds his own armored train out of old scythes and armaments and wants to travel with it to fight in the war of independence, but gets smacked by his father.

1924   Orav sees a *tibla** for the first time: Arnold Sommerling, a participant in the failed December uprising, is found hiding in the branches of an apple tree. Orav brings him down with a stone.

1926   Orav passes his blacksmith's exam and shaves for the first time. Two months in the hospital.

1928   Orav travels by train to Tallinn to buy matches and meets the politician Konstantin Päts in the station's canteen. It is friendship at first sight. After that he never returns to his father's farm.

1929   When coming home one night, Orav finds a drunken man in his bed. This is the beginning of his friendship with Jaan Tõnisson.

---

*   A derogatory slang word for Soviet Russians.

1930   General Johan Laidoner brings his horse for Orav to fix. The horse, Suksu, gets new legs and kidneys. The beginning of a life-long friendship.

1933   Orav does dentistry for the first time and pulls Tammsaare's tooth out.

1940   Orav is arrested and sent to a cold land. He successfully escapes, but later finds himself in the clutches of the devil's vodka.

1944   Orav gets sober and returns to Estonia.

1945   Orav heads to the forest and commits himself to victory against the tiblas.

1948   A short romance with one mushroom picker,

1949   A short romance with one berry picker.

1952   A summer filled with mosquitoes. Orav comes out of the forest.

1953   Stalin's death fills Orav with such joy that he proposes to his manager's granddaughter. Orav becomes a domesticated man.

1957   The first tiblas arrive in Orav's yard. He ensnares them in a trap.

1961   Orav leaves a dead hamster under the Johannes Käbin cabinet's floorboard.

1963   A sick cosmonaut falls in Orav's yard. Orav nurses him back to health so he can fly again.

1968   Orav goes to the song festival jubilee with three pigs dressed up as lions because the tiblas don't have the strength to arrest "three lions."

1974   Orav listens to the Voice of America so loudly that all of the windows on his street are shattered.

1982 During Brezhnev's funeral, Orav teaches his dog and cat to dance and puts on a circus in Nõmme.

1988 Orav doesn't spend one night at home. Instead he goes from one meeting to the next. His legs become 5 centimeters shorter and his pants are too loose.

1991 Orav helps to carry the Russian Army's bags over the Narva River.

1994 Orav finds in his yard the last slightly rotten and worm-eaten tibla.

1997 Orav receives four medals from the president at one time and makes them into a ladle for his sauna in his blacksmith shop.

2001 Orav is really sick, but when he sees Vladimir Putin on TV, he goes looking in the attic for his old machine gun.

Tibla was a derogatory term for a Russian and/or Communist dating back to the interwar years. It came from the Russian term, "*ti, bliad*," which meant "you bitch," but was still in use among the country's older generation. Tibla. There was the rhyme of a joke to it. Not every Russian was a tibla. Tchaikovsky wasn't. Pushkin wasn't. Dostoevsky wasn't a tibla. But Brezhnev? He was the King Tibla. That bitter old man at the market? Tibla.

Epp had told me once how she had first heard the word tibla from her cousin Helina, who had heard it from an older relative during the Singing Revolution.

"And do you know, they aren't really Russians? My auntie says that they are actually tiblas!" That's what Estonian teenage girls were whispering in 1988.

And so the great secret of the *tibla*-word was passed on to me, that gauzy veil of hatred that could be appreciated by even a novice reader of Estonian, as I was at the time, and could make me laugh out loud, as I did at the library, prompting a very stern stone face from the lady librarian, who demanded absolute silence.

"I'm sorry, sir, but if you cannot contain your laughter in here, I must ask you to please leave."

In the stairwell of the library, beneath the haunting portraits of Loone Ots, Elo Viiding, and Viivi Luik, I thought of Val Koso, the Eskimo who had been locked in the basement of the embassy in Washington, and how he had *hated* Kivrähk. Why? Maybe it was because Ivan Orav's Memoirs were a satire of the great national conservative narrative about Estonia. And that perspective, best articulated in those days by Val's old drinking buddy Mart Laar, seemed to be beyond satire.

For most Westerners at the murky intersection of the diplomatic, intelligence, and media worlds, the national conservative politician Mart Laar *was* Estonia. There were three men in this Estonian Holy Trinity: Lennart Meri (The Father), Mart Laar (The Son) and Toomas Hendrik Ilves (The Holy Ghost). Yes, the bearded, bespectacled Laar was clearly Jesus. He, of them all, was the resurrected patriot who would come again to judge the living and the dead and his kingdom (Estonia) would have no end, forever and ever. Amen.

As for the writer Andrus Kivirähk? He was probably Lucifer, that cynical jester. Naughty devil.

Maybe that's why Vello had spoken so fondly of him.

"Because if the conservatives and everybody else hate him, he must be doing something right."

Kivirähk pissed everybody off, but the memoirs of the fictional curmudgeonly pensioner Ivan Orav were particularly offensive to some conservatives, whose ideology was based on a very powerful myth. It went something like this. Estonia and Finland had been more or less on equal economic footing before World War II. Had Estonia retained its independence after 1944, it would have been just as wealthy and free as its brother nation. The mission of the conservative movement in Estonia was to restore the country to this idyll. All symbols and public references to socialism were to be erased or relocated, and in their place monuments to the state that had existed in the 1920s and 1930s would arise. This would eventually give one the feeling that Communism had never existed, as the old collective farm buildings were one by one molded by the invisible hand of the free market into spas or casinos.

I liked to think of this attitude as raising the Titanic. The restorationists like Laar wanted to return to pre-war splendor. Not only would they raise the sunken relic of the golden age, but they would restore it to its former glory. And add free WiFi.

What Kivirähk did in *Ivan Orav* was piss all over this piety. He chose the most popular format – the personal memoir – as the vehicle for his satire of the Good Old Days. Half of Estonia might have hated Kivirähk for it, but I didn't hate him for it. I learned from him.

As much as Vello's words could sting, I took them in stride and continued quietly with my work. I always had this feeling that I was getting somewhere, digging down to somewhere, ascending up to somewhere, and that nothing I wrote would ever be my very best, but that everything I wrote would be better than what had come before, or at least would remind me and others of previous glories, as if I had once touched the sun and returned with a handful of burning light. It was a deeply religious pursuit, a smoldering within, that kept me writing on. Whenever I had a successful day writing, I would be happy, and also my wife would seem to love me more.

It was around this time that I got sick. I came down with something infectious out in Karksi, where my father-in-law lived, something that made the throat swell and the joints ache, something that had Epp's relatives packing me off, so that I could partake of the special Estonian cure – sea buckthorn berries, onions, garlic, and honey. A few teaspoons of the pungent stuff went down all right but I was still bed-ridden for a week and growing weaker, with *Ivan Orav* as my only companion. Epp's grandparents heard I was sick, and soon they were calling the house to inquire about my condition and to advise their own natural cures. Did he put goose fat on his feet? Did he gurgle with baking soda and water? This was really odd to me. Did they think I was going to die?

"Warm milk with honey," said Grandpa Karl. "And drink plenty of hot tea," added Grandma Laine.

I had felt invisible for so long, but suddenly my Estonian relatives cared about me, though their folk cures still didn't manage to restore my health. In the end, the doctor was called. She came with her white uniform and kit, felt my throat and put me on antibiotics, and I got better in days with *Ivan Orav* always at my side to keep me company.

"1971 – Tiblas gave Orav a toe infection in a public sauna. Sick for a little while."

WITH TAAGEPERA IN KAUNAS

With the great Rein Taagepera in Kaunas, I felt that I had found some kind of soul brother, if soul brothers could look like elves.

He did! He looked just like one! Vello was always grumbling to me about how I shouldn't write off the Estonians as Tolkien characters, that it was "cliche" and that their well-honed "Hobbit" image allowed them to escape more penetrating scrutiny but, you know what, Vello wasn't always right.

Every time I looked at Taagepera, I saw elf. The curly white hair, the pointy ears, the eyes that curled up into the finest of slits. He dressed all in black like Johnny Cash and walked like he was going somewhere important. That somewhere was probably just the Sokos Hotel restaurant for the breakfast buffet. We met there, introduced by Andres Kasekamp, who had come to seem like some kind of guardian angel to me. Not that I ever confessed my deepest feelings to Kasekamp, but he just seemed to appear at the right moments, like that microsecond when my elbow bumped into Taagepera's as he went for a second helping of sliced tomatoes and cucumbers in Kaunas.

"Rein, I want you to meet Justin Petrone. He's studying Baltic Studies with us at Tartu."

"Ah, yes, Justin. I read the abstract for your talk," Taagepera said and his eyes folded up into those elvish slits. "Sounds kind of interesting."

He was a political scientist who had once run for president. We treated his volumes, *Estonia: Return to Independence*, and *The Baltic States, Years of Dependence 1940–1990*, as holy texts in class. He split his time teaching between Tartu and Irvine, California. It seemed an ideal life for anybody.

Taagepera was born in 1933 in Estonia, but left with many others in 1944, graduated from high school in Morocco, and eventually moved to the US. When I asked him later how his family had managed to survive both the Soviet and German occupations, he answered: "The Communists instructed my father to build a Red corner at the university library, but he took his time building it. Each time they came to check on it, he said, 'It's just not ready yet,' because everybody knew the Germans were coming."

In exile, Taagepera had found his home in academia. He had even authored a paper in 1971 where he proposed a 30-year plan under which Estonia and its neighbors would regain independence by 2001. This was obviously out of date. But that's where Baltic independence existed during the Soviet era. Other than in the exile societies, it lived on in university Baltic Studies programs.

Each year, these Baltic Studies programs would arrange a grand conference, a meeting of the Baltic minds. That year's event was in Kaunas, Lithuania, and I was invited too.

I took the Eurolines bus straight down from the Tartu bus station, stopping in Riga, and then on toward flat and humid Lithuania. In all my Estonian years, I had been once to Latvia and never to Lithuania, even though the world thought of them as a contiguous unit. While hilly, birch-tree dotted northern Latvia bore some resemblance to the land I left behind, but with far more terrifying roads, that all changed once we passed the Daugava River.

Beyond the Daugava was the prairie-like humidity of southern Latvia and then Lithuania with its Catholic shrines along the roads. The saunas disappeared from the homesteads, and everything – the houses, the fields, even the air – seemed golden yellow and warm. There was less of that cool and remote northern blue you encountered in Estonia, maybe in the trim of a house, or just in the sky above the islands. The cities changed, too, from the sturdy, geometric, Puritannical whites and grays of the northern towns to the swanky, gold and red New Orleans-like lanes of curvy balconies, iron lamps, and gangs of locals gathered around bar fronts speaking loudly in a language that could have been Polish or Russian or even Czech based on its sounds.

It was said that Lithuanians still spoke Russian well, even though they had the tiniest of Russian minorities and their greatest ethnic dilemmas and Internet hatred pile-ons revolved around Vilnius Poles who wanted to use Polish letters in their Lithuanian passports. It sounded like a Monty Python sketch, but it was true and caused big problems. Sometimes the Lithuanians and Poles didn't get along at all. Lithuanian, while removed from Russian on the Indo-European family tree and not a Slavic tongue, was still Indo-European, and the sounds of the two languages, their boisterous cadences, were more similar to each other than to Estonian.

More than ever, in hot June in dusty Kaunas, I felt as if Estonia was truly alone on its perch in the world. Estonia, the solitary island. I felt alone when I rolled up with my bag to the hotel, and then went to buy some pirogies from the Maxima across the street. I felt alone when I paid a cashier named Daumantas, and alone as I took the elevator to the eighth floor and shoveled the greasy dumplings into my mouth while I reviewed the PowerPoint slides for the next day's big talk.

The first slide had impressive portraits of King Charles XII of Sweden, *Karl Kaksteist*, as he was called in Estonian, and Peter the Great of Russia, *Peeter Suur*, who had fought each other in the Great Northern War, a bloody conflict that raged for the first two decades of the 18th century, from Narva in Estonia to the fields of Poltava in Ukraine. It resulted in the Baltic German nobility capitulating to *Peeter Suur* and Estonia becoming part of the Russian Empire, an event that somehow made some Russians believe they had a real estate claim to the country to this day.

When it came to the retelling of the great war between the great powers, the Estonians were very obviously on the side of Sweden. The era of Swedish rule was known as "The Good Old Swedish Time." There were Swedish monuments all over Estonia – to Gustaf Adolf outside the University of Tartu as well as the famous Swedish Lion sculpture in Narva. Even President Ilves' birth, in Stockholm in 1953 to exile parents, seemed but more fruit of this long-standing uncle-nephew relationship between Sweden and Estonia.

When President Ilves would meet with Swedish Foreign Minister Carl Bildt or King Carl XVI Gustaf, he would wear a bow tie sewn from Swedish blue and gold. There were even a few parishes in Western Estonia that had Swedish signs, even though there were but a handful of Swedes living there nowadays. In Narva, most of the signs were in Estonian, even though there were but handful of Estonians there. When the Narva City Government tried to erect a statue to Peter the Great, Prime Minister Ansip intervened and the plan was nixed.

Estonia was apparently still Swedish territory.

I had relied on Rein Taagepera's books for my anti-Russian perspective in the presentation, which I was told could become my master's thesis. It was Taagepera who had provided the most scathing indictment of Peter the Great's actions in his newly won Baltic Provinces. "The usual plunder and murder were aggravated by a systemic scorched earth policy ordered by the Russian tsar," he wrote. "The entire burgher population of Tartu was deported to Vologda and Kostroma in northern Russia, foreshadowing Soviet mass deportations." Taagepera watched me from the front row as I gave my Power-Point presentation to a room full of students and professors, his slits of eyes smarting with amusement. Then the elf in black got up and gave his own presentation, which challenged almost everything I had just said.

"It's been very interesting to see some of my old words up here, but let me tell you there was more to the story."

That's how Taagepera started. There was a slight murmuring of muffled, academic laughs. "Now, Estonia, as you know, is the windy land. It is today known for its lovely windmills and now its wind energy turbines."

There was a bit of an old creakiness to the man's voice and a softness about the consonants.

Taagepera paced back and forth before a projected silhouette of Peter the Great. Or maybe there was no silhouette. Maybe it was Peter the Great's ghost I saw there. It was he who had wrested Estonia from the Swedes in the Great Northern War. If Peter had not won Estonia, the past 300 years would have been different.

You could see Peter up there behind Taagepera, that old-fashioned cavalier hat, the outline of his nose and mustache and long hair, and then the chest that sloped down to some fairytale boots. When Taagepera's eye slits opened a bit, you could see the irises, which were an otherworldly intelligent blue. All of the skin on his face seemed to fold into itself, like the wrinkled and puckered peel of a yellow baby potato boiled away in sea salt.

"What is good about this wind is that while it blows empires in," the old man circled his hands in a wind-like movement, "it also blows them away. While I may have argued in the past that Peter the Great's influence on Estonia was a mostly negative one, I'm not so sure now that this is entirely the case. The reforms of the absolutist Charles XI of Sweden at the end of the 17th Century were aimed at ending serfdom for once and for all and putting the Estonians on the path to full citizenship within the Swedish Empire. But had they ended serfdom at that time, when all education was in German, and all public life was in German, then the Estonians surely within a few generations would have completely Germanized and I would not be standing here speaking to you about any Estonian-speaking people with funny names like Taagepera."

A few more faint laughs. A cough.

"The Estonian wind continued to blow," he circled his hands again, "and it blew in Peter the Great, who reversed the Swedish reforms, allowing serfdom to continue for another century. So this great risk to Estonian identity, of Germanization, was avoided, and Estonian identity was allowed to survive into the Romantic period."

Taagepera stood still and looked directly into my eyes. "It thus could be argued that without Peter the Great, there would be no Estonian State."

I felt every laser eye in that auditorium on the nape of my neck. Taagepera was just too damn good.

Instead of thinking of points I could use to argue my case back against the Godfather of Baltic Studies, I was scribbling madly, jotting down other thoughts in my notebook.

I was thinking of a conversation I had once had with an American fellow named Rick, about what to do when your 90-day tourist period in Estonia ran out, and your life was such that you had to stay for a longer time.

I was writing my first book, *My Estonia 1*.

My dream of becoming the next Taagepera or Kasekamp had already died its death weeks before.

It had died south of Stockholm, where there was a college that offered a PhD program in Baltic Studies. It had died when one of the professors, a clean, sharp, older woman with shoulder-length gray hair and a collared shirt, enlightened me as to what my duties would be as a PhD student.

"So, if I am accepted, we were thinking of getting an apartment somewhere in Stockholm," I said.

"Oh, no!" her eyes lit up. "You will be living here, on campus, in one of the university dormitories."

"But I have a family."

"*You* have a family?"

"Yes, I have a family. I have two daughters. And a wife."

"*You* have two daughters? And a wife?"

"What? Is that so hard to believe?"

"You just look so young."

"I'm going to be 30 soon. Is that young?"

"How old are your children?"

"Five and almost two."

"I have a seven year old," the dignified lady said.

There was an uncomfortable pause.

"Do you have university living places for PhD students with families?" I asked.

"I don't really know. Most of the PhD students who come to us do not have such responsibilities."

"But it is still possible to live off campus. We could rent a place."

"With what income?" she poked at a piece of paper with the back of a pen. "Your stipend will be too small for a rental in Stockholm. Besides, the waiting lists for good flats are notoriously long."

"I have a job, too, you know. I work as a biotech journalist. And I am writing a book." I had been doing both, even that same day. I was expected back at a genetics conference north of the city, where the attendees had no idea that I might also be a Baltic Studies student, or a wannabe Kerouac.

"You won't have time for working as a journalist or writing books if you are in the PhD program."

"I won't?"

"You absolutely will not."

I looked at the woman, at her clean, sharp Swedish face, her gray hair, and then I looked at all of those books around her, the Ikea shelves, and the construction of the building itself, all of its metal and cement and glass, the futuristic-looking Scandinavian design chairs and lamps.

I used to worship these people, and maybe I still did. I admired their welfare state, I admired their egalitarianism. I admired their pretty people on bicycles. But down there in the university building I started to feel those walls close in around me, that suffocating feeling. If I wasn't careful, I could get stuck here and those walls would take over all my thinking.

I cleared my throat. "The Estonian school we wanted to put the kids in is in the old town of Stockholm. So it would make much more sense for us to live somewhere closer to that area. Surely, we might be able to arrange a place."

"You won't be in Stockholm very much."

"But won't I be going to school right here? Doing the PhD work right here?"

"You most certainly will not. You will be all over. You will be taking some classes in Örebro, too. In fact, we'll have to see if we can arrange a room for you to stay there as well, because you will be in Örebro as often as you will be here. Maybe three days a week you will be out teaching in Örebro."

But how the hell am I supposed to take care of my family in Stockholm if I'm in goddamn Örebro?

"Okay."

"By the way, what academic books have you been reading?" she crossed her legs and eyed me.

And now the big lie. I had a Haruki Murakami novel in my bag. But the last academic work I had read was...?

"*Daughter of the Baltic* by Matti Klinge. It's about the history of Helsin..."

"I know it very well. What did you think of that book?"

I hadn't actually read it. I had skimmed its dense contents about 19th century Finnish living standards and put it back on the shelf. It had been a gift from the Finnish foreign ministry to its foreign correspondence program students, and I only consulted it during periods of intense boredom.

"It was highly detailed," I said.

"How so?"

"It was about Finnish living standards at that time. What kinds of food they ate." I tried not to yawn.

"That is how Matti works. He produces highly informative texts. Did you have any other opinions?"

The Ikea clock thundered on the wall.

"Not really."

"None at all?"

"Nope."

"Oh," she squinted at me. It was then that I knew that she knew.

I was an imposter.

Give an academic a book and they will break it down and discuss it like machines. This woman seemed like a machine. If you filed your application and got your recommendation letters, if you signed your life over to her, you could become part of the proud machinery. She would tell you what you could and could not do, where you could and could not be. She could tell you that classes were more important than family. Because family was an afterthought when you had the program. That would all come before you earned the gold medal of a PhD and were Deemed Worthy. But what would you do with that PhD once you won it? Work more, teach more? I wanted to *write* more. I wanted to finish the book and start another. I had ideas.

So that was how our plans changed. There would be no Sweden, no PhD studies for me.

Epp had thrown herself into this Swedish dream with her typical jungle cat restlessness. Not only had she spent time looking up apartments in the Stockholm area, she had found a Swedish course for us in Tartu where we sat around playing bingo in Swedish. *Sjuttiosju? Sjuttiosju**. She had taken the vocabulary words from our lessons, written them out on brown construction paper and posted them on the wall of the Cold Room. She had rented Swedish movies and been in touch with the Estonian school in Stockholm's Old Town. It was all falling into place, our vibrant Swedish academic future.

I stood in the stairwell of the college and made a phone call. My hands were shaking even though it wasn't cold. The stairwell smelled of an overflowing toilet or a chemistry experiment that had employed sulphur. Some ungodly student-like stink. God, why did I ever think that academic life was right for me? Hadn't I worked so hard in my college years so that I would graduate and never go to school again?

"Hey, it's me."

"Oh," Epp sounded cheerful. "We are having a beautiful day in Tartu. We are at the park and Anna is picking flowers. What is the weather like in Stockholm?"

"Gray."

"Did you have your meeting with the head of the program?"

"We met."

"Did you get any kind of feeling? Would they take you? Did you like it there?"

"It's..."

"Did you ask her about getting a place to live in the city center, near the kids' school?"

---

* Seventy-seven in Swedish.

"I don't think this is the right future for me."

"What?"

"Not the right way. I'm really sorry. I can explain more later."

"Really? Oh, wow. Okay. Look, I have to go. Anna is eating sand. ANNA!"

When the session in Kaunas was over, Taagepera pulled me aside in the corridor.

"That was a very interesting talk you gave there. You should keep up with that topic. Have you considered pursuing that for your master's thesis? It seems like the way to go."

"Maybe. But I thought you were an Estonian. I thought you were supposed to be on the side of *Karl Kaksteist*."

Taagepera chuckled a little. "Charles XII was a very ambitious young ruler. He was only 18 years old when he led the forces at Narva, during the first battle, which the Swedes won. If he had stopped there, he could have kept Estonia. But his ambition, and recklessness, got the best of him. You know how he died, right?"

"He was shot in the head in battle."

"Correct. I've even seen the image of his mortal wound. They took a photo of Karl's body when they re-interred it about a hundred years ago. It was ugly. But, you know, he led his men deep into Ukraine, and got way too many of them killed. Then he invaded Norway, which is where he died. There was always the question if the bullet that killed Charles

XII came from a Danish soldier's musket, or if it came from one of his own men."

"Really? You think one of his own men might have killed him?"

"Well, you know," Taagepera leaned in and whispered as if he had been there. "It was an awfully close shot."

Taagepera and the other professors didn't take the Eurolines bus back to Tartu. They all drove to Vilnius and took a plane up to Tallinn and then caught another bus down to Tartu. It was another fine example of how unconnected the three Baltic States really were.

When my bus arrived in Tartu it was still light. There were men and women in folk costumes walking back from a festival. I could see them through the leaves of the trees and I could hear them, because even though the festival was over, they were still singing. The air in Tartu was nice and cool, a breeze carried the scent of blossoms. Tartu felt like home that night. We moved away one year later.

VILJANDI SEDUCTION

It was Tagaq who seduced me.

Tanya Tagaq of Nunavut, world-renowned Inuit throat singer, a big, brown, beautiful woman who with her *ha* grunts and *ugh* sighs and *urra* physical heaving and rolling gave birth to something bloody and thrilling each night. When Tagaq the throat singer came to Estonia she gave two performances. One was in Tallinn somewhere. The other was at the Viljandi *Pärimusmuusika Ait*.

An *Ait* in Estonian means a barn, but in English they called this building the Estonian Traditional Music Center. Yet it was neither a barn nor a center. It was a beating, pulsating, living muscle built out of bloody red bricks. Originally, it was part of an old manor complex, built in the mid-18th century as part of a gift from the Czarina to a local Dame. But the Ait transcended time. To be inside its crimson walls was to feel oneself in the gullet of a whale, or the womb of a sea lioness. It was within this chasm that the throat singing seduction took place. "So erotic," a girl beside me whispered.

Set atop a hill, the Ait overlooked grassy ravines, remnants of the Teutonic Order Castle that had been blasted to smithereens by Polish cannon in 1603, its leftover stones carted away by do-it-yourself Estonians so that they could build sturdier barns for their firewood and good latrines.

I can imagine those guys were even *happy* the Poles blew up the castle because of all the free rocks. They were rolling their wheelbarrows over that wooden bridge and whistling.

"Hi ho, hi ho, it's off to work we go." I could almost hear them singing it to themselves.

The region of the castle ruins, including the Ait, was known to all Viljandi children as Lossikad. The windows of the cafe on the second floor of the Ait looked out on the ancient fortifications of Lossikad and when you looked out of them at night, especially in winter, and saw the yellow lights of the lanterns on the snow, the shadows of the ruined castle walls looming over them, and heard the conversations of the good-looking young people in their loose, old-fashioned clothing, you felt blessed. You felt lucky to see such real beauty, and all of it for free. It seemed sometimes as if anybody who was anybody in the world of culture made his or her presence felt at the Ait. On the night of the Tagaq concert I even saw Peeter Volkonski[*], the high and supreme cultural instigator of all Estonian hepcats, come walking down the aisles, slowly, gracefully, with his gray and white beard, beatnik cap, flowing cloak, and cane.

---

[*]   Peeter Volkonski is an Estonian actor, rock musician, and composer. He is a descendant of the Rurik dynasty, and an influential art figure in Estonia.

It was like a coronation.

There were several spaces within the Ait, and in one of them on the night of the Tagaq concert the 1922 silent film *Nanook of the North* was projected on the wall as the students from the local academy of arts provided musical accompaniment with voice and strings and percussion, some approximation of indigenous music. Eerie. Young musicians, a young audience, all of them beautiful in every way, in the sloppiness of their hair, in the absence of cynicism on their pale pretty faces. The old documentary about Eskimos on the eastern shore of Canada's Hudson Bay played out on the wall.

"A sentinel is always on watch for while walrus are ferocious on water, they are helpless on land."

The Eskimo, who looked exactly like Val Koso, laid his ear to the ice until he pulled a seal out of a crack and wrestled it to death, seeming to offer words of comfort in its ear. And so it surrendered its life, its meat, its blood, to the man who lived in an ice house. The muffled beat carried it along, *plum plum plam* with each pale pretty face holding its pale, pretty breath, while the plucks of the strings cascaded over the rhythms like shards of broken ice cracking in the sunlight.

It was winter, and all of Viljandi was packed in white, so that you came to think of the Ait as an igloo, and as Tagaq as a witch who managed to capture the good-evil duality of womanhood that you had always known but could never describe. There was something about the whole bewitching spectacle that made me feel as if Viljandi and I were of the same dimension. We were both trying to touch something spiritual, something sensual, something elusive. The town had already started to feel like home, although I had come there only for a concert.

It was one year later when the ice melted and collected in clear pools between the cobblestones of the most treacherous and wild remnant of Viljandi Old Town: Lower Pikk Street. I remember that day very clearly: the water between the mossy rocks, how it mirrored the blue above, and if you looked closely enough at it, you could also see the reflection of the white moon in the daytime sky. It was the oldest street in Viljandi Old Town, a thousand years old, they said. It started out trustworthy enough with Upper Pikk Street behind the liquor store that would one day become Cafe Fellin, and proceeded under the watch of Saint John's Church, the Ingrian-Finnish Society's yellowy cream building, then beyond the Kondas Centre of Naive and Outsider Art and those strawberry sculptures. It flowed down a bit more past leaning homes with laundry strung out to dry, children running and hiding and *Kuri koer* (Angry Dog) signs, with curious dogs barking, until you reached the crest of the hill and had the air sucked out of your lungs by the great awesome view of the lake.

I remember how I paused to look with wind tussling my hair and peace settling in to a more slowly beating heart.

"You know, you're really lucky," I told Epp.

She finished her phone conversation and cocked an eyebrow at me. "Wait, what did you say? Why am I lucky?"

"Because you were born in such a beautiful place."

"Oh," she blushed a bit. "Yeah. It is really nice here, especially now in spring." She stretched her arms. "When I was a child my parents would take me to swim right down there, on that beach," she gestured. "It hasn't changed since then. So much of it is the same."

"It reminds me of Centerport. My first childhood memories."

"Because of the water?"

"And because of the hills, all of these narrow streets. That's just what it was like when I was a kid."

I missed Long Island a bit when I said it, but I knew I could never live back there where I grew up, not unless I abandoned my writer's dreams and was willing to take on infinite debt to fund a lifestyle we could never afford, because that's is how life went in my America. But we weren't in my hometown. We were in her hometown. Our childhoods were intermeshing, all of the shared and now common memories. That's what happens when you live with the same person for a long time.

Beyond that point, Lower Pikk Street, was neither street nor path. On most maps it was a thin gray line, curving down toward the lake showing that it could, in theory, be traversed.

The houses on this thin gray line bore Pikk Street addresses but they seemed to exist in their own dimension. This was the region of the lake-front villas. At the crest of the hill next to the Waldorf School, stood a green and yellow mansion that was supposedly haunted. Later, a couple who had lived there on the second floor told me the ghost stories were true, and how they had heard noises and seen a figure at night, and also seen doors open and shut themselves.

After that flow of information, I never felt comfortable walking beneath those windows at night. I did see an apparition in the house across the street though, an old wooden dwelling with multiple families within and toys and broken-down gardening equipment in the yard. It was on Halloween night, years later. I remember looking up at the second floor window, through gobs of marshmallow-like fog circulating in unpredictable ways.

I was just confused. *What the hell is that thing?*

These two haunted houses flanked the opening to Lower Pikk Street, which, as I have said, wasn't really a street. I guess at some point, it had all been functional with cobblestones, but the earth had shifted beneath it over the centuries, so that the stones had collapsed into each other, and someone had tried to fix this by pouring concrete and asphalt in the ditches and holes but these broke into pieces, too.

It was useless as a street.

Only jeeps could make it down Lower Pikk Street without trouble, and the local taxi company had one certain car that it would send to fetch passengers from the so-called *Muksimaja*, Muks' House halfway down the hill, and sometimes, when it was too icy, they would refuse to send anyone at all. Then you would have to haul your bags to the top of the hill.

Muks' House was the nickname of the three-story, yellow and white Bavarian-looking castle that towered over Lower

Pikk Street. It was officially referred to as the Villa Rosenberg. If you scanned the lakefront of Viljandi you saw a lot of these gorgeous villas, but Muks' House was the most welcoming, the most impressive of them. Something about its structure stayed with you. It had been named after the painter Juhan Muks, who had lived in the house for decades painting images of the lovely lake. According to the plaque on the wall outside, he died in 1983, which meant we both could have met him as children. Maybe a much younger Epp crossed paths with Muks while he was swimming down at the lake.

Epp and I came down the steep incline of Lower Pikk Street with "Looking for a Nest" fliers in our hands and encountered a young woman with black hair and a blue dress and white stockings, like an Estonian flag standing right before us. She had fine features and dark eyes and seemed beautiful enough to belong to the pretty surroundings.

"Excuse me, can we trouble you for a minute?" Epp asked.

The woman stopped and looked at us with alert eyes but did not respond.

"We were wondering – are there any free apartments left in this house that you know of?"

"There are no free apartments," she said quickly, without blinking.

"Are you sure?" Epp said. "It seems like such a beautiful place."

"There are no free apartments," she repeated. Then she turned and hurried up the steps into her own.

I watched the woman walk away and noticed that she seemed less beautiful than she had at first.

Something about the reticence, the standoffishness, that Estonian distrust of strangers. Viljandi was like that. You fell for its pretty people, its pretty painted doors, its pretty views. Like an Inuit throat singer, Viljandi danced for you and tantalized you and seduced you, so that you thought it was true love. Only after you had spent the night in her watery embrace, after the sun had gone down and risen again and cast its light across her puffy, weary, ugly morning face did you at last get a sense of how tormented she was and who she really was inside.

"Let's put our fliers into the mailboxes anyway," Epp said. "Who knows, maybe we'll get lucky!"

We stuffed the mailboxes in the corridor, which was very cool and painted a light blue that seemed to reflect the heaviness of the lake and had a maritime feel that reminded me of my first home on Long Island.

The two of us had had so many fights over what should be our next and hopefully permanent home. She offered ten options, I said no or don't know to them all. She was frustrated with my unwillingness and pessimism, I was frustrated with her future fixation and new plans. How could I tell what I wanted to do when there were too many impossible people to please? I had told relatives in the US we would return one day. Yet it seemed like we were never going to return because all the winds were against it. The winds blew us here to Estonia and kept us here. It was what Taagepera had been talking about in Kaunas, that windy land that blew in empires and blew them out with a strong gust.

Around that time, I had a dream that I was on a plane from Tartu to New York, and I was so excited that planes now flew from Tartu to New York. Terrific! I took the car out to the Tartu Airport and got on the plane and watched Estonia roll along below me until we got to Tallinn. The plane went to ascend, but no matter how much fuel the captain burned, no matter how hard he pulled back on the yoke, the plane would just not rise above Toompea. So it landed there. The captain refused to fly any further and a new crew was called in, but nobody could figure out how to get off Toompea. There wasn't enough room to take off, with all of those ancient churches and government buildings.

So there I was. Stuck in Estonia.

I remember feeling perplexed in the dream. Not sad, not angry, not happy – just confused. Why couldn't they get the plane off Toompea? Why were we stuck in this country? We were stranded here and it seemed to be our destiny, our inescapable future.

That was the tricky thing about the future: you only got one. No matter how much you planned, or theorized, or backtracked, or tried to imagine how it might have been had one detail gone differently, it was a mostly meaningless exercise. You only got one future and our one future seemed to be here. That's how it was *supposed* to be.

I lived day to day in guilt though, as if it had been my grand conspiracy to leave my relatives dissatisfied. It nipped at my heels like an underfed dog. "Abandoned" was the word from America. "Dumped."

"Have you noticed that you look really miserable some-times?" Epp asked as we walked around Muks' House for the first time. We came down the driveway and then traversed some boulders down into the gardens, old green terraces against the slant of the hill.

"Oh, I just got another letter from home this morning," I said. "That's all."

"You have to live your own life," she said, but did not look at me. "Not other people's lives."

The windy land wouldn't yet blow us out of Estonia, that was for certain. But it did blow us out of Tartu as quickly as it had drawn us in. It blew us for different reasons. Maybe it was those wild and ugly neighborhood cats in Tartu, who used to piss all over our yard, so that the firewood stank like urine, or the fact that our aging rental house was slowly crumbling from within, and that we would have to move anyway, becau-se our three-year lease was up. But the house we had identi-fied as a potential new home in the neighborhood would not be ready in time, and the Waldorf School we liked was on the other side of the city, which meant a life of driving and car-pooling, while we wanted some European ideal of living and walking.

Tartu stopped adding up, the life mathematics went all wrong. We tinkered with the idea of moving down to Põlva, to live near the *Johannese Kool*, a Waldorf school of wide repute. It was another beautiful place, a long grand house painted Swedish red, surrounding by pastoral peace, men raking hay and women picking cucumbers. Põlva was one of Estonia's better country towns, with clean streets, well-kept buildings, and a great lake at its center with rolling hills all around.

We even stuffed the mailboxes there, around the school. No one responded.

I was secretly happy about it. Something didn't feel right to me about the place. There had been no Estonian Trad- itional Music Center in Põlva. There had been no Tagaq. There had been no Peeter Volkonski or other folk culture royalty. No Culture Academy. The Ait was in Viljandi and maybe Viljandi was the place where two weirdos like us would at last fit in.

So I was the one who told Epp: "Forget about Põlva. Let's try to find home in Viljandi!"

Epp seemed surprised. "Viljandi?! You think we should go live in Viljandi? Well, it does have a Waldorf School. And it is my birth town. And it is Estonia's cultural capital."

And it felt right.

"Looking for a nest!"

The following night after our flier trip one of the owners of Muks' House called us. He said that there was an apart- ment that might work. Three rooms, plus a kitchen, a bath- room, and a lake view.

"It's odd that girl from the same house didn't know about it."

"Maybe she didn't like us," Epp shrugged. "Who knows?"

Later we found out that the last free apartment in Muks' House was built into the ground floor and accessible by a separate door on the street. The girl just thought it was a basement room or something. That was the thing about Muks' House. It was full of interesting compartments and characters, and it was a startlingly beautiful house. No matter where you were in Viljandi, if you looked at the hill from across the lake or from above, its image would hit you in the face. It was put together like a layer cake – the bottom was made of enormous field stones, the second, ground floor, was painted yellow, and the third was white and adorned with grand balconies.

Sometimes we would see our neighbors up on those balconies, studying the clouds above the lake. They were musicians and directors, I was told, artists like us. We should fit right in, I was told.

Not too long after that, we left Tartu and its *vaim* behind and moved to Viljandi, into the apartment in Muks' House, a fine space with a wonderful lake view. The Ait where I had first glimpsed Tagaq was two minutes away. We had come to Tartu with six suitcases. This time around, it took three trips with a van to move our possessions 76 kilometers to the west.

A clay house in Viljandi, built by a student from the local Culture Academy. When the door is removed from the ladder, the owner is at home. When the door is placed on the ladder, the house is "locked."

My favorite view of Tartu, taken from the fourth floor
of the downtown library.

Kassitoome or Cat's Dome Park in the middle of Tartu.
These ancient green hills pack powerful energy.

War of Independence hero Julius Kuperjanov's sarcophagus at Raadi Cemetery in Tartu, a place for my secret confessions. A visit to his grave during the Soviet era might have gotten you expelled from the university.

The house of the Estonian Students' Society in Tartu, where some of the country's most influential men gather. "You wouldn't believe the things I have seen go on down here," a friend told me.

Renovation! This is how we used many people's help
to reach the promised land: our own renovated house
in the Tähtvere district of Tartu

Three-year-old Marta playing in the middle of
construction debris outside her future home.

This was the reason we took the house: its romantic orchard. As it turned out, managing a dozen apple trees was a mixed blessing.

Our white, Greek-inspired facade in winter.

Estonians never let a good apple go to waste. First, they scour the ground for any salvageable ones that may have dropped overnight, and then they pick the trees.

Shredding another apple. At first, the process seems tedious, but soon you come to find your own inner juice-making rhythm, and keep on making juice, even in your sleep.

An old-fashioned apple press. The pulp is spread out in layers, which are then pressed by a vise.

Raw juice. It is delicious, but I wouldn't drink it too much. You probably know why.

Digging out after another storm. There were times when
I felt like a paleontologist, exhuming a woolly mammoth
encased in ice.

Marta and Anna on sleds, with Epp pulling. In winter, it is
common for children to go to preschool on sleds.

Marta learns a new skill. Skiing is compulsory in Estonian schools.

Winter delivered new pets. First we got a mouse and then we got a cat who didn't want to catch that mouse.

A moment on Sepa Street when a music video for a local
folk group "Naised köögis" ("Women in the Kitchen")
was shot in and outside of our home.

The Kondas Centre of Naive Art, with our youngest daughter, Maria,
leaning on the iconic strawberry sculpture in front. Those strawberries,
inspired by one of Paul Kondas' paintings, are spread all over town.

Viljandi's famous Roheline Maja (Green House Cafe) on the corner of Tartu and Koidu Streets. Stop by and if you're lucky, you might run into Green House Enn.

Cafe Fellin, with its bold blue door. We were lucky to move to Viljandi at a time when there was a renaissance of cafe culture.

Our friend Gea walking on Lower Pikk Street, with our first home in Viljandi, Muks' House, visible behind her. The street has recently been renovated with new cobblestones.

Sepa Street, our second home address in Viljandi, also known as "that hole" before it was excavated by archaeologists and renovated.

An inside peek at folkie life in Viljandi: a folkie scene through a folkie window.

Viljandi is thick with wild kids. Here, my friend Elias, the Swedish chef, is besieged in a hammock by a bunch of them.

A real Waldorf education. Marta's class prepares
to plant their own rye to make their own bread.
But first they have to plow the field.

The girls like to get
their hands dirty!

Waldorf kids learn from nature: how to make dolls out of flowers.

Young girls in Estonian folk costumes serenade passersby during the annual Viljandi Folk Music Festival.

Viljandi holds several events, the best ones are the Hanseatic Days in June and the Folk Music Festival in July. Attendees braid headbands and do a lot of other traditional things.

Folkie kids barely sleep during Viljandi Folk and they attend night concerts too. Here, our daughter Anna climbs a lantern pole to enjoy her favorite group, Zetod.

TWO MINUTES AWAY

From our door at Muks' House or officially the Villa Rosenberg, our new home, it was just a two-minute walk to the Viljandi Free Waldorf School.

The walk was straight up, a 45-degree angle, and there were no sidewalks, so you kept to the side of the street, even if it was muddy. When it was winter, then you could walk right up the middle of the cobblestones of Lower Pikk Street. You had to be careful and concentrate. Once I came down that street in winter and started thinking about genetics and slipped with my groceries in my hands. A dozen eggs went flying into the air and rolled down the hill.

Other than the ice, the street was safe because very few cars ever came down, and if they did, they drove carefully, because the back lanes of Viljandi were thick with wild children.

Our six-year-old Marta was one of these street children now, and she would climb the bumpy hill not only to go to school, but to visit new friends like Ragne and Anita. Ragne was a bit older and had long straw-colored hair that fell around her shoulders. She seemed quiet enough and peaceful enough, and had placid blue eyes, and the girls would play with dolls in the front yard of her home together, but sometimes there would be a spat with Ragne, which left Marta heading straight over to Anita's house. Anita lived with her mother and some cats in a small house beside the haunted green villa, at the crest of the hill where Lower Pikk met Upper Pikk. She had a cheerful, freckled face with big dimples and blonde braids, and she lived in a fantasy world which she and Marta shared.

Sometimes I would see the two girls on the hill speaking gibberish to each other and laughing.

"What are you talking about?" I asked.

"We're speaking fairy language, Daddy," Marta answered.

"Ookachookachoolooohoo," Anita would cry out and smile. "Bookalookchooleeleewoo!"

"Harraleeharrapuu!" Marta answered her. "Roorooohaaaaaaaaaplong."

"Nukknukkpadukkdukkkalukklukk."

"Where are you two fairies going?"

"We're going to the lake now, Daddy. See you!"

You learned to let your children go in Viljandi. It had a cozy, free air, and you knew that if they went down to the lake, even out onto the pier to climb on its cupola, it would all be just fine, that they would return. Sometimes Anita and Marta caught baby frogs in the hills and played with them. Anita would hold one up gently in her hand and Marta the other.

"I now pronounce you man and wife," Anita said. "You can kiss the bride!"

They would press the frogs against each other as if they were kissing at their wedding, but then one frog would slip free and hop away and the two of them would pursue it down the hill into the woods behind the school.

"Runaway bride! Runaway bride! Get her!"

Anita did not go to the Waldorf School. She went to a regular school across town. "Why is Marta going to Waldorf school?" Anita wanted to know. "Why doesn't she go to school with me?"

Yes, why? We tried to explain it to her, but the truth was that it just felt right and natural for us.

Marta had begged us to go to school, because she didn't want to attend kindergarten anymore. That little girl hated the perfunctory nap time. This was too *titekas*, as they said, baby-like, and the thought of a six-year-old girl who looked like a nine year old snuggling up every naptime until she was nearly eight years old and therefore legally the correct age to start school seemed preposterous. But the Waldorf School had a reputation for giving its children room to breathe, room to think, room to develop on their own. They learned to recite poetry and play instruments and put on plays. It seemed perfect for precocious little girl who hated preschool, but probably was too young for hardcore academics. And she could walk to school by herself, although it was the kind of hill that stretched out your legs.

"You know what our neighbors say," Epp had told me. "If you live in Muks' House, you can never get fat."

It was like the Estonian San Francisco, all of those new age hippies, all of those steep inclines. You came up and down the hills and felt your calf muscles bulge, and sometimes they ached at the end of the day. After Marta had climbed up the hill to school, I would hoist Anna on my shoulders and take her to the Waldorf kindergarten on Oru Street, which was a bit further.

Anna. She had matured in just a few years into a little girl with blonde pig-tails and lots of questions. We bundled her up in Marta's old pink and gold sweater and took her away to the one-story house where golden-haired Jaanika and dark-haired Anu were waiting outside. They were both sympathetic, effervescent, sparkling women and tried their best to manage a dozen or so wild Viljandi children. Once a week, they would go on a *matk*, a hike, sometimes to Lossi-kad, sometimes down to the lake. The children walked the great hills of Viljandi, many kilometers in a row. On these days the parents were expected to bring to the kindergarten a *matkavõileib*, "hike sandwich." I put one together for Anna, just like my mother had made for me.

My sandwiches were not always up to local standards.

"Justin, what did you give Anna today for her hike sandwich?" asked Jaanika. She was as pretty as a Disney princess, but could also be quite austere if she needed to be.

"Some bread with mozzarella and tomatoes. And olive oil."

Jaanika squinted at me like I was among the more hopeless children she'd had to deal with. "Olive oil? Justin, it's called a *võileib*. *Või – leib*. Butter – bread. All you need is butter and bread. *Võileib*. Simple. Okay?"

"Okay, Jaanika. Next time I will just put butter and bread."

She gave me another one of those doting, "What a silly man" looks. "You can put other things in too. Like ham, or cucumber. Cheese."

"Okay, Jaanika."

Something happened to me in Viljandi, at the kindergarten on Oru Street. I began to pay attention to children more. I began to take them more seriously, as if they were adults. There was Urmas Volmer, the big photographer, and Ekke Karu, his tiny son, who liked to wear a hat that looked like a rooster. To me, those two guys were equals, the same. I began to see the adults around me in Viljandi as if they were big children. I knew that the teacher Jaanika was the same age as me. We could have played together as children, just as her daughter Marii played with our Anna. They played as princesses, they played with yarn and painted, they dug for hours in the sandbox.

"They are classic children," Epp said of our street kids. "And they are having a great childhood."

We became so enamored with children, so in love with our free life, that one more decided to join our family.

And so we had to leave Muks' House behind after only one year. We needed more space for our growing family – and we had become so accustomed to the warm fires and comforting wood floors of the Waldorf kindergarten and other great Viljandi homes that the laminated floors in our apartment and the central heating came to feel stifling and dry.

So we moved up the street to a house on Sepa Street, where the floors were made of good, worn wood and the walls were painted with ecologically safe *kohupiimavärv*, a blend of dyes, natural chemicals and *kohupiim*, soft quark cheese. The place breathed, and when the air filtered through the cracks in the floorboards and caught the lingering scent of the kohupiim on the walls, the whole space smelled like a pastry.

It was delicious.

We packed our things again and moved up the hill to the Sepa Street apartment. I don't think it was a big change for the girls. They could run free in the same streets and play with their friends. The school and kindergarten were still just a two-minute walk away.

Every time we moved, old friends like Triin and David would arrive bearing gifts of bread and salt. It happened when we moved into Muks' House, and again at the house on Sepa Street. You would get a thick loaf of the dark rye bread, the leib, and then a paper or plastic bag of salt, or *sool*. Often, the bread was homemade and delicious with some soft butter or *sõir* cheese, the kind that was common in the southeast, with caraway seeds. This was the local custom, the *soolaleib*, the salt and bread as a house warming gift. I guess that's all you really needed in life: bread, salt, and water, plus maybe a passport and a credit card.

But in Viljandi, things were so loose that at times it seemed as if documents and money were no longer necessary.

What you needed was a good folk instrument – a harmonica or a zither – and an old-timey song and dance act. What you needed was a nickname, like "*Habe*" (Beard) or "Jimbeano." What you needed was a cool wardrobe. In Viljandi, I started to wear a Greek fisherman's cap and ethnic shirts, just to fit in. I started playing music again and bought an acoustic bass, just so I could join my new friend Silver Sepp in one of his impromptu street jams.

Once, I even wound up backing a folk group during the Viljandi Folk Music Festival, which was held each year in the center of town. The band was called "Küi" from the Sõrve Peninsula out on Saaremaa. They called themselves *sõrulased* – as if the peninsula had its own language and culture. Maybe it did. A woman with a handkerchief on her head played fiddle, and a man with shoulder-length black hair and glasses strummed his guitar, while the singer, a robust fellow, with a shorn head and a barrel-like chest, spat Sõrve poetry. Silver played a bass drum and I tried to hold it together with some bass lines.

When we finished, I felt about 15 years younger and my daughters ran up to me, their eyes glowing, as if for the first time, after all those years of writing, I had actually done something of merit, something worthy of respect in their Finno-Ugric eyes.

"Daddy!" Marta said, almost out of breath. "I can't believe it! You can play that big thing!"

You could say that folkie life suited me particularly well, that I was built for it, that it made all of my teenage hippie dreams come true. With my new reputation as an eccentric and as a writer, I should have slid slickly into place among Enn and Kaari at the Green House Cafe or the Ukrainian trombonist Ruslan of the band "Svjata Vatra," who would pull out a flute in the cafe and serenade us while the ladies blushed and the fires roared. There were more people in that scene: Elias, the Swedish chef philosopher, and his wife Gea, the energetic cafe culture instigator, and then there were the two blond elves: Silver Sepp the musician and Kristiina Ehin the poet.

And there were children, children everywhere. Enn and Kaari had half a dozen of them, and Elias and Gea would have half that amount, the third coming, and soon we would have that amount, too. So would Ruslan and Terje. Something about Viljandi made people make babies. As soon as one was born, another was in the pipe. Down every supermarket aisle there was a folk lady with a babe in a sling. You would walk into the Green House Cafe and try not to notice all of the breastfeeding and focus on the wonderful selection of high-end organic produce. Tomatoes, avocados, melons, bananas, and babies. It was like a documentary about African tribesmen, except happening in Estonia, with crumbling, *chateau*-like villas all around, leftovers from Viljandi's heyday as a summer resort, when August Maramaa was mayor in the 1920s.

Each morning when I took Anna to preschool we would pass the statue of the legendary Mayor Maramaa beside the white modernist Town Hall. His metal form held a cane and faced the sculpture of a dog, and if you looked closely you could see a pleased look on Maramaa's face.

I often paused to read the plaque about Maramaa's life, about how he had tried to develop Viljandi as a summer resort in the 1920s and 1930s and how the Soviets had arrested him and sent him to die in a work camp in 1941. Anna knew that Maramaa was dead, and almost every morning she asked me again how he had died. I tried to explain it to the inquisitive four year old but it never made sense. She didn't seem to have any interest in the Nazis or the Soviets or the Deportations.

But one morning she became interested in the other, furrier part of the memorial.

"Daddy, how did the dog die?" she asked.

"The dog? Well, Maramaa's dog died happy," I decided quickly. "He lived a long, fulfilling life."

"He?" she raised an eyebrow. "Don't you mean she?"

"Well, maybe..."

"Yeah, I thought it looked more like a girl dog than a boy dog," Anna said. "I could just tell."

That was Viljandi. We lived there for three years, before the tsunami hit.

GREEN HOUSE ENN

Even today, if I pull into Viljandi, I immediately head for its famous Green House Cafe, that charming old building on the corner of Koidu and Tartu Streets.

It has its own Mecca-like gravitation that pulls in people in need. In need of what? Good soup, or good coffee maybe. Or just good company. These days, the cafe is open seven days a week, and runs like a fine machine. I no longer know all of the staff. But years ago, from our attic office above what would become the cafe, we came to witness its genesis, its false starts, to smell its first pastries, and taste its first coffees.

For me, it was hard to distinguish between the cafe and Enn and Kaari's home, where it incubated.

Enn was the older statesman of hip culture. He had actually been a hippie in the Sixties when he lived in the US and had his many adventures. One story was that his friend ditched him in Puerto Rico, and Enn spent months sleeping beneath palm trees and working carpentry jobs before he could get enough money together to travel back to New York. He carried with him secret knowledge of that more ideal and bohemian time. He wore a bandana around his neck, and his hair, reduced by heat and weather to wisps of gray and brown, was never combed and yet always seemed perfect. His face was not of this side of the planet. The eyes were a bit too thin, the skin too ruddy. He looked like one of those tribes in western China that swear they are descended from a lost Roman legion. Enn was a builder, so he usually had some sawdust on him. He had – and still has – a terrific grin, an easygoing gait, and the gift of gab.

"Hey, yo, Justin. What gives? I thought I saw you going into the A ja O to buy bread last week. How come you didn't buy your bread here, from us, man?"

"Uh, it wasn't me, Enn. It must have been somebody else."

"Some other guy in Viljandi who looks just like you? Nice try. Come on, you can't eat the stuff they sell in there! You eat that crappy factory-made bread and you will be dead in, like, two weeks."

"Okay, Enn. I'll only buy bread from you from now on."

Kaari was – and still is – Enn's wife. A fine Finnish girl's face, with rosy freckled cheeks and light, comforting blue eyes. Kaari never seemed to be in a hurry to go anywhere and didn't even own a mobile phone. If you wanted to talk to Kaari, you either called the house number or you called Enn. But usually you didn't need to call Kaari, you just saw her hanging laundry in the yard.

To get up to our Petrone Print Viljandi office, you had to enter the yard from Koidu Street and then step past the children's toys and boxes of potatoes until you ducked through a small green ivy-covered gate into Hela's yard.

Hela was Enn's older sister who kept a small flowerbed and was mother to many cats. You usually encountered one of these cats on the way up the back staircase which led into the office.

You would nudge the cat out of the way with your boot and make it to the door, fumble with your keys, and let yourself in. It was a brightly-lit space, with exposed beams, and Epp and I had two desks where we would sit and work. Epp would often listen to Indian raga music and the whole room would be filled with the incantations of yogis and their followers. Next to my desk was a small balcony, where you could go out and stretch your arms and relax.

Once I looked down from that balcony and saw Miko, who was the youngest of Enn and Kaari's brood at the time, ascend a ladder and leap from the roof onto a trampoline. Miko was a scrappy four year old, with blond-streaky hair and dirt all over his face. But instead of being relieved that he had survived the jump, he climbed back up the ladder to the roof and was about to fly again.

This time, though, his mother caught him.

"Miko, are you crazy?" I heard Kaari's voice from back stage, her kitchen. "What are you doing? Get down from up there!"

Miko. He was the most likely of their offspring to become a stuntman.

He was also already an Estonian nationalist. I knew that Miko understood English, because that's all Enn spoke to him – it was Enn's decision, to ensure his children could speak both languages fluently. But whenever I spoke English to Miko, he would squint and sneer at me.

"Speak Estonian, Justin," Miko would growl. "*Räägi eesti keeles.*"

Enn and Kaari had many children. When we came to Viljandi, there were four. When we left, there were five, and now there are six, according to the most recent data. But in some weird way all of the children only helped to make Kaari seem younger and younger. When she wore her hair in two braids, she looked like a young girl herself, with her tall slim figure.

Enn and Kaari fathered and mothered people who weren't even their children. If I was hungry, Kaari would bring me a slice of *karask,* a baked treat, with some butter and honey on it. If I was tired, Enn would invite me in to sit on an an old stool by the fire and talk to me about anything. He read a lot for a man who was constantly building and making customers cappuccinos. Enn loved Raymond Chandler, those old Los Angeles detective stories, and he liked Paul Auster, too. Vello, my writer friend up in Nõmme, typically did not have a kind word for anybody, least of all another *väliseestlane*, a foreign Estonian, who were usually considered to have taken the arrogance and self-helping individualism of the Estonians to astronomical new American levels.

Yet my friendship with the Green House cappuccino maestro met with his blessing.

"Is this the mason from New Jersey?" Vello grumbled to me when I told him about Viljandi. "Believe it or not, I hear he's okay. Still a *väliseestlane*, but… decent. One of the few, I guess."

When we first moved to Viljandi there was no Green House Cafe, which meant there was no good place to get coffee. I still remember how I woke up in our apartment in Muks' House on our first morning, a really hot July day, and went to find some, because we didn't have a kitchen yet. We didn't have a kitchen because the owner of the house insisted that we design and install our own, which would take months. It didn't bother him though.

"A kitchen is such a personal decision," he explained. We liked the views so much we agreed to build our own and got on the workmen's waiting list.

In Tartu, getting your hands on a cup of coffee was simple. You could go to Pierre on the Town Hall Square, or to Kohvipaus on Rüütli Street, and so on. But Viljandi was new, foreign territory for me. I came up crumbling Lower Pikk Street and walked the residential part of Upper Pikk Street, passed that house with the warning sign, where the dog snarled at me, as he would every single time I walked by him for the next three years, and I cursed at him, as I always did. Then I felt bad for cursing at the dog because I knew Epp would never do a thing like that.

Not Epp. She was a country girl. When she passed the dog, she didn't curse at him, she said, "Hello there, doggy, how are you doing?" She would never hesitate to put her hand under the fence and let the dog sniff it. She'd let the children go near the dog. She was crazy but I loved her.

And I took her need for morning coffee seriously.

On that first Viljandi morning, with the boxes stacked up in our apartment, including the one that had our coffee machine hidden somewhere inside it, we both took it seriously.

I came to Lossi Street and turned right, heading for the only cafe I knew that might be open at 9 a.m., the vaunted Cafe Viljandi. Epp said the place hadn't changed at all since she was a girl. The same old beige wallpaper, the same old dark wooden furniture, the same old servings of breakfast *omlett* or hot porridge. The servers wore vaguely retro shirts and skirts, and the radio only played Retro FM, so that you might hear Laura Branigan singing, "Gloria," or, if you were really lucky, "The Safety Dance."

I walked into the cafe, stood at the counter, drummed my fingers on the glass and waited for the server to come. When she did she gave me a frustrated look, as if I had annoyed her by being there. She stood behind the counter and waited for my order, but she still didn't say anything. I studied her face. It wasn't a bad face. Even with the blue mascara.

There was a heart down in there, somewhere deep below the nametag. There had to be.

Then I said, "Tere."

She didn't answer.

"Two coffees with milk," I told her.

She turned to begin making them.

"And... "

She froze and peered back at me.

"Is it possible to get them to go?" I asked her in Estonian.

"To go?" She wrinkled her nose. "I think so." This answer was given cautiously, as if I had just asked a NASA engineer if it was theoretically possible to put a man on Mars.

She dug around in a cabinet until she produced a small Styrofoam cup. "This is all we have," she said. "And we don't have any plastic lids left." A careless shrug.

I paid for the one hot coffee and walked back down Lossi Street, stepping very carefully down the misplaced cobblestones and chunks of asphalt and concrete, so as not to spill one drop of the precious brown liquid, which now contained an additional few dots of orange flower pollen that had floated in while I walked. Epp was very grateful for the coffee that had remained in the cup. She drank it with one gulp.

That's how it was in Viljandi before the advent of the Green House Cafe. During those first weeks I felt a desperation simmering inside. I had been promised the 1922 Arctic of *Nanook from the North* and the sensual Tagaq concert, and wound up back in the 1980s, except not even the 1980s I knew as a child, but a different 1980s – the 1980s of Viljandi. Epp said nothing had changed at Cafe Viljandi, and she was right. Nothing had changed. Maybe it was elitist of me to want coffee just like that. But back then I thought Viljandi was just another town in Europe. If you could get coffee on the street in Paris, then why not get the same in Viljandi? Something didn't add up.

I had been tricked.

I never could tell Epp about this treacherous trickery though because she had been born here, in that white clapboard house, an old hospital since turned into a hostel, overlooking the lake in the middle of the Old Town. In Viljandi, Epp just swam right back into place. She was friends with people at the Lion's Club, at the library, at the theater, even at the candy store. Most of them had known her mother or aunt or father or grandfather. Within weeks, she had several friends named Tiina or Piret, while I was still mixing up our neighbors Hillar and Tiit at Muks' House. They looked the same to me. It would take months before I was confident that the soft-spoken theater director who lived upstairs was Hillar and the starry-eyed composer and musician who lived in the apartment across the hall from him was Tiit.

There were women in Muks' House, too, but they were even harder to tell apart. One of them, later known to me as Kristiina, who became theater director after Hillar and his family moved over to Tallinn, was identified by her curls and freckles and her white jeep, which she drove with gusto up and down the ruin of Lower Pikk Street. For this reason, I called her "white jeep." Liina was the "blonde with the dog" who worked for the folk music festival. Jaanus, the decorator of the local theater, was "the guy with the bike." Fitness freak Janek was "that guy who is always running around the lake." And Peep? Peep wore a black leather jacket and, on colder days, a wool cap. He drove a yellow jeep that had the 'J' on the emblem slightly altered so that it read: "Peep." He looked so much like an old hippie with his gray hair, bushy mustache and cool jacket that I called him "Wild Bill" after Dennis Hopper's character in *Easy Rider*. When I told him this he seemed to ponder it a bit and then mumbled something incomprehensible to me. *Möh möh möh. Noh, jah.* Most of our conversations were like this.

Soon after that Peep offered me something alcoholic out of an old jar. I drank it and it was strong. No idea what it was. I also had no idea for quite some time what Peep was actually doing for a living other than driving his jeep around. I found out that he was in the business of building steel structures. As for Janek, it took time before I found out that when not running around Lake Viljandi he was the director of a vodka factory.

Most of the residents of Muks' House seemed to remember my name quickly. I stood out I guess, in a town that most of them had known their whole lives, and which they regarded with a certain nostalgia. For them, the fact that Cafe Viljandi hadn't changed in 30 years was just wonderful.

But change was coming, and one day, soon after we moved in, I met two of Epp's many new friends.

They were called Kaari and Enn.

I remember clearly those days in Viljandi, how I walked from Muks' House to our office in the Green House Cafe... I came up to a green wooden fence, so tall that I could barely see over it, opened the gate, and entered the courtyard, half of which was taken up by a giant trampoline. Once or twice I saw Enn doing back-flips on it and winking at me mid-jump. You would see his head above the fence and then he would disappear below it and then be up above it again. And don't forget he was more than 60 years old.

Enn was playing the harmonica that night we first met him with a scarf around his neck. He seemed to have children crawling all over him. Born to Estonian parents in a German refugee camp while the nuclear fallout was still fresh over Hiroshima, he was raised at least partially in New Jersey in the US. He spoke English with an old-fashioned New Jersey accent, too, and not the whiny, suburban mall rat speak you hear in the movies, I mean an old-timer's accent, the way the old fishermen on Long Island where I grew up used to speak. It was almost British, but from the coves of the West Country, not the Queen's English.

There was a cool warp in time and space. In a house in Viljandi, I heard the English of my grandfathers coming out of the mouth of this man. Enn spoke Estonian with that old-timer's accent. The night I met Enn, he brought us deep into the kitchen and he made us cappuccinos on an Italian-made machine.

"You like living here in Viljandi?" I asked.

"Well, you know," Enn shrugged, "it's home now. I got a family here, a new business. My older kids are still in the States. But they are grown now, and they have their own lives."

"Tell him about Vietnam, Dad," Enn's eldest son Mano said. Mano was about 10 or 11 back then. He was a free-thinking young man, with the wiry build of Enn and the softer looks of Kaari. He spoke English with a bit of hesitancy, the same way he would put his school trumpet to his lips and blow through the mouthpiece a bit before producing any sounds. His was a new form of "Euro English," Enn remarked with a shrug. But Mano was a prodigious learner. He was always reading, and thinking, and listening to adults' conversations. Later, he would try to convince me that the moon landing in 1969 had been staged in a desert and that he read all about it on the Internet.

"Go on, Daddy. Tell him about the war."

"Mano," Enn groaned.

"You were in Vietnam?" I asked quickly.

"Yeah, I was."

"When?"

"Oh, 1967, 1968." He looked away to tinker with the cappuccino machine, like he did not want to talk about it.

"Where?"

"On the border with Laos."

"Ho Chi Minh Trail?"

Oh, I knew about that place. One of the most dangerous areas in Vietnam during the conflict. It was the logistical network from which the North Vietnamese supported the Southern Vietnamese Viet Cong. All my childhood I had heard nightmare stories of Vietnam, about men who died their first day on active duty, men who stepped on mines, whose heads got ripped off by booby traps. And then there were the "tunnel rats" – the men who had been sent into the Viet Cong's tunnels.

My friend's father had been a sniper in Vietnam. He never spoke about the war. Sometimes his son would prod him. "How many Viet Cong fighters did you kill, Dad?" – "I don't want to talk about it." – "Come on, Dad, tell me." – "How do I have to say it? I don't want to talk about it!"

When I was a kid, you would see veterans outside the liquor stores in wheelchairs. Another friend's father never was able to adapt back to civilian life. He went to live in the woods with his gun.

"If they had sent me there, to Vietnam," my father told me once, "You simply would not exist."

"...Yeah, that's right. The Ho Chi Minh Trail," Enn said in the kitchen as if it was no big deal. "But don't go believing those movies. It was a bunch of bullshit. All wars are bullshit."

"Were you drafted?"

"That's right. They took me into Uncle Sam's Army, the day after my 21st birthday. It was the end of summer 1966. They processed us in Manhattan, put us on trains, and sent us south for training. Actually," he rubbed his fingers against his lips and then pointed at me, "this is kind of weird, but I remember this name, Petrone, from when I was doing basic training at Fort Jackson."

"The training camp in Fort Jackson, South Carolina?" I had heard the name from my father.

"Yeah, good old Fort Jackson. Damn it was hot down there. You sweat 24 hours a day. I still have nightmares that I am back there, marching around with all those guys. Anyway, I grew up around Estonians, I had never really met Italians before, so I remember that new name. Petrone. Did your father serve?"

"Yeah, he was also drafted."

"What year?"

"1966."

"Get out of town! That's when I joined! I remember there were a bunch of Italians singing doo wop songs down the hall. And one of them was called Petrone."

The hair really did stick up on the back of my neck. "It probably was my father."

"See, we have almost met before," Enn shrugged and showed his teeth in a grin. "The world is funny like that."

I hesitated a moment before I asked. "Hope you don't mind me asking this, Enn. but how come you are still normal?"

"Me? Normal? Ha! I live here in friggin' Estonia and I'm starting an organic shop and cafe. You call that normal? Believe me, I could have had a very normal, very boring life. I could be back there in the US, watching TV right now."

"I mean, how come you're not a drunk? Or you didn't blow your brains out?"

Enn shook his head. "I got back from the war and I went back to work in construction. I had no time to start feeling sorry for myself. Besides, most of the guys I knew had been in a war, and I was no different from them. So that's just how it was."

Then he served me a cappuccino, a good cappuccino, in a white ceramic cup. I took a sip.

"How's the coffee?" he asked me.

"It's good," I said.

"Damn right, it's good. I import it straight from this place in Greenwich Village. They have the best coffee, the very best.

You want to live long? You want to be happy? Don't dwell on your problems, your ailments. Drink the best coffee. You have to eat well, make your own bread. Here, look at this," he showed me a candy bar wrapper. "I found this on the ground outside. This is what kids eat these days," and then he ran his finger along the line of dozens of artificial ingredients. "And that's what's in it." He looked away, overcome by disgust.

Enn's first cafe opened that autumn right there in the kitchen, with the fire roaring. Even upstairs in our office you could smell the hot stews bubbling and the loaves of bread baking. Dozens of people squeezed in along the wooden tables for organic beet soup or chicken and couscous or whatever it was that the friendly chef Elias had prepared for the day.

The place had a nice bohemian vibe. Ruslan would come in and play his trombone and growl in Ukrainian. He was assisted by Arno, the lanky singer and actor, who always seemed like he was in character, so that even when he brought you a glass of yellow tangy sea-buckthorn juice, *astelpaju mahl*, he did it with dramatic gestures.

The cafe quickly became a magnet for Viljandi's many dancers, actors, and folk musicians because of its alternative vibe. Sometimes Epp and I would sit in the corners writing, soaking up the energy. We would eat the daily special, maybe spicy lentil soup, and Enn's bread would come on the side, hunks of black rye baked in an industrial oven in the back, with butter melting all over the top.

Cappuccinos were served on demand, finessed by Enn himself, who manned the machines like a seasoned bartender. Children climbed over everything. At that time, Enn and Kaari had Mano, Miia, Maari, and Miko. Then baby Mingo came along and they closed the cafe for a while, then reopened it in the house next door, right under our office. They painted the old apothecary interior a vibrant yellow and imported organic foods and marked the prices up as high as I would pay, which was plenty because good food like that could be found nowhere else in Viljandi. And, like Enn said, if you ate any other food, you might be dead in two weeks. I didn't want to take any chances.

They made coffees right on the same counter where pharmacists used to bottle drugs. The cafe staff was friendly and really beautiful. They would talk to you and ask you about your life and what you were writing while you drank the good coffee up, then maybe another. You could even order coffees to go, in cups made of recycled paper. There was a whole stack of them and they never seemed to run out of cups at the Green House Cafe. The cups had lids. You could order two cappuccinos and walk down to Muks' House without spilling a drop.

It wasn't too long after that though that another cafe opened up in Viljandi's Old Town, so we had two places to go when we wanted coffee. By that time, our kitchen in Muks' House was installed, so we could have coffee at home too.

We didn't know it then, but Viljandi was undergoing a renaissance of cafe culture. There were other people with ideas for its neglected buildings. For years, the corner brick house at the entrance to the Old Town was occupied by a plain, boring liquor store. It sold the local brands, along with some cheaper imports, cigarettes, chocolates, cookies, and ice cream. Sometimes, when the girls were hungry, we would stop in there and buy a chocolate or an ice cream cone, but it did make me somewhat sad that our corner shop specialized in keeping the locals inebriated.

Then one day the store was closed. We heard at Kaari's birthday party that a new cafe was planned on the site, something a bit more classically European and elegant. The light blue wallpaper went up, and the white wooden furniture went in. There were some nice couches, bookshelves, delicious and interesting cakes, and a friendly and considerate staff.

When the organizers were searching for a name for the new cafe, Epp suggested Fellin, the old German name for Viljandi. And soon it was written there, on the window, in gold. Cafe Fellin. I had to split my time between two wonderful cafes then, without letting the owners know that I had been eating at their competitor's. So if I saw Enn and he said, "Hey, dude, long time no see. Where have you been?" I would just shrug and tell him I had been eating at home.

TWO TRIBES

Viljandi was then, as it is now, a town of tribes. There were probably many tribes in the town, but the only two that mattered to me were the groupings I personally refered to as the folkies and the hoi polloi.

The folkies were identifiable by their values, *joie de vivre*, their commitment to the romantic ideals of 19th century life, their hip, old-timey wardrobe. In their world, all would be much better if the clocks had stopped ticking in 1899.

When you walked into our new friends Gea and Elias' apartment, whichever one they happened to be living in at the time, and the smell of all of that old wood hit your nostrils, rolled around in your olfactory system, and you huffed that cool breathability of the air, you felt at once comforted and displaced. Comforted in that it was so familiar to you as a human being, and yet displaced because it was an environment you had seldom known in your own short life, outside of open air farm museums. Elias always seemed to be out to enjoy life when he wasn't sweating over a stove fire or putting up vintage wallpaper, and he would invite you in for a Swedish *fika*, the ceremonial taking of the coffee, preferably with some chocolate or pastries.

"You've got to have something sweet for a proper *fika*," he would say, very, very seriously.

After Enn, Elias was the second English-speaking friend I made in Viljandi, and he probably understood me better than Enn because we were both true foreigners. We joked to each other about how the women would praise highly skilled men as *asjalik*, an odd word that translated literally as "thing-oriented," and the strange Estonian mating rituals that went on whenever a man installed some shelves in the living room. This was never done with the easy-going pace of the American or the Swede. No, no, no. You had to sweat a bit, you had to throw your arms dramatically into the drilling and grunt, if only so that your woman would see you working. Then she would kiss you and say, "Darling, you are so *asjalik*!" and give you some soup.

"Ugh, asjalik, asjalik, enough asjalik," Elias would say and roll his eyes. "'He's so handy.'"

He took his *fika* seriously, though, and he took his roast pork even more seriously, baking it in the oven at 100 degrees Celsius for eight hours until it achieved the proper temperature and juicy consistency. Then he would show you his latest triumph: a soup. "I had some onions laying around, some carrots, potatoes, wild mushrooms, a little leftover moose sausage," he raised his eyebrow to note the delicacy. "And half a bottle of lager, so I thought, why not make a soup?"

The murky broth, the cracked bowl, the old bent spoon. The way the beer taste lingered and meshed with the pungent mushrooms and the red onions, and then that special taste, the musty moose sausage.

"How long have you been cooking?" I asked.

"Since he could walk," Gea chimed in and beamed. She was so proud of Elias and his soup. In his own way, the Swedish chef was *asjalik* too.

Both of our new friends looked like fairies, they were both young, well younger than us. Once Elias made a joke about people born in the Nineties and I had to inform him that Epp and I felt the same way about the elegant, young, angst-less *Kaheksakümendikud*, as they were called in Estonian, the Eighties-born people whose entire personal histories could be perused by browsing through old text messages.

Gea was pretty and girlish and slim, she wore her light brown hair long, and an old-fashioned sewn gray dress that ended just above the knees. Sometimes she wore black stockings, other times, especially at home, she was barefoot. It felt good to walk on the old wooden floorboards, to feel the grain of the well-walked wood on the soles on your feet. But in Viljandi, you could also walk barefoot around town, dodging the shards of drunks' broken vodka bottles.

"Viljandi," Gea would say, "is the only town in Estonia where you can walk around barefoot and it's totally normal."

Or, as the locals called it, *paljajalu*.

Gea. She was another one of these hardworking farm daughters, the kind who never lets her husband rest even a minute when he is around because she knows how much work there is to be done. If Elias was not off at money-making gigs, preparing soup at some ski resort in Sweden, or on the Norwegian oil rigs in the North Sea, then he was in his home, covered with drops of paint, wallpaper glue, sawdust. "I would love to hang out," he would say, "but Gea has me working. Working, working. There's always so much work to do."

It wasn't a complaint. But Elias didn't feel guilty watching a hockey game at 9 p.m., whereas an Estonian man, like my neighbor on Sepa Street, Veiko, didn't watch games, as far as I knew. He sawed wood, and when he wasn't sawing wood he was fixing the chimney. Wild Bill Peep down at Muks' House had been the same. At midnight, I would hear the saw running in the workshop below our apartment. Epp thought nothing of it. "Normal," she said.

"What's wrong with these Estonians?" Elias would say when he visited. "Always working."

"They like it. That's what the Estonians do with their free time. It's what makes them happy."

"Why don't they just watch a hockey game or some-thing?" Then he would pour me coffee. *"Ska vi fika?"*

It wasn't always easy to get your hands on a good treat for *fika*. Sometimes, I would grab chocolate cake from the Green House Cafe, but usually I popped into the A ja O to get a big chocolate bar, an Anneke, or maybe one of those Kalev specialities, white chocolate with blueberry or dark chocolate with cherry. And then the big Mesikäpp bars, with the little pieces of cookie inside. We could go through three bars of chocolate in one afternoon *fika*.

---

*   „Let's have coffee?" (in Swedish)

The A ja O was the discount supermarket in Old Town, a single-story building with the bare essentials: bananas, potato chips, beer, toilet paper. Its full name was *Alati ja Odavalt*, which translated as "Always and Cheaply." It was in the A ja O that you usually encountered the other tribe that mattered in Viljandi's Old Town, the hoi polloi. I should make it clear that hard-working Estonian men like Veiko or Peep were not the hoi polloi. Nor were the folkies like Gea and Elias by any means wealthier than those next door deserving of the label, and being partly Swedish had nothing to do with it either. The juxtaposition between the two tribes was not international-local, or rich-poor.

And yet you could just tell a hoi polloi from a folkie on sight. You could tell them apart by what they bought at the A ja O discount supermarket. The folkie bought three chocolates for a Swedish fika. Actually, a true folkie didn't shop at the A ja O to begin with. He only bought his organic cakes from the Green House Cafe, or, even better, made them all from scratch. The hoi polloi depended on the A ja O though. He bought a pack of cigarettes and a 2-liter plastic bottle of Bear Beer.

There was no political division of which to speak between these groupings though. As far as I could tell, the folkies were apolitical, or perhaps mildly progressive, though when Ando Kiviberg, the good-humored, fuzzy-faced, bagpipe-playing founder of the annual folk music festival and practical king of the folkies ran for mayor in 2013, he did so under the auspices of the national conservative party Isamaa ja Res Publica Liit, or IRL.

And the hoi polloi? I'm not sure if the hoi polloi even bothered to vote. They wouldn't speak to you, wouldn't look you in the eye as you crossed paths in the street. You were just invisible to them, not of their special world.

Clothing was an important tribe identifier too. A proper member of the folkies had at least a full ethno outfit hanging in his closet, and a musical instrument on hand for jamming, just in case. They never wore mainstream clothes anyway. It was funny to imagine them, with their long, natural hair and unkempt beards, walking around in trendy European fashions. A person from this tribe would always wear their ethno design hats and flax shirts, for example when going to the events at the Ait, the annual *Lõikuspidu* in September, the Harvest Party, a celebration that opened up the Ait for a full season of music, or the big folk music festival itself at the end of July. For those days, Viljandi seemed to overflow with the folkies. But the hoi polloi, they didn't seem to care. They were inside of their houses somewhere, drinking beer and watching television. Just like a program that didn't interest them, when a gang of folkies came walking by, jamming on some guitars and flutes, they turned them off. Even on the most ecstatic folkie nights, you would pass under the windows of Viljandi houses and see the blue light from the TV screen reflected in the glass and you knew that they were on the other side, because folkies didn't own TV sets.

As much as the hoi polloi tried to ignore the spectacle around them they certainly saw the folkies. And they resented us. They didn't like us, and they showed it. A folkie would never slam his shoulder into a fellow pedestrian outside the supermarket. But I nearly got knocked down a handful of times. Because of that I started to hate them back. I hated the buffoons who would dig through the trash cans at the various musical events so that they could harness the empty bottles for a trip to the bottle depository to gather enough jing together for some cheap vodka. I hated the packs of young men who would hang around the stores on a Sunday morning drinking beer as soon as the doors opened.

What made me angriest was that my children saw this too. Marta would come running home with a fearful quiver in her voice. "We were playing at Lossikad, and then some drunks came."

I had walked accidentally into bitter class warfare playing out on the streets of Old Town Viljandi. I joined in too. I privately hoped that the hip folkies, moving in from Tallinn and Tartu and elsewhere, would eventually crowd out the other tribe, who didn't have the money or desire to paint their ruined homes because the mother was too often a drunk and the father was in jail for larceny. Meantime, the folkies were stripping the interiors of all their plaster. They were like me, painting the walls of our new apartment on Sepa Street with the special paint, an ecofriendly mix of natural dye and quark cheese.

The hoi polloi tribe's children ran free, but kept to their own. They would also huddle on street corners, but they wouldn't even talk to the Waldorf students, the children of the folkies. The lines were drawn.

I felt bad for despising the hoi polloi sometimes, for seeing them as a nuisance, as something I was up against. I felt bad for hating all of those drunkards that lived up the crooked staircases of the old villas, or in the cat-urine-doused cellars on the water, as they lined up at the supermarket to get their evening's stash of booze before they closed shop and the cashiers humored them.

But my friend Enn, who was as rough edged as they come, held no such sympathies.

"I don't get it. In Tallinn, Tartu, Pärnu, the old towns are prime real estate," he said to me one fine spring morning as we watched some of our fellow villagers guzzle beer at 11 o'clock. "But in Viljandi, it's different. In Viljandi, the sun brings out all of the slugs. Just look at them."

THE ORDER OF THINGS

For foreign Estonians like Enn, it was perhaps easier to slip back into Estonian life, with a knowledge of the language, and even more importantly, an understanding of how things were ordered in the Estonian mind.

Once, when I had got back from a trip overseas, and the weather was grim, rainy, and miserable, I called him up just to see how he was doing.

"Hey dude, what's happening, bro?" he said. "How were things back in the States?"

"I'm doing all right," I said. "The States were good. Loaded up on Mexican food."

"Oh, man, I could go for an *enchilada* right now. An *enchilada*, a *chimichanga*, and a *cerveza*." With each Spanish word, I recognized a desperate creak in his voice.

"What are you doing?"

"Ah, shit. I'm down in the cellar right now. Sorting potatoes." *Sortin' pa-tay-tas.*

After I got off the phone, I remarked to Epp about how Estonian Enn had become in Viljandi.

"What do you mean?"

"Not only is he handling potatoes, but he's *sorting* them."

I came from a family where the tomato was the *prima frutta* held in highest regard, so the Estonian devotion to the potato, which I regarded as a starchy, tasteless, superfluous crop, was fascinating. In early autumn, when the spuds were ready, Estonians would hold so-called *talgud*, when friends and neighbors would be invited to take part in a harvest.

At Enn and Kaari's country house out of Viljandi, in Metsküla, a tiny enclave of farmsteads set back in the woods, the tractor drove down the beds of potatoes, firing them out into the air and then down into the dirt. Then we went after them with sacks and paint buckets, loading them up onto a small truck that took them away. You picked every potato you could find, combed through every last patch of dirt. Even the small ones were treated with respect, and you felt a tiny thrill when you felt through the soil and pulled a baby potato out, one that had been left behind accidentally by the others.

After hours spent in the fields, you received your pay off: three sacks of potatoes for you to carry home on your back.

The muscles on the insides of your thighs ached for days after *talgud* though. You had to walk around town bowlegged, as if you had just ridden your horse across the Eurasian Steppe.

Down in Setomaa, we repeated the *talgud* experience with our neighbors Meelis and Kadri, only there they had a bottle of Sovetskoye Shampanskoye to quench our thirst. Every time you filled a bucket up with new potatoes, it seemed like an excuse to take another bubbly sip.

I remember Epp on that fall day. How beautiful she looked surrounded by potatoes, in her natural Estonian habitat. Her hair was a brilliant red-gold-brown and flowed wildly over her shoulders.

"Justin, pass the, uh, Sovetskoye Shampanskoye. That's what's so great about *talgud*, you know... *hiccup*... you get to work in the outdoors [wiping sweat from face with soiled hand] and get sun on your face and ...*gluglugglug* ... Hey, give me another sip of that, wouldya?"

And then back to work!

Apple picking in autumn was carried out with the same industry. The Estonians had a certain starvation mentality when it came to food. Nothing was wasted, even though the labor that went into picking all the half-rotten apples from the muddy ground might have been better spent on ascending a ladder to pluck the largest, ripest fruit from the boughs of the trees. But nobody would ever permit me to do this. The "picking" began on the ground and seldom left it.

When the Waldorf families would gather at the teacher Sulev's house to pick his orchard, you might see a dozen forms crouching in the grass, examining fruit for salvage-ability.

Sulev. White hair, white beard, jolly – but thoughtful – disposition. Sulev had been a teacher forever. He also was a vegetarian, and would be served a few boiled eggs when the Waldorf School students ate in the grand hall, on wooden benches around tables, and were served organic pork or organic ground beef with sauerkraut and – of course –

organic potatoes. Before they ate, they would all sing together, with sweetest, highest, angelic voices.

Marta was there, too, with the other first grade students. In the Waldorf School she learned to sing, to knit, to recite poetry, to play tunes on the recorder. Every month there was a party, a *kuupidu*, when the children and teachers performed for the parents. Sulev would stand in the corner, watching, with arms folded, a happy, thoughtful man.

Just as he stood outside his house during the apple-picking *talgud* to survey the scene. But he wasn't alone. His wife Virgi was there too. So was his mother. Given Sulev's white hair and beard, I was surprised that Sulev's mother was alive. But she was. And picking apples.

She went after that half-rotten fruit like a grain-harvesting combine. Crouched down low, in the dirt, fingers curled, curly white hair bobbing along, she seemed to be able to go through five apples at a time, examining each one for worthiness. When she saw me climbing a ladder to pull some fruit from the tree, she looked up from her perch in the mud and scolded me.

"Young man, get down! You have to pick the apples off the ground before you do the trees."

"But the better quality fruit is up here!"

"No, no. That's not how it goes. You pick the apples from the ground first. Then the trees!"

And so I climbed down, started to pick through the grass, and got stung by some nettles.

Most of my frustrations with Estonia grew out of such experiences. That feeling of being a square peg hammered through a circular hole. On the face of it, the differences were nothing, harmless, even admirable. It was admirable that the Estonians never let a potato or apple go to waste. It was admirable that they were working all of the time. But that rigid devotion to how things went, *kuidas asjad käivad*, that's what irked me.

There was no room for what made sense to me, should I have a different opinion or ideal. There was only how things went and it was expected of me that I embrace that mental order rather than try to see the world on my own terms. You just had to pick the half-rotten apples off the ground first. Then you picked the trees. *Lihtne!* Simple!

They had their own order of things. Who knows what my order was? For all the talk of Italian roots, hadn't I left my relatives behind in the name of love, adventure, and independence? Real Italians weren't supposed to leave home, they were supposed to live right next door to Mama and Papa forever. But that Italian peasant mentality, it persisted in some ways. So what if you picked the apples off the tree first. Who really cared? Why was it so important? It was this casual disdain for authority that was bred into me as an Italian. Of course we had no regard for rules. Hadn't Italy been ruled by foreign tyrants and corrupt powerful families forever? To hell with them! If there was a system, it existed only to be outsmarted and flouted. My grandfather's most beloved hobby was betting illegally on horses.

Both of my grandfather's fathers had sold bootleg alcohol during Prohibition. In essence, they were criminals. I came from a time-honored Italian tradition of rule breaking and criminality.

But the Estonians? They respected order. They worked hard to hone and perfect their system, to make it accessible online via identity card. Andrei, the blogger, once bragged that he never in his life had crossed a street unless he was given the green light to go or there was a crosswalk.

"But what if there are no cars around?" I had asked.

"It doesn't matter," he shook his head. "I wait until I get the green light."

"But what if other people cross the street and there's a red light? Don't you feel ridiculous?"

"Then they are breaking the rules and they are all idiots."

So simple!

MARIA AND THE BIRD

When Maria came it was September.

The autumn had not yet arrived officially, but in Estonia the ends and beginnings of seasons were open to question. The year Maria came, summer was already gone, dead, and finished.

Carried away by the September wind.

You could hear it, rattling the wood, gusting down the streets near our new home. The trees shimmied and the laundry flapped in the air. The wind brought with it new life, but also clouds, some fluffy and harmless, the others brooding, ripe with rain. It rained every day that September, and it was also sunny every day. The morning before Maria came, it had been sunny three times and had rained four times. I had counted it. Then the rain stopped and the gray fogged in. But you knew the sun would return to settle things. Such moody days, those days in Viljandi. I felt as if I was living in Ireland.

And it was green like Ireland. The grass was lush and verdant. Moss grew everywhere, on the sides of houses, on the tops of roofs, up telephone poles. Moss and rot and rust. My cheeks were moist with the rain. I didn't use an umbrella anymore. I didn't mind getting wet. I set out across town to the supermarket to buy a few things because we both knew it would be soon.

When I entered the parking lot of the shopping center, I noticed Eints, one of the local builders I knew. He was there walking across the parking lot, but hunched a bit and with a limp, too. When he came nearer to me, I could see his eyes focused ahead, a bit of deadness in them. His white fuzzy mustache. Stained blue overalls. He had some dark red above his eye, almost black, that I recognized as dried blood.

"Tere, Eints," I called out.

No response.

"It's Justin. Remember me? How are you doing, man?"

But there was no response from Eints. He traipsed forward, eyes front. Enn had warned me about Eints. He never referred to him by his given name either. He always called him, "The Drunk." "Oh, The Drunk. He's a mean son of a bitch. Only nice to people when he's drunk."

The Drunk.

When you came up behind the supermarket, you encountered the bottle return, the infamous *Taarapunkt*. There were two other drunks seated outside, sorting through big bags of empty beer bottles. They wore worn, weather-fatigued jackets, with messy hair that seemed to be glued into place. I never made eye contact with these kinds of men. I averted my gaze and checked my pocket for the list of pertinent goods. Just then, the gray sliced open and it began to drizzle down on all of us. Epp had reminded me to take the umbrella along, but I had forgotten. But by the time I had finished shopping, the rain had finished and the sun had come out again as well as a cool chill that remained.

That's one thing I remember about that September when Maria came, that cool gray blue chill that seemed to come off the lake and stay and stay. That soothing, crisp airy feeling. The way the children's voices echoed off the ancient houses. It felt good to wear pants again and it felt good to wear sweatshirts.

Maria was born on Sepa Street. She was born in the bathroom, beside the *tünnivann*. This was a bathtub, a *vann*, fashioned from wood and metal, just like a *tünn*, a barrel. The bathroom had clay walls painted with flower flourishes, wooden shelves suspended by ropes, a sink built into an antique dresser, and another great old trunk you could sit on. The toilet room had as wallpaper old copies of *Rahva Hääl* and *Edasi* – Soviet-era newspapers. You could sit a while and enjoy stories about tractorists and exciting days in Pioneer camps, or Comrade Chernenko's latest address. The hall led to the main room, which had a re-upholstered "snail couch," built in 1940. It was called a snail couch because its arms curled at the ends, resembling the shell of a snail. We had found the couch online, and I had driven up to Türi one day to fetch it from a crumbling garage.

I remember the old man who walked by, guzzling straight from a plastic bottle of beer. He had a long white beard and a flat cap. Looked like a misplaced fisherman. No fish in Türi. No sea.

The world into which Maria came was a long way from the prewar chic of snail couches. Instead of singing peaceful folk songs, my daughter Marta and her Waldorf friends would hold hands and skip down the bumpy back lanes of Viljandi singing Nicki Minaj. *"Have a drink, clink..."* I could never get mad at Marta and her friends for singing the lyrics, even the bad ones. They were so young. I remember watching them sing that song in their puffy September vests.

"Daddy, is it okay if me and Loretta go to climb on the castle ruins?"

"That's okay with me, but be careful, honey!"

"Don't worry. If we see any drunks we'll turn to the other path."

Rugged streets of Viljandi, hard on the legs, our Sepa Street the hardest. It used to have cobblestones too, but at some point in the past, someone had dug them up and sold them. On that September day when Maria was born, there was just sand and puddles there. Our home was single-story, serpentine, wooden, green, with a red tiled roof. It was a few hundred years old and had long lost any sense of geometry. Sometimes I thought this house resembled an old drunk, like Eints, staggering across a parking lot.

Our neighbors were a pack of youths. I wasn't sure if they were students or not. By that point I didn't care. Once I met them out in the streets in winter. They were all naked, standing around in towels. It was minus 15 degrees Celsius. "What are you doing out here like this? It's freezing!"

"Sauna," came the reply.

They were drinking too. *Normaalne.*

Sometimes when I looked at the ruined houses across the street through our window at night, I imagined that I was a scuba diver examining a shipwreck. There had once been more houses on Sepa Street, but one of the local lunatics burned them down. Nobody ever wanted to discuss who he was or what happened to him. I assumed he was in jail or dead.

In Tallinn, another old man was arrested for bomb making. For years, explosives would go off, wounding passersby, shattering glass. This was the September world into which our Maria was born.

An Estonian face. Pudgy as a seal pup's. But too round. *It looks like a foreigner*, a friend said.

A few days later we took Maria on her first sojourn, to Heimtali manor, one of those Baltic German castles out in the forests, with towers and narrow windows, like a medieval movie set. We forgot to take the mushrooming knife but we had a pair of scissors in the car's First-Aid kit, and so we used the scissors to cut the mushrooms. Maie-ly, our wonderful, gray-haired jolly cheerful babysitter, who never seemed to shy from love, even though her husband had just died, made an apple cake for us. We ate all of it at Heimtali estate park with our hands.

When we came home, we encountered the gangs of children, the Viljandi street urchins. They roamed the dirty streets, playing games I could not understand. One of them knew that I was an American, and had taught the others to greet me with, "Hello! Hi!"

Once I found three of the street kids in my kitchen. Our front door was locked, so the trio had crawled through an open window in the same bathroom where Maria was born. When I asked them why they had broken into my house, the youngsters explained that they were hungry and saw from the window that we had some food. I told them that they should leave and never come back. The thought did cross my mind that we were living in a ghetto.

Maria was born in a wooden ghetto. That was my thought.

We had given Maria the name of my great grandmother, who moved to America and yet always longed to go back home to Italy, where she thought she still belonged. But where did this new little Maria belong? To this place? This rain-soaked muddy street where she was born?

Obviously, I was depressed, even with a new baby.

Epp, on the other hand, was convinced that the place had potential.

"Someone will buy the burned house across the street and fix it up, Justin. New cobblestones will be outside our window soon! It's been in the town plans for seven years," she said. "Sooner or later the city will get around to doing it." She wouldn't admit it, but she was proud of the place. She remembered when the hair salon used to be a bookstore, and the doctor's office was an ice cream depot, or something like that. She was born here.

And maybe Epp and Maria were lucky. You couldn't pick a more beautiful place to be born. Viljandi was situated on pretty bluffs overlooking a lovely lake, a gash of glacial blue among rolling forest green hills, like the soft entrance to a womb. Sometimes when I saw this town in the morning mist, I was taken aback by it. I felt lucky to live there too, lucky to be alive.

Then one day, while I was holding Maria in the chill air and pale autumn sunlight, a bird flew around my head.

The small gray bird dropped down from the sky, circled my head, and took off. Just like that.

"Huh, did you see that?" Epp said in the doorway. "A bird just flew around your head!"

"I know. Weird, right?"

But it wasn't just weird. It was a sign. Something was going to happen.

One of my history professors at the university, Heiki Valk, had told a story in class about how a bird had flown into his house following a funeral, extinguished the candle lit for the dead person's soul on the window sill with its wing, and flown out the same way, all in about three seconds. It was the old Nordic pagan beliefs, the ancient superstitions that persisted.

Some people in class looked at the bearded historian like he was insane. But I knew he wasn't. I had lived in Estonia long enough to know that when a bird flew around your head on a September morning with a newborn daughter in your arms it meant something really big.

You were marked.

But marked for what? I had no wise Heiki leaning over my shoulder at that moment, no Estonian shaman who was fluent in bird signs.

I could only wager that something out of the ordinary was about to happen to me, to happen to us. I did not know what it was. I felt unsettled.

HOLY BIRCH

She wanted to put it in the garden, but I didn't think so.

For one, it was more like our neighbor's garden. For two, they were eating dinner nearby. It was all in plain sight, and, for some reason, I didn't feel like sharing this intimate moment with anybody.

"But Toomas the witch said that there is an energy point over there, next to the stone wall," Epp said.

"Okay. But why don't we wait until after dinner?"

"But if we wait that long it will be too dark and I need to put the ice cream into the freezer."

This was homemade ice cream, Viljandi recipe. Gea had provided the instructions. Most of it was condensed milk and egg yolks, the rest nuts and raisins.

But before the great tub of homemade ice cream went in, something else had to come out.

It was my mistake that I put the placenta in the freezer.

Anna's placenta sat in the freezer in Tartu for years before it found its final resting place in Setomaa beside a sapling. But the instructions for Maria's placenta were actually to put it in the refrigerator and plant it sooner

I cannot really describe what a placenta looks like. Epp described it as looking like a liver. To me, it resembled the heart of a walrus. Whatever, it had a distinct form. Our midwife Siiri had left it in a bowl in the barrel where Maria was born.

We agreed to bury it in the front lot. At first, Epp suggested the *kibuvitsa** bush, a genuine Estonian moment, because I didn't even know what a *kibuvitsa* bush was in English and, up into that point, I was unaware we had an entire *kibuvitsa* bush growing right in our front yard.

We decided on the foot of a birch instead. It was easier to dig there and there was a rock before it, too. A headstone for the placenta.

"I was looking at this birch during labor," said Epp. "It's a holy tree, I think."

I preferred the birch too, so I could do my business out of sight. The last thing I wanted to see was our neighbors strolling and whistling along while I dumped that placenta into the ground.

"Dumped? You can tell we have a different way of looking at it when you use that word!"

"I'm sorry. I meant placed, not dumped."

---

* Rose hip in English.

"To me this is a sacred thing – this placenta gave Maria food and nourishment for months."

"I understand. I really do."

"I don't get it. Why do you have to be such a mainstream asshole?"

"I'm not a mainstream asshole, damn it! I just have never dump, er, placed a placenta, okay?" Marta's placenta had really been dumped at the Tallinn Central Hospital and Epp said she regretted it later. As for Anna's, it was Epp herself who planted the sacred deep frozen placenta in Setomaa.

This time it was my turn to do the work.

It happened in the orange light of the street lamps, with the ripe smoke of the neighbors' chimneys sooting and smogging up the street, so that you felt like you were lost in London of old, transported into a Charles Dickens novel. Between short coughs I dug out a hole large enough for the placenta at the foot of the birch. Not a soul stirred. I thought I was in the clear.

But then, just as I was about to sneak back to the house to retrieve the frozen placenta, I saw a small group of shadowy people moving down the road. It was Enn and Kaari, Maari, Miko, and baby Mingo.

Maari and Miko were on bikes. Enn had baby Mingo in a sling. Kaari had a great smile. She was like a folk saint, immune from all the poisons of the world. Her toothy smile was visible from halfway down the street. They really were something out of *Oliver Twist*. The rumpled, worn clothes. A little dirt on the cheeks from manual labor. I laid my shovel against the tree and stepped back.

"Hey, dude. What's happening?" Enn called out.

"Hello there. Um. Nothing, just doing a little gardening here."

"Gardening? At this hour? Isn't it a bit dark and cold?"

"Yeah, it is, now that you mention it."

"Can we see the baby?" Maari asked with a scratchy young voice, looking up at me with her little twinkling blue eyes. Maari understood English but always spoke to me in Estonian.

"Oh, I'm sorry, Maari, the baby's asleep."

"It's too early?" said Enn, nodding. "Maybe tomorrow?"

"Yes, mh... Why don't you come back the day after tomorrow. Then you can see the baby."

From within the house, I heard screams and sounds of physical violence. Through the window I could see one of my children standing over another. A chair lay on the kitchen floor.

Enn nodded toward the window. "Everything all right, dude?"

"Oh, that's just Marta and Anna," I said. "They are always fighting. Italian blood, you know."

Kaari continued to smile, but there was a slight reticence in her lips.

Epp was now at the window. Maari and Miko peered in, trying to catch a glimpse of the baby. Epp saw them and came outside.

"Oh, this is so nice you happened to come here for our special moment," Epp gestured to me. "We are just about to plant Maria's placenta under that birch tree."

All the heads turned to me, as I rested an elbow on the shovel, smiled and said nothing.

"Ah, Miko's is still in our freezer," said Kaari. "I think Maari's is too. Isn't it, Enn?"

"Yeah, I think it is."

Wait, these people kept their placentas in the freezer, too? Were we actually normal? At least among the tribe of folkies? Maybe. I had read in my time amongst the folkies that placentas, these sacred bloody givers of life, could prove beneficial in the future, should the child need a bone marrow transplant. As for burying rituals, I was a novice. So I tried to crack a joke.

"Heh. I've heard some people even eat it."

"I've eaten placenta before," Kaari blurted out. "They say it is a very good traditional remedy against postnatal depression."

"Really?" I said.

"It was only one mouthful, I swear," she giggled.

"Whose was it?"

"Who cares? Just fry it up with some butter, salt and pepper," Enn said. "Tastes like chicken."

"Everything tastes like chicken," I said.

"Just delicious!"

When they were gone, I finished the task and placed the placenta into the hole before the holy birch.

I did think of it from time to time when I walked by, though I'm sure it degraded into dirt within a few weeks. But it had given that holy birch nourishment, just as it had given sustenance to our daughter. We came to love that tree, as if it was our own tree-daughter. It was sad when the construction crews cut it down when they were renovating the road. But that birch still lives in my memory.

INDIAN DREAM

All through the dark hole that was November, I prayed for winter to come and slay the rain with ice and whiteness.

And then it came to Viljandi, the cold. Brilliant minus 25 degree Celsius weather. The cold took away the fog and replaced it with white sunlight that caught on the faces of the icicles. The air was fresh because there was no moisture to case the smoke as it escaped from the Old Town chimneys. It curled straight up into the sky.

Still, there were other dangers. In that kind of weather, the Estonians said, you must have a fire in your furnace two or even three times a day, otherwise the cold "might come into the house."

I had never thought of the cold as something that could *move* like that before. To me, it was a solid block of air that came in and sailed away. It didn't have a mind of its own. But, as I experienced it that winter, when it got cold enough, you really could feel it, coming up through the beams of the floor. If you left the office, you had to let the water drip, to keep the pipes moving. You had to shut the door tight, or else the cold might come in. It might burst a pipe. Then everything would smell like a toilet.

You hung thick blankets on the doors, and insulated the windows with puffs of cotton from the apothecary and tape, to keep it out. You had to poke the cotton into the cracks between the windows and the frames with a butter knife.

All of this was done so that the cold *would not come in.*

But the cold, it conspired against you, tested every weakness in your home.

The cold would find a way.

On that morning, I resumed my role as ship's stoker on our wood-burning craft. I got up at 5 a.m. in the cold and went to the kitchen and worked on a book. As it got colder still, I went to make a fire.

And then I saw that there was no more wood.

This meant one thing. I would have to go outside in the dark and get it. I had to 'suit up' as I liked to say, like a diver of old or an astronaut, with thick wool socks, insulated pants, a shirt, a sweater, a scarf, thick gloves, a hat, and shin-high boots, fit for trench warfare.

But before I went out I had to have breakfast to give me strength, three eggs fried in butter, three mandarins, some whole grain bread, some cheese, a glass of orange juice.

When I looked at the egg frying in the pan, with its yellow orange yolk at the center, I thought of my vegan friends who would mock such food as the menstrual cycle of a chicken. "Would you eat something from my menstrual cycle?" one asked. My answer that morning was this: when it is minus

25 degrees Celsius out and it's 5 a.m., I'll eat just about anything. I needed energy to survive that trip to the barn.

The differences between the interior and exterior were vast. The outside had become a different planet. The way the starchy snow crumpled beneath your boots. How the moisture of your breath clung to your whiskers and nostril hairs and eyebrows. Each movement was slow, deliberate, and stiff. My muscles ached from days of hauling wood in minus temperatures. I had asked Hevel the neighbor if her muscles also hurt from moving wood in the cold, but she said no, she was used to it. I had asked my friend Mart, too, and he also denied this phenomenon. Were they both stoic and lying or was my body just not built for this climate? The cold did keep the muscles constricted, I read. I took a pill to ease the pain.

The vital sign out there was the smoke from neighboring chimneys. I looked up at Hevel's chimney for that slight movement of transparent gray. It was already going, at quarter past five. In fact as far as I knew, she never stopped her fires during that extra cold patch. She and her husband would use a wheelbarrow to cart the wood to their apartment. The fires never stopped because they had a fireplace, and not a proper furnace.

Outside, in the morning dark, all was silent. What other creatures could live in this? There were no birds, no insects, and at that hour no people. Only the sound of my boots and the lights from our kitchen window.

I moved three bundles of wood from the small barn. There were two whole walls stacked to the ceiling with wood. When it had been delivered, I had thought it was too much. Now I feared that it might not be enough.

The bundles got dragged to the door.

My car was frosted over, like some kind of woolly mammoth encased in ice. Inside, I saw the little red light from the car alarm blinking like a heartbeat. *The damn thing is still alive.*

I opened the big barn and turned on the light, brought out one bag of the "fluffy stuff," soft blocks of sawdust that light easily, and then two bundles of the wood for the central furnace.

When I was in the barn, I started to feel the eyes on me. This reminded me of ghost stories I'd read. "I was standing in a cold barn at 5.15 a.m. and then I felt someone, or something, watching me." Who is watching me? Who's there? I waited for some apparition of a deceased Estonian to loom up out of the wood and lecture me about heating. There is nothing an Estonian, even a dead one, loves more than giving a good lecture to a foreigner on how to keep a house warm. Instead there was nothing. I turned to the house and saw that Epp was looking at me from the kitchen window. I waved to her and she waved back.

"I was worried. I looked in the bedroom, in the bathroom. I couldn't find you," she said when I came inside, stomping my boots to clear them of snow.

"It was cold and we were out of wood," I said, bringing the wood inside. She lifted the big bag of sawdust blocks. A strong woman.

"Early morning exercise, eh?"

"I'm sick again," she sniffled. "Did you see the links I sent you last night?"

For days, Epp had been trying to convince me that we should move to Goa, India, for the next winter, and the winters after that. Goa is the richest, most visited state in West India, and was until 1961 part of Portuguese India. So it was vaguely European. Epp even located a Waldorf school there. There were images on its website of European-colored children in ethnic Indian clothes holding hands. Another possible future.

"Let this be our very last winter in Estonia," she said, pouring the coffee. "I love springs, summers and early falls in this latitude... but winter! I am not made for this winter."

"But you were born here."

"When I was young I dreamed of beaches and palm trees. I don't even know where I got those images. They just came to me."

"Maybe you saw them on television?"

"They didn't show palm trees and beaches on Soviet television."

"Didn't the Soviets have any client states in the South Pacific? The People's Republic of Polynesia?"

"I don't remember where my palm tree dreams came from. What about you? Where did you want to live when you were a child?"

"I do remember one cartoon. A cruise ship docked at night in Nome, Alaska. It was so beautiful, white and black. The lights from all the houses looked like stars. The snow sheeting down all around. Then the little Eskimos started dancing! It was so cute."

Epp glared at me over her morning coffee.

"So you're the one," she said at last. "It is your fault we suffer here."

"What do you mean?"

She nodded at me. "You're the one who likes this climate."

"But you were born here."

"But you're the reason we're still here!"

"No! It's not like that at all," I said and walked over to bring in the last bundle of wood. "I just thought that Alaska would be a neat place to visit. All of that snow and those dancing Eskimos. I didn't actually want to spend the rest of my life up there."

Just then, I heard a sort of rustling sound come from the cabinet behind me. I trained my ears to pick up any more sounds but there were none. I don't think Epp paid attention to the sound either. She was still dreaming of palm trees.

ONE ARROGANT MOUSE

It became a savage tale of life and death, as are most stories of mice and men.

I don't remember the first time I suspected that we may have had a mouse in the Viljandi apartment. Maybe it was those telling black pellets that surrounded the garbage can in our kitchen, or the continuous squeaking I would hear from the cabinets above the stove while I worked late, or maybe that strange smell Epp was complaining about.

"Do you smell it?" she sniffed at the air. "It's the nastiest thing in the world."

Our Seto neighbor, Kadri, had warned me about mice. They would come in, she said, when the weather got cold. We would have to poison them, she said. After they died, their bodies would stink for a while. Then they would be forgotten.

It sounded sad. But Kadri was used to killing things. No matter the animal, Meelis and Kadri had killed it. Sheep, chickens, pigs... they were Seto country people, murder was second nature for them, right up there with mushrooming and *karmoška*[*] playing.

---

[*] The garmon (called the *karmoška* in Seto language), is a Russian button accordion.

But I didn't want to kill our mouse. For me, his sounds were welcome. I did not fear him. As I saw it, our mouse was a poor vagabond, without an item of furniture or clothing to his name. And he was in danger! The outside temperature had dropped too low. The wall between our kitchen and our bathroom was the only place where he could stay warm.

And let's not forget, he had chosen our old home because it was so cozy. As I was told, mice never went into the new-fangled constructions of sheetrock and laminate and dry central heating, oh no, they adored old homes with warm, wood-heated furnaces.

Another part of me, a cowardly part, didn't want to believe that we really had a mouse, or that I would have to do something about it. If I pretended not to hear him, if I imagined his turds were actually black pepper or chocolate flakes, maybe there wouldn't have to be a confrontation. He could sleep well behind our wall, peacefully, quietly, happily.

Christmas was almost upon us. Any day, President Too-mas Hendrik Ilves would declare the Christmas peace and there would be a moratorium on conflicts in Estonia. All conflicts. Even those between species.

I didn't want what took place next to happen.

But I could not lie to myself any more. The area behind the cabinets began to stink like urine, a hot, foul stench. And one evening, while I was typing away at the kitchen table, I saw a tail swing down between the cabinet and cabinet door, as its owner squeaked its way through another mouthful of our food.

Dangling like a worm on a hook.

I watched that hypnotizing little tail twitch for three minutes. Then I went into the other room, where Epp and Marta were curled up on the couch.

"I hate to have to tell you this," I said to Epp and Marta. "But I just saw his tail."

"You did?" Marta perked up.

"When?" Epp put her book aside. "Where?"

"Just now. In the kitchen."

"Really?"

Epp leaped up and tiptoed into the kitchen where she got on a chair and opened up one of the cabinets. When she did it, that fresh hot fecal odor reached our noses and lingered. But the mouse wasn't there. Until Epp opened up the other cabinet.

"Aha! There he is!" she pointed at some mugs. "I can see your nose, little mouse!"

"You can?" Marta said. "Hey, I want to see, too."

Epp helped Marta up. "Look, he's hiding. He thinks we can't see him!"

"Silly mouse!"

"Shh! I don't want him to run away."

I squinted between the two brave women. Sure enough, there was the mouse's little nose poking out between two cups.

It's a shame what happened to that mouse later.

The next morning, I removed all of the food from the cabinet. The boxes of garlic thins and bags of flour. The container of cocoa and the dried peas. At last, I removed the half-chewed-through bag of oat flakes, pushing it into a metal pot with a hand brush. I swept up the little black turds that lay about and washed the surface down with soapy water.

After all this preparation I put an open plastic dish of poisoned mouse food into the cabinet and closed the door and waited. I hoped the mouse would eat it and die somewhere behind the wall. Maybe it would be so cold where he died that he would simply freeze and we wouldn't smell his corpse as Kadri predicted.

I also decided to set up another trap: a container of water for the mouse, deep enough that should he happen to get thirsty and then perch on its wobbly edge and fall in, it would look like an accident.

These things happen.

Endel, the handyman who knew everything and was very reliable when he wasn't "in Vietnam" (his term for a drinking binge, so that if you called him and he was tight he would tell you, "I can't come today. I'm fighting in Vietnam") heard about the mouse and urged us to pursue a scorched earth policy and take no prisoners. We should use traps instead, he said.

"But the mouse is not actually causing us harm," I lamented. "He just eats our garbage. Is that really a reason to kill him that way?"

"That mouse is eating your food, right?" Endel said. He was an older fellow, white hair, mustache, had an answer for everything, always one thumb tucked away in his blue workman's overalls. "And you should be eating your food, right? Tell you what you do. Get yourself some strong mouse traps and grease them up with sausage or cheese. The mouse comes sniffing and them – bammo! – goodbye, mouse!"

I relented and acquired several old-fashioned mouse traps and coated them in sausage grease just like Endel had advised us.

But mouse traps are not as easy as they look, especially when you are a big man with big hands. The mechanics behind the traps are governed by tiny, moving metal parts. Trying to get the trap to catch is like trying to thread a needle, except when you thread a needle, you might only prick a finger. If you weren't careful with the traps enough force to splatter a mouse's brains across a cabinet would come down hard on your fingers.

I set those traps, and opened the cabinet slowly the next morning... but we never caught any mouse. Which is why I put out more poison and water. Anyway, better a poisoning or a drowning than a splattering. Not only was it easier on my fingers, it was more convenient for the mouse. Just a bellyache or a lung full of water and... bammo!

All night long, after putting out the poison and water again, I lay in bed with one eye open, my ears attentive to any sounds of struggle coming from the kitchen. In the morning, I ever so carefully opened the cabinet door, bracing myself to find the mouse's corpse floating in the container of water, or to see it sprawled out beside the container, grasping at its throat.

Instead, I only saw a trail of tiny shits leading away from the poison, which had been shat all over itself. The tiny mice turds lay about in the poisoned mix like plump peppercorns.

The mouse hadn't taken the bait. He had shit all over it instead. He was laughing at us.

"Do you know what the word *ülbik* means?" Epp asked me when I showed her the scene.

I shook my head.

"It means arrogant," she said. "What we have here is one really, really *ülbik* mouse."

Of course we tried to get a cat in to do our dirty work. We researched the problem and solution online and decided to take a mature female feline from the local animal shelter who supposedly had once lived on the streets, which almost guaranteed that she would be a great mouse killer. And yet when we brought the gray striped cat into our home, she just licked her paws and purred and slept and didn't seem bothered by the presence of the mouse at all. Probably she had been taken from the streets to live in the shelter when she was still a small kitten, and so she never learned to catch the mice for a living. That was our hypothesis.

From then on we seemed to have two pets. A cat and a mouse.

I saw our mouse one more time. It was when I was cleaning out the cabinet next to the one that housed the untouched container of water and the plastic dish of poison, which continued to sit there, turds and all, with the hope that he would eventually get so hungry that he would be forced to consume it.

As I opened the door, I saw the ball of gray fur looking and squeaking at me before he disappeared behind the back ledge of the shelf. I imagined that if mice squeaks meant anything, he was basically telling me to go to hell in mouse talk with a great mouse smile.

"Hey you! Giant person! This is what I think of your poison!" Turd, turd, turd.

The mouse's defiance grew as the winter went on. I could hear him rustling around in our bedroom. One time a TV crew came to film our family for a Christmas special and caught a mouse running across the floor. "We got your mouse on video!" the camera man exclaimed.

Enough was enough. That was the same day that Epp acquired the sticky mouse poison that a seller in the gardening store had suggested as the most efficient way to catch the creatures.

And that's when things started to get weird.

Sticky mouse poison is a kind of glue that is set out on a piece of cardboard. Red and gooey, the mouse becomes trapped, with the poison eventually sinking into the mouse's skin and stopping its tiny heartbeat.

The following morning, Epp came into the bedroom to inform me that there had been two mice – both had been stuck to the cardboard.

"Oh, so we have two, not one!" I said. "Good, they're both dead."

"No, Justin," she whispered. "They are still alive."
Still alive?!?

"Well, what should we do with them?" she asked.

"Put them in the garbage," I said.

"But they are still alive!"

It was true. The poison had not yet worked its magic on the two mice in the cabinet above the stove. There they lay wriggling, trying to get themselves free beside the mouse traps that were set and still. Their tails spasmed with each attempt to free themselves.

"Maybe we should put them outside," I said. "They shouldn't last long in this weather."

It was 15 below zero, Celsius.

Epp stood on a chair and moved the cardboard in one quick movement into the open bag of kitchen trash. But there was a tiny problem. The other mouse had managed to crawl away. It was now stuck to the shelf. Epp threw a paper towel over it, her hand shaking.

"What should we do now?" she said and looked back at me.

That's when I dug the palette knife out of my toolbox and got up on the chair. I made a few stabs at the moving creature beneath the sheet. At last, the mouse seemed to stick to the edge of the palette knife, and I ferried it quickly into the trash.

I laughed when I did it too. The kind of laugh you hear in a horror film.

"Is it wrong that I laughed?" I asked Epp after, when the mice were dying outside.

"I think sometimes people laugh when very horrible things happen," she said, still shaking a little.

I remembered that when I had first heard of the Oklahoma City Bombing in 1995, I had laughed. Not because there was anything humorous about that many innocent people being killed, but because I didn't know how else to react. It was just so terrible.

The saddest part came the next morning when we found more mice "attached" to the sticky cardboard that we had left out, just in case.

And there would be more mice. And more mice. And more.

I originally thought we had one arrogant mouse. But soon there were ten frozen corpses lying in the trash outside our apartment. Then there were the two who drowned, but not in my water trap. Epp had seen them running across the floor and both times trapped them with a gloved hand. Like a real jungle cat.

"What should we do with it?" she said when she caught the first one.

"Put it outside," I said.

"But it could come back inside."

"Then flush it down the toilet."

"Oh my God..."

Both times we flushed the mice, they spread out their little arms and legs until the gushing tidal wave of cold winter toilet water came down on them from above, pushing them down below. These were terrible things to witness, but we soon forgot about them...

Or tried to.

The fact is that is that I could never forget.

This period of our life presaged the nastiness and guilt. I did not want to kill anything but what were we supposed to do? It seemed that the mice and the killing of them came with the country lifestyle we had chosen. You had to make up your mind, you had to keep choosing. Either you were a Buddhist pacifist, or you were a countryman, a peasant. I thought of my roots, my great grandfathers in Italy. They probably would not even have understood why I felt so bad about killing the mice.

"Have you ever seen *The Godfather*?" I asked Epp one night. "I have these mice corpses in front of me every time I close my eyes. It's like the final scene. When Michael Corleone takes out all of the family's enemies."

"Dying by freezing is probably not so bad," Epp answered sadly. "You just get kind of tired."

"Numb. Sleepy. Yes, I have heard that this is one of the most convenient ways to die."

"But getting flushed down the toilet?" She looked up at me.

I shrugged. "Then you drown."

"But which is worse, freezing to death or drowning?"

"I don't know," I said. "I've never drowned."

In the end, 38 mice met their end in the Viljandi apartment. And I had thought it was one mouse. If there was one thing I learned, it was that there never is only one mouse. Maybe there are two at the beginning. Maybe we should have taken Endel's advice and gotten rid of them as soon as possible, before they had time to replicate. Think of it, 38 was what I could count. I am still not sure how many might have nibbled the poison and died behind the wall.

At some point though, there were no more mice. We left the glue and poison out, but none appeared. A whole colony of them had been wiped out, massacred, erased from history by another, competitive species. They were captured in glue and transported outside to freeze to death. It usually took a few minutes for this to happen, I think... Then I would put them in the trash and they were sent to the landfill on the edge of town. It was as if they had never existed.

Sometimes I thought about Stalin as I did this dirty work and of his famous saying, "No man, no problem," except I thought, "No mouse, no problem."

Someone once suggested to me (long after it all happened) that we might have used traps to capture the Viljandi mice live, then taken them someplace safe and let them go.

But it was minus 15 degrees Celsius outside. Where could we have taken them? Unless we had left them outside somebody else's house. But wouldn't they have then suffered a similar fate? It was troubling, our experience with those mice. Both of us felt bad about what we had done.

"It's the law of the jungle," Epp said, trying to justify what had happened. "Two species competing against each other. They wanted our house, they wanted our food. It was either us or them."

At one point we just stopped talking about it.

A few weeks later, Epp did find an ornament at the second-hand items shop. It was a painting of a mouse with a red hat and a cheerful "Season's Greetings!" look on its face.

We hung it on the wall in remembrance of all of those poor souls who lost their lives.

FIRE-BREATHING SALMON

I still cannot identify the moment when the bitterness leaked into me totally and made everything wrong.

But I do remember feeling frustrated with the direction things were going, ticked off by all the strange incidents that left me clutching for my American heart. Not like America was the promised land, but sometimes I did feel some things were weird in Estonia. When I saw a man standing ahead of me in a supermarket with a black t-shirt on it that showed the lightning-shaped letters of the *SS*, I couldn't understand why the cashier would even speak to him, or why someone didn't grab his bottle of vodka and crack it over his shaved head. But nobody paid him any attention. To them he was just another *jobu*, a jerk. When I told Epp at home about it, she shrugged. *Just a jerk. What can you do?*

If it wasn't the supermarket neo-Nazis who irritated me, then it was the drunks, guzzling their liters of cheap beer right in front of the bottle return so they could get some quick coins to buy another bottle. I complained to my niece Simona about the drunks but she shrugged too.

"What makes you think they are drunks?" asked adolescent Simona, brushing at her blonde locks.

"They are grown men drinking beer outside a super-market at 11 a.m.," I said. "Of course they are drunks."

"Then I guess there are a lot of drunks in Estonia."

"They should round them all up. All the Estonian drunks. Exile them to Piirisaare to dry out."

"Piirisaare? Is it that little place in Peipsi järv?"

"Yeah."

"Oh. I think you're going to need a bigger island," Simona remarked in a somber voice. "Most of the men I know drink too much."

So maybe it wasn't a good idea, but at least I didn't just shrug my shoulders and move on. If I was ever proud to be an American, in the flag-waving, song-singing way, then it was a long time ago. But my ideal of Americanness, that abrasive, honest aspect, lived on. Europeans were too accustomed to averting their gaze. But Americans? We were truth tellers. In Viljandi, I imagined myself as a train-hopping vagabond writer like Jack Kerouac clad in dirty clothes and muddy boots, with a truthy journal in hand. If nobody else was going to write about the skinheads and the drunks of Viljandi, I would. Thanks to Viljandi, my clothes were dirty and my boots muddy. And I did have a journal in hand.

I came down Sepa Street, turned left, and then hooked a quick right over the wooden bridge to the Ait and the castle ruins. I came out to the edge of the ruins that looked out over the lake and reached for my pen of truth.

But instead of grasping the pen I itched at my scalp. And kept itching. And itching. And itching. And itching.

When Epp was shocked, her face would flatten out a bit and her skin would turn from a ruddy pink to gray white. I had seen this face when she got the call that Aunt Salme had died, and also when Papa, her grandfather Karl, had passed away in Viljandi Hospital.

I saw it again that day in the kitchen. Her eyes tripled in size and her mouth lay agape.

"What happened?" I asked.

No answer.

"What's going on?"

Epp set the phone down slowly.

"Did somebody die?"

"That was Jaanika, from the kindergarten," Epp said. "She says they have *täid*."

"Oh, no."

Täid. It was the Estonian word for lice and it was never said without a bit of a shudder. There were plenty of things to fear in that land, neo-Nazis, drunks, Russian soldiers, but nothing seemed to put true terror into the hearts of the Estonians as the word for lice.

Täid.

Lice called for a complete cleansing of the home. All the sheets and blankets would have to be washed at high temperatures. The clothes lines in the yard looked like the sails of ocean-going ships. All of that white and yellow, flapping in the wind. You can imagine what the neighbors thought.

We read that tea tree oil was feared by all Estonian lice, so we mixed it with water and sprayed it on all of the furniture.

"Even if one egg survives on a couch, we could still have a problem," Epp informed.

Then we vacuumed and scrubbed every surface, wiping it down with the oil as well. Any cast aside grain of sand or rice was inspected for similarity to a lice egg. It was impossible to tell if it was an egg or dead skin. You held it between your fingernails in the light and studied it.

Täid. Lice. There was an urgency to the word, to the situation. The email home from the the Viljandi Free Waldorf School that week had as a subject line *Kiire ja tähtis!* – Quick and important!

"Dear parents,

Many of you have already been informed of this and acted on it, but we will add the same information to the list. Several children in our kindergartens and school have been found to have lice. Several families have already undergone delousing. Even today, several children were sent home when they were discovered to have lice or eggs. We ask you to immediately, today, inspect your children's head and hair and, if necessary, to delouse them!!! In the apothecary, there are solutions for this. We ask you to keep the lice from spreading. Certainly, you should inspect the hair of all family members. From our side in the kindergartens and the school, we will do the same."

We were under siege. You could almost hear the lice's helicopters circling above the pointy roofs of Viljandi's Old Town. The lice paratroopers were parachuting down, at night when you least suspected it, into the blond tresses of the innocent children.

Something had to be done. Another dispatch from the school arrived with the subject line, "Check your children's heads because there might be…"

"Dear lovely parents,

In our school, head lice are on the move. Please check your children's hair.

When your children have long hair, then it MUST be properly secured – combed and styled – with a ponytail or in braids, etc. Just having a headband is not a solution. You should check if your children's hair is really clean. Remember to fasten long bangs, also for boys, up with a hair elastic or a hair clip, because that way the children can see well and the bangs will not create any problems with their vision. It is nice when a child has the kind of hairstyle that does not require special maintenance and with which a child can manage in school by his or herself. Unclean hair is a breeding ground for lice.

Be vigilant and we will maintain order as well."

We were vigilant. At the apothecary in town, they sold kits for lice removal, little bottles of strange smelling liquids, with metallic, thin combs, for removal of the insects. You sprayed your hair at night and then slept with it in a plastic bag until morning when you first combed it out and then rinsed it.

And yet there were no lice to be found. But we did it anyway. Just in case. Because we were told.

We also tried some home remedies we had identified on the Internet. A mix of mayonnaise and tea trea oil, to suffocate the tiny creatures we could not find. You mixed it up in a metal bowl and then applied it to your head and then the children's heads and wrapped them up in plastic. Then you slept again, hoping they would at last die, if they were there. Or maybe they weren't?

The issue was that the more you thought about the lice, the more you read about treatments, the more you saw the close-up images of their translucent little bodies, tiny legs, and curious poking antennae, the more you itched, and itched and itched, until you became positive that you *had* to have them, even though you had found none at all.

When the supermarket skinheads, morning drunks, and lice and mice of Viljandi hadn't driven me to absolute despair, my second daughter's monolingualism sunk me to the bottom. Marta, our seven year old, had learned to switch smoothly, and even spoke English with a New York accent. But four-year-old Anna rarely used English words any more, and I had begun to catch myself speaking to her in Estonian just out of convenience because maintaining the golden rule of bilingualism – one parent, one language – was just exhausting.

Supposedly, David the whiskey sipping rare metals dealer up in Sillamäe and all around globe-hopping hero (who once set up a meeting with a Japanese client on a Wednesday, flew to Tokyo the same evening direct from Helsinki, took a quick shower, and negotiated the deal and flew back on Friday) had never ever slipped into speaking Estonian to his daughter Teele and son Toomas. Ever. Not one word.

"If they speak to me in Estonian, I just pretend to not understand them," David said confidently. „Only English with me, that's the rule!"

At the same time, both of his children spoke Estonian to each other and it was their mother tongue.

When my relatives understood over Christmas in America that the three-year-old towhead Anna only said things in her mother tongue, that to them must have sounded peculiar, there were curious looks and whispers. I remember how my grandmother looked up at my uncle and said, "That child does not speak a word of English."

"But she understands everything you say, Grandma," I said. "She *does* understand English. I swear. Just give her time!"

Anna. I felt a very special bond with our second daughter. Most of the things she would say and do seemed to reflect dim memories of my own childhood. When Anna hid behind my leg at birthday parties, I remembered how intimidated I also felt at parties when I was small. And it did make me feel a bit proud, and just a bit confused, when Anna asked me specifically to play the Rolling Stones in the car, when I drove her over to the kindergarten on rainy days.

But our special communication was beginning to break. One night in the tub, she handed me a bar of soap and asked me to pretend that it was, what I heard as the word *lõhe*: salmon.

"Oh, okay," I said, making the soapy salmon swim along.

"No, no," she said. "*Lohe*. You know, it is big and green and it breathes fire?"

"You must be confused. A *lõhe* is a fish. We just had *lõhe* for dinner last night."

"Are you crazy? We didn't have *lohe* for dinner! They have big wings. They are ferocious!"

"But salmon don't have wings! They have little fins!"

Epp explained later that we were both right. *Lohe*, pronounced something like "loh-heh," was the word for dragon. *Lõhe*, with that special tight õ sound, sounded more like "luh-heh," and was the word for salmon. Everybody I told the *lohe-lõhe* story to thought it was just hilarious. It ranked right up there with my old joke about how I thought Väino in Tartu had built the apartment for Endel, but he was really telling me that he had renovated it for himself, or how I was being interviewed once for my health insurance policy and when I was asked "*kas olete sooritanud enesetapukatset*" – Have you ever tried to commit suicide? – I thought the woman asked "*kas olete söönud hapukapsast,*" Have you ever eaten sauerkraut? Of course I answered her: "Yes, every week!"

But I didn't think it was funny. I couldn't even play with my own daughter without having language problems.

Back then, I could never have imagined that in one year we would find ourselves in the exact opposite situation, on the other side of the planet, where Anna wanted to speak only English and refused to speak Estonian anymore.

WHAT HAPPENED?

*There are storms and upheavals for which you can pre-
pare and then there are those that rise up out of nowhere
like a tidal wave of ill feeling and take you down and all
your bliss with it.*

You never see it coming, no more than you can sense that
gray line on the horizon is a land-bound tsunami, but when
it does come, you begin to ask yourself what happened and
what you could have done differently. Maybe you should
have stayed on higher ground. Or maybe you should have listened to your friends and vacationed in the Canary Islands
and not Thailand. But when you see the gray line on the horizon, the truth is that it is already too late.

There is nothing left to do but run.

The road connecting the villages of Ardu and Mäo in central
Estonia was among the country's most treacherous. It was
snake-like in its ominousness, curving and wriggling off and
out in unexpected directions, lined by dark, conspiring trees.

The first thing I remember saying to myself when the
police pulled me over that night was: "Damn, I'm tired."

Then I heard the Estonian equivalent of "License and registration, please."

Actually, no, stop. It wasn't like this. He didn't say "please." He just wanted the documents. Now.

I fumbled the documents over, and one of the officers returned to his car. I think he did. Everything about that night is mist. The rain and fog, the trucks carrying wood zooming by. I was the only driver on that road who wasn't driving over the speed limit. Another truck went by and I watched the orange blur of its lights. Half a forest in its back. Then it was gone.

The other policeman, the one with the German name, had me blow into one of those devices.

I gave a puff, but he waved me on. "You have to do it longer and blow harder," he instructed.

I did as told. As much air as I could force out. Then the reading came back.

"*Uskumatu, normis,*" he said to himself. "Unbelievable, it's normal."

"What seems to be the problem, officer?"

"Huh?" He stepped back as if confused by the question.

"Why did you pull me over?"

"Oh?" Still puzzled. "Uh... Your driving was *ebaühtlane*."

"*Ebaühtlane.*" I ran the word through my inner translator. Something like unusual, inconsistent.

"Yeah, you know, I'm really tired," I told them. "I was hoping to get some coffee at the cafe over there."

After that, I cannot exactly recall what happened. I do remember I was asked to come and sit in the back of the police car. There was something comforting and lullaby-like about the back of that Estonian police car, so I did not worry. In the other car before us, Simona and Marta slept peacefully, covered in the Estonian flags they had waved for Robbie Williams in Tallinn. But we weren't in Tallinn anymore. Where were we? I glanced out the window at the bus stop sign. Kükita.

More trucks barrelled by. "Hey," I said.

"What?" the one with the German name grunted.

"Can we move my car to the parking lot? I'm a bit worried about the kids in the dark car. With all the high-speed traffic around here, I mean."

The one with the German name looked at the one with the Estonian name and whispered a while. "We don't think that's necessary," the officer with the German name told me. "We have our lights on."

The officers were dressed in the blue uniform of the *politsei*, with yellow vests to make them visible to traffic. The one with the German name conferred with the one with the Estonian name some more. I wondered what the other drivers thought as they passed us. Speeder? Alcoholic?

Something else. American.

All through that period leading up to what happened, I felt an incredible sense of loss and lonesomeness. Sure, the good-humored antics of Elias or Silver or Enn, or esoteric conversations with blue-eyed poet Kristiina Ehin would distract me from it, but some kind of blackness was swallowing me. Little things set off my edginess: the Nazi in the supermarket, the local drunks, the unforgiving rigidness of Estonian life that seemed to permeate most person-to-person relationships. But the real culprit in this swirling Van Gogh-like nightmare that was sweeping over me was the work.

The work was choking every last drop of love out of my life. I secretly cursed the advent of portable devices that had made it possible for the mercurial founder of Petrone Print to work all of the time. Whole gray days would pass in Viljandi where I sat in one room and she in the other, just typing. We used to sit in London drawing pictures together or listening to music or talking. But there was no longer time for that. Work just seemed to come to you in Estonia, like oxygen. There was always more of it. Our neighbor labored outside from morning til midnight, hammering and sawing and sanding and smoking, and this was very much approved of, even coveted. But I was just not built the same way.

I could have worked hard too, even enjoyed the physical labor, but there was some fundamental joy missing. When I worked in construction, during my college summers, we told jokes and took breaks and ate sandwiches together. But most Estonian workers didn't talk. If I asked the neighbor something I would get a terse reply.

"Lifelong renovation, eh?" I tried sometimes.

A very long, contemplative pause. "It is." Then back to drilling.

The Estonians were workaholics and so I became one, too. My work was writing. I wrote and wrote more. The problem was that I reached my breaking point where it seemed like I was incapable of analytical thought. Some call this burning out.

I swear, at some moment in those hellbound workaholic years, staring at that mess of backlit screens, some piece of my brain ceased to work. Increasingly, on some gray days I was dumber than a sun-soaked, pot-dealing California surfer boy.

There had been harbingers of the doom that was to come. David had warned me first, Vello second.

David warned me at Christmas when his family came to visit us and we sat around watching YouTube clips. David was both alert and exhausted. Alert because of the coffee, exhausted from planes. Japan, Brazil, flight hours, time zones: our lives had become too similar. I had also tried to mesh international travel to conferences with the day-to-day hum of Estonian town life. You'd tell people you had to go somewhere tomorrow, and when they asked where, you told them: "Beijing," and they thought you were joking.

I had been doing that for six years, the trips, the late night articles, the university, the book writing, the promotion. Somehow in the middle of all this I had forgotten to get an Estonian license or an International Driver's Permit.

"But how can you drive?" asked Triin.

I shrugged. "With my car keys."

"You know you're going to have to get the right documents?" David said. "They used to be loose about it but the word on the street these days is that they are cracking down on foreign drivers."

I spoke about it with some of my American friends but they scoffed. "Yo, I've been driving here since '95 with an American license, dude, and I have had no trouble with the law," a certain foreign Estonian who used to stop in at the Green House Cafe said. "That law is like the speed limit, man. Nobody in Estonia follows it."

Vello had also begun to hear murmurings of something amiss. Vello had been driving without an Estonian license since 1992. But now having a Canadian document only was a liability. Vello was coming out of the Solaris shopping center in Tallinn on a late August day when he warned me. He was walking his bicycle along while his young son Robert sat in the seat. It had been a while since I slept on his couch, though I heard that both Tom Bissell, the writer, and Val Koso, the Eskimo, had been there.

"How is Val?" I inquired.

"Val's good," Vello answered. "His Alaskan burger place in New York City is supposedly doing great."

"Good, good. Where are you off to?"

"Well, I've actually got to go take a test soon. I've decided to go get an Estonian driver's license. And they don't just give you one if you know how to drive. You have to take exams and it is pretty complicated, theoretical crap."

"What? Why? Haven't you been driving for 20 years without one?"

"I have indeed. But the word on the street these days is that they are cracking down on foreign drivers. They catch you without the right document and you've got to walk home."

"No, you don't."

"It happened to a businessman I know, from Toronto, out in East Estonia."

"How are you getting around, then?"

"Oh, I'm still driving. Just quietly, just trying not to run any red lights or speed before the license comes. Tell all your buddies in Tartu and Viljandi to look out, get their documents in order, *et cetera*."

I took his warning seriously and even wrote it down to my notebook to look into things. But before that, there would be more deadlines, more renovation.

And there would be the Robbie Williams concert.

August 20, 2013. 2013 minus 1993 equalled 20.

Could it really have been already two decades since the British singing sensation and I had last crossed paths?

"Kids, we have a special treat for you today, a new pop group from England called Take That!"

There was silence and a few groans. Who could take a boy band seriously after New Kids on the Block broke up? The boy band era was finished in the US. We had been rechristened by Nirvana. Flannel shirts, ripped blue jeans. The Eighties were over.

It was a bright and crisp early autumn morning in 1993. I was shepherded with my classmates into a junior high school gymnasium. I was an ugly teenager. Big braces, short hair – and I vowed later to never cut it that short again – pimples on every inch of my body, an aroma of sweat that never seemed to fade. I was probably in love with some girl who had no interest in me. Which one? I can't remember. In the afternoons, I took my aggression out on the football field. I really enjoyed hurting people. Football was a rough sport. I got hit in the head so many times I couldn't remember the games.

Funny then that I remember that concert. A teacher stood at the center of a basketball court that day, five young men milling around behind him. They were all about five years older than us, late teens. These wannabe New Kids on the Block had stylish haircuts, buzzed underneath, long on top, one had an earring, another wore blue jean overalls, but with one strap loose, a sign of his disregard for authority.

The Englishmen began to perform and they beckoned us to join them on the floor. Two girls at last went down to the basketball court and began to dance, moving from side to side and jerking their hands in the air, all while smiling to their friends in the crowd to show they were joking. The girls both had purple hair and black clothes. They listened to The Smiths and smoked dope. One of the performers was particularly energetic. It's funny, I don't remember what their music sounded like, and I don't remember any of the other singers. But I remember that one man.

Everybody called him "Robbie."

After the group had performed, we went back to class. It wasn't too long after that I turned 16 and began to drive. The following summer I got my full license and I forgot all about Take That, and that their short, forgotten tour of American junior high schools had paid a stop at ours. They went on to much greater things and most likely forgot all about us too.

But it wasn't the last time that Robbie Williams and I would come into contact. The next time I saw Robbie, he was draped in an Estonian blue, black, and white flag at the Tallinn Song Festival Grounds.

I just knew that Robbie would wear the Estonian flag when he came out mid-show and began pointing at the thousands of audience members. It was August 20, 2013, the 22nd anniversary of re-declared independence, a national holiday. "Oh, you're beautiful. And you're beautiful, too," Robbie strutted around the stage with the microphone in his hand. "My, when they ask me how things were, how was Estonia, what the people were like, I'll say, they were really, really beautiful."

Robbie Williams. He was a pop star, a song and dance man, an entertainer. He was Cool Britannia in the flesh.

I had gone to that concert mostly for my niece, Simona, who wanted so badly to go, but also for Marta, so that one day she could say she saw Robbie Williams, the same way that I still bragged about that Ringo Starr concert when I was 10 years old. But something troubled me about the show. It was all about *him*. Robbie Williams. Everything was about *his* name and *his* face. Looking out on all those thousands of people waving flags, I found myself wondering how many of them knew my name and my face. A lot of them must have known me. My first book, *My Estonia 1* had been the number one book in the country for months, and the second one, *My Estonia 2*, for just as long.

It was a self-centered thought, yes, but by this time, I had become so full of myself that my "self" seemed to blot out the sun. In Estonia, I had become somebody, a writer, but this only led me deeper into darker, unexplored territory. And all this time I had been trying to please everyone, to *be* everyone, like an image-conscious pop star. I was writing articles for the world, books for Estonia, a master's paper for Tartu, painting a house facade for Viljandi, and then I was trying to soothe rattled nerves on Long Island writing long letters to my relatives, so that America would at last be pleased by my strange life. Then there was the Setomaa renovation.

I was no longer the sensitive man I had started out as, the one who had met Epp on those sunny Helsinki docks. I had become something dreadful, something dead. I had changed for the worse. I knew she knew it. But it seemed like there was no way back. Instead there were only deadlines. Deadlines after deadlines.

In the windy land, the time had come at last for me to die. Not a real physical death, but a spiritual one, a bonfire of the ghost, like one of those big Saint John's Day fires. Only through this burning might I rise once again as something better, be reborn into something true, reincarnated back into who I had been before I fell in love with those pretty images of myself.

I knew all of this that night as I watched thousands singing along with Robbie Williams. I had no idea what would happen but I felt that a change was about to come. Things just couldn't go on like that.

The next morning was the morning that the scandal broke and I would be afraid even to leave my house.

The police handed me the yellow sheet of paper that said I couldn't drive anywhere with a New York State license unless I had an International Driving Permit or an Estonian license. At last, I was permitted to move the car to the parking lot of the cafe.

I remember asking them how I was supposed to get home if I couldn't drive.

"Don't you have a friend who can come and drive you home?" the one with the German name said.

"No." I glimpsed at the radio clock in police car. It was 2:30 a.m.

"You can wait until morning and take the bus," the one with the Estonian name offered.

I tried to imagine myself sleeping in the cold car all night, and then taking a local bus into Paide, to catch a connection to Viljandi to get someone to accompany me back to the car in Kükita. Oh, and the first part of this trip would be with sleepy kids.

"Or you could go to Paide?" the one with the Estonian name suggested. "It's not too far. Just a few kilometers."

"How can we get there?"

The one with the German name motioned at the road. "You can walk."

"But I have two sleeping kids with me. Can't I just get some coffee and drive it home now? Please. I will work with my license thing tomorrow. I swear, I've learned my lesson."

"No," the one with the German name said. "According to Estonian law, you cannot drive on the Estonian roads."

And I really couldn't, not even illegally, because the police decided to park in the same parking lot and have breakfast in the cafe, with a clear line of vision to me and my car for what seemed like hours. Maybe they were waiting for me to try to escape. Then they could chase me down and put me in jail for the night. From the perspective of a cold parking lot, an Estonian jail suddenly didn't sound bad. A warm, dry bed. But what to do with the kids? Could they come to jail with me too?

At last I called Epp, hoping that the unaccented voice of one of their people might move the police to reconsider. Epp was usually persuasive. I walked into the cafe and handed the phone over to the one with the German name, but he told her the same.

Then the line went dead. I tried to call her back but for some reason it would not connect.

331

Better let her sleep, I thought. I knew what a hard time my wife had going back to sleep. Once I had accidentally woken her up when I called from Los Angeles, making a mistake in time difference math, and she was upset and sleepless for hours. Instead I called to a hotel in Paide. They said they had a room, and I said we could come, but then I learned that we had no way of getting there because there is no taxi in Paide at that hour.

And then, just after I had hung up, I heard the tell-tale ring of a phone running out of power and its screen went black.

So that was that. The end. I was stuck in a soggy parking lot in Kükita, Estonia, at 3 a.m. with no way out and two kids.

Epp had actually sent me some phone messages while we were at the concert. She said that we should take a hotel and not try to drive home so late. She had even booked a hotel room in Tallinn for us.

I did not get any of these messages though because there were so many people at the Tallinn Song Festival Grounds, the telecommunication networks went haywire. I was probably near Kükita when the messages came. But – what the hell – just some coffee and I'll make it, I thought. I had driven like this before, with some coffee to fix me up.

Real Estonian men didn't get tired. Real Estonian men just had some coffee, right? Right?

While I was waiting in that hell of a parking lot, like Jean-Paul Sartre's condemned characters in *No Exit*, Epp was turning to Facebook. She said that I had been stopped by the police and she asked that if anybody from the after-concert crowds was passing through Kükita could they please help us to get home safely.

At the same moment, somebody from the newspaper *Õhtuleht* was searching for some important front page news.

The headline on the popular tabloid the next day read: „Police Stopped Justin Petrone's Car at Night: A US License Is No Good!"

There was a picture, too, a picture that looked just like me.

The next day, I watched a woman in a supermarket look at that picture of me on the newspaper and then look up at me and realize I was the person with the word "police" next to his name.

It had begun.

I knew I had been caught and I knew it was my responsibility and I knew I had made a mistake. Simple. When you are wrong you must take responsibility for it and tell others that you are responsible.

If I had just had the correct document, order would have been upheld.

What bothered me was not the law, but the hopelessness of being a foreigner trapped in a place he cannot get out of. I tried to stop two travelers in the dark parking lot, but they both ignored me. Maybe they were tired and maybe they couldn't hear the man speaking beside them. In the middle of that night I felt that whoever I asked for help would ignore me, because I was a stranger, because I had an accent, and because I might even be a Muslim or something.

What also bothered me was the unreadability of the eyes of the police officer with the German name and the one with the Estonian name. I couldn't understand anything they were doing with their eyes, with their bodies. Their body language was impenetrable to me, and so I felt doubly blind. As the rain came down and I paced that parking lot trying to figure out what to do, I kept thinking about Mertelsmann's class and all of those stories about the NKVD troikas and the Forest Brothers.

How would it feel to be detained in the middle of nowhere by strangers?

Even if the police in New York could be brutal, perhaps even murderous, at least you were aware of this and might be able to anticipate their actions based on the tones of their voices or the way in which they walked toward you. But in Estonia, there were no such signals, or if there were, I could not decipher them. I was just a foreigner, a stranger. I was outside the majority, unaccustomed to their mindset.

I decided to ask one more fellow traveler for some help. A big man got out of a big truck and spat on the ground beside me and went to the window at the cafe to order a pork sandwich with extra mayonnaise. I tried to speak to him but he ignored me and smoked his cigarette. So I did the only thing I knew. I got out my journal and started to write.

On the Internet the following day, strange things were happening. People were arguing vehemently about me. They were arguing with each other about the actions of the police. They were just arguing.

"It is good to know that the police are enforcing the rules. In the given situation I think the police acted correctly. Driving without a valid license in the Estonian Republic is not allowed and this order is for everyone. Similarly, it is well known all over the world that in difficult situations, such as driving at night, one should have a communications device (in this case, a charged phone!). This is every driver's own responsibility! When children are sleeping in the car, then it is very irresponsible to drive at night with an uncharged telephone and an invalid license!"

"I agree. An Estonian license in Yankeeland is not valid! There you must get another license. Every country has its own order. Although driving is similar all over the world, every state has its own traffic system, and therefore it is correct to get it right, when one lives there regularly. For me, this is elementary."

"Thoughtless and sick bureaucracy. The laws do not protect, they just harass normal citizens. Disgusting."

"Justin should be grateful. When his driving appeared to be dangerous then he was apparently tired and endangering his children. The police finally woke him up. And the police were even considerate. Epp should shut up and be grateful.

And how is it possible that a person is traveling with children and he doesn't have a phone charger in his car? All of this time, with children in Estonia already, and he still doesn't know what documents are necessary!"

It was as if there were 1.3 million index fingers raised in my face. There was no defense, and even a long apology on my blog in Estonian could not sate the beast.

I'd been shocked in many ways in Estonia, by supermarket neo-Nazis, by flagrant alcoholism, and yet the one thing that could motivate hundreds of people to rush to their computers and beat me and each other up with comments and emails was that some American got stopped for driving without an Estonian license late at night. In a land where young men happily ascended rickety, handmade ladders to paint second-floor windows, I was suddenly the poster boy for irresponsibility. It seemed surreal.

Who were these people? What happened?

But this track of mind led nowhere. You just had to apologize. It had been my responsibility. I had been tired. It was dangerous.

"Look, whatever you do, you can't treat officials as humans," Vello told me on the phone as we were packing our things. "Police, bureaucrats – they're just not like us. They should be regarded as vending machines, because they will never dispense more compassion than a soda machine. I do think schadenfreude is a big part of their lives."

Deciding to leave hurt. Estonia by that time had come to feel like home. The weather in those August days was magnificent: warm, sunny, a light breeze coming in off the lake. The sound of the wind as it winded and crumpled through the branches of the trees soothed you like a natural lullaby. The parks around the castle ruins were lush and green. Shadows danced along and down the long, winding cobblestone lanes of Viljandi. Even the stoic statue of General Johan Laidoner outside the Ait looked welcoming. I had finally come to accept my place in Viljandi. And then...

Beyond our windows, our cursed street was finally getting it together. Soon one would be able to drive from one end of Sepa Street to the other without crashing into a hole. The burned rubble across the way was starting to look like a real house again. Men worked in the August warmth assembling a new roof. The mossed-over foundation beside it, which had stood barren since the war, was still littered with weeds but there were rumors that soon it would be used as a concert stage. Good feelings were everywhere. But I was hunched and speechless. The tickets had been bought, and with that big sum, the knowledge that we would have to use them. Suitcases were being packed, new tenants found, and a friend agreed to take our cat. We were leaving.

For how long?

Not too long, I said. Just as I had told my family in America that we would be back soon, I now told our friends in Viljandi that we would return. "We'll be back. You'll see."

During the year after I got my fine I would not be allowed to apply for an Estonian driving license, and I could get into new trouble if I tried to drive with an international one. This is what I was told, and during those panicky days, it seemed the most logical and responsible way: to leave the country for one year. Moreover, we had to decide quickly, because the school year was about to start. The decision had to be fast.

"But we will be back! We will, honestly."

Few believed me. For them, the name of America carried the ring of finality. America was the place to which Europeans had always gone and from which they usually did not return.

Like a black hole, but with shopping malls.

Leaving Estonia contained treason and treachery. The local term was "*jätsite Eesti maha*" – which doesn't translate well into English. "*Maha,*" indicates a downward motion. "*Jätsite*" means "you left it." So people were telling us, literally, "you left Estonia down," as if we had crumpled up the whole country into a ball of rubbish and tossed it away.

And as for our Estonian relatives, well, the only thing my sister-in-law said was: "Such a quick decision!"

Epp's sister Eva the confectioner was the steadiest, most deliberate and dependable girl you could find. Like other members of the family, I had initially mistaken her bashfulness for coldness. My relatives were not emotionally cold people, they were just introverts. If you gave Eva a hug, she would blush. And I never dared to kiss her on the cheek as we used to with our Italian-American family members. She would just combust after that.

When I did drive with Eva to the car dealership to see if they could make a new key for my car in two hours, she said very little. But I sensed her concern for me, for us. She didn't have to say anything. When my brother-in-law Aap drove us to the ferry terminal, these days with a big bushy head of reddish brown hair and wild beard to match, his silence seemed to share an equal concern.

I hoped they didn't blame me for this mess, but in a way, I was all to blame. If I had got my license, if I hadn't been American. And Italian. And irresponsible. And stupid. If I had not been all those things, everything would be "normaalne."

Moving anywhere is unpleasant, but I remember that last day in Estonia was particularly unpleasant because of the car key situation.

What happened?

Our car – the one I was prohibited from driving – had only one functional key. When we bought it from the car lot, I was handed one old key. "That's what it came with," they told me. I had a copy made of that key, but there was something odd about it. It would start the car for a second and then it would die. This, I learned, was because the other key contained some kind of software that allowed the car to start and continue to run. The new key didn't have it. I do recall that, according to the locksmith in Viljandi, it would be difficult for him to replicate such a key and would cost over 100 euros. He had asked me if I really needed a copy of such a special key and I said I didn't think so.

So I drove with one key for years, until the Kükita Police ended my Estonian driving career. Epp couldn't drive at all. Her Estonian driving licence was not renewed either.

But in the middle of sorting and moving, you need to transport things.

That's when my friend Elias started driving with my one key, and my brother-in-law Aap started driving with my one key, and our babysitter Maie-Ly, too, and somewhere in the midst of all of these surrogate drivers, my special one key got lost on the day we needed it most.

Thursday, August 29. Scheduled departure from Viljandi to Tallinn's ferry terminal, 2:30 p.m.. Key: necessary.

Time at the moment: 11 a.m. Key: missing.

Decision: to call to Mulgi Motoäri, the famous Viljandi automotive shop. Elias had introduced me to them. I had never been disappointed with Tarmo or Rasmus or their crew of go-at-it grease monkeys.

Tarmo answered this time. Tarmo was the big guy with the big shiny wristwatch who wanted to bring me a Mercedes Benz from Germany, as if I would desire such a car, or even look appropriate driving it around Viljandi. "Don't buy a car in Estonia," Tarmo said. "All of the dealers crack into the dashboard and reset the odometers. If it says 80,000 km, it probably has 280,000 km on it." He had tolerated the purchase of our Volkswagen Sharan, even though we had got it in a lot in Tartu, because it had come from Germany and was still in good shape, but his eyes still wore a "what could have been" look when he glanced in my direction.

I could tell it was Tarmo on the phone because of his deep, slightly sluggish manner of speech that was hard to follow. I recalled how the Mulgi Motoäri men knew somebody in town with a magic computer that could be linked into my car to perform all kinds of miracles. Maybe this same magic man could help me.

Tarmo called back two minutes later and said I should go to a certain car dealership, and that they might be able to fix it very soon. Resourceful Mulgi Motoäri had saved the day again.

I got my sister-in-law Eva to take me in her car to the dealership. She waited while I engaged the dark-haired woman at the desk. Our conversation went something like this.

"I have a problem. I have a car, a Volkswagen, and I have lost one of the keys. But the other key doesn't have the right software in it, and I can't start the car. I heard that you might be able to fix something like that quickly. I need it today. We have to catch a ferry in Tallinn in a few hours."

"Where is the car?"

"It's at my house."

"Then we can't help you."

"What do you mean?"

"If the car isn't here, we can't help."

"But how am I supposed to get my car here? Remember what I said? It doesn't have a functioning key."

"I'm sorry, we can't help you."

She sustained eye contact for half a second then returned her gaze to her laptop.

"Maybe your manager can help? My friend said that you do these kinds of things."

The woman tried to get the attention of the rotund bald man seated beside her. He was also staring intently at the computer.

"Raivo," she reached out to touch his arm. "Raivo?"

"D-don't b-bother me!" he stuttered shaking his arms in the air. "Can't you see? I'm working."

The woman looked up at me again and shrugged. "We can't help you."

I was about to give up, but I decided to call to Mulgi Motoäri's Tarmo instead. I felt a bit ashamed that Big Daddy Tarmo would have to bail out Poor Foreigner Justin again, but it was my last option.

"My friend would like to talk to you," I said, and handed her the phone. She took it and winced a bit when he began talking to her in his sluggish but confident know-it-all, Estonian-man way. Then, after saying "okay" a few times, she handed the phone back to me.

"Stand outside," Tarmo said on the phone. "We'll be by to pick you up in a few minutes."

Meantime my sister-in-law Eva had come inside. I explained what was going on. "Does this mean that I can go?" she asked. "Yes," I said. "You are free to go. Freedom!"

Eva got in her little blue car, put her sunglasses on, checked her mirrors and drove away. I felt a stirring of tenderness when I watched it. I had known Eva for years. I had known many of these people for a long time. They were relatives, friends, no matter what language they spoke with me, no matter their nationality. And it would be one full year before I saw them again?

Tarmo arrived in his white truck, and another mechanic, who never introduced himself to me and generally avoided eye contact, moved to the back of the van to sit on the floor. It was illegal, but it seemed other people could do all kinds of illegal things and not get caught. Not me. Not this time. You only got so much good fortune. And when it was gone?

While Tarmo was driving me to pick up my car he said, "I heard about what happened to you in Kükita."

"You mean with the police?"

"Yeah. I read it online and in the papers. Pretty *matslik* if you ask me." He rolled his eyes.

"*Matslik*?" I ran it through my head. It should mean "rude," I decided.

"I've been stopped in Germany," Tarmo continued. "In Poland, for speeding or running a red light. Nobody ever bothered me about my license, and even if they did, they didn't tell me I couldn't leave."

"But you have a European license."

"Who cares what kind of license it is? If you know how to drive a car and have a license, then you know how to drive a car and have a license. Obviously, you know how to drive a vehicle."

"They didn't think so."

"Pssh. And you were stopped before by police, and they didn't tell you?"

"I've been stopped several times and they didn't tell me. I registered the car with that license, drove into and out of the country several times with that license, had the car inspected with that license. I knew that I had to do something, but my license seemed to work fine for everyone."

He leaned in. "I read in some Internet comments that you were driving slow, and skidding on the turns."

"I was tired. It's a pretty dangerous road. I didn't feel like speeding in the dark."

"I would have told you to drink some coffee ," he snorted. "It's not rocket science."

"Why do you need to borrow my car?" Elias asked.

"Because we lost our car key. And we have to catch the 6 p.m. ferry to Stockholm, you know that..."

"Don't you have another key?"

"Yes, but it doesn't have the right software."

"What?"

"It just doesn't work."

Elias was putting some wallpaper in his children's room. In the kitchen, his mother's sister sat reading a newspaper, calling out to him in Swedish from time to time. I understood some of it. This was my world. Swedish, Estonian, English. Elias and I even lapsed into Estonian sometimes between each other. What would my high school friends think of that?

„Kuradi kole!" Elias cursed in Estonian, standing back and looking at the wall. "This wallpaper looks like crap!"

"It's just wet," I said. "It'll look better when it dries."

"Yeah, that side dried, it looks okay now. But this side, I just can't get it right. Anyway, you need a key, you said."

"I need your car and your car key, yes."

"You know it's a sign, don't you?" he folded his arms. "A sign that you should stay. You should read the signs more often, Justin."

"Don't say that!" I screamed at him. "Don't talk to me about fucking signs anymore!"

"I'm just saying ..."

"Tell you what, if we miss the ferry, then I'll take it as a sign! But I have to try to make this boat! We already have a new home waiting for us over there, a new school for our children. I have to try to make this boat, do you hear me..."

"Okay."

We almost did miss that ferry, with Aap driving quickly, but coolly, with Elias's car, to D-Terminal, and me inside cursing the Estonian engineers who had drawn up so few left turns.

"Everybody knows you're supposed to turn at Mere Puiestee!" Epp was screaming from the back seat. "Didn't you see the sign and the picture of the ferry?"

"But there was a big traffic jam up there," I yelled back, wondering what would happen if we missed the ferry and then what would happen if we missed the plane to New York. How many misses would it take to get us to change our plans? We had spent all that time finding a place to live in the States. And work! And my parents! We had rented our home out! We had given our cat away! What would we do if we were just stuck in Europe? "Maybe move to Tallinn, or Pärnu," Epp had

345

sung the day before in jest. "In fact, this weather really makes me wish I was in Pärnu on the beach."

"Me, too," I told her. "Me, too."

There was no time to talk when the car pulled up beside the ferry terminal. We had three minutes to get to the counter and get our tickets. Then they would close the counter and there would be no further negotiations. Even 30 seconds too late and we would miss that important ship. Aap let Epp out and she ran upstairs, clutching Maria in her arms, and the rest of us followed, pulling heavy suitcases. In these kinds of situations I usually developed super strength, and could pull three giant bags at the same time.

And I needed that strength. Once we got our tickets, we still had to run to catch the ship before it left port.

I looked at Tallinn as I lugged those huge, heavy bags down the kilometer-long ramp that led to the ship. My shoulders ached, sweat was running down my face. As the alarms rang and I rushed to get aboard the ship that would take us to Stockholm and then North America, I looked at Tallinn one last time, the liquor stores and parking lots and medieval-looking port restaurants, and I did have that thought that comes to us all at some bottom point in our lives.

I'm really getting too old for this.

Later, when I sat in our room on the ship, writing on the small desk and watching the last dark green strip of land vanish from vision, I did wonder how, after all of this craziness, we could ever come back.

Would we?

SPRING FATIGUE

There was a moment, zooming through the country roads of my Long Island home, passing through those villages with their Algonquian Indian names – Cutchogue, Mattituck, Amagansett, Montauk – that I swore I would never go back to Estonia.

When the late afternoon American sun hit your eyes and you turned your head a bit and saw all of those vineyards and cornfields on the sides of the road, you wished you had died before you had ever set foot anywhere else. An ocean evaporated off your back, and you never wanted to do a thing again. Not anything. Forget your ambitions, forget your dreams. Who needed dreams? Just talk, eat, and sleep. Turn the ignition to the car, drive along the coast, get some coffee, go see a movie, maybe go to the beach.

Be normal.

But never write. Not seriously. You couldn't be a writer and be serious about it here, unless you were paid big money to do it. You needed big money to stay. There were always more important things to do for us on that island: deadlines and birthday parties and trips and endless routes to the shopping centers to buy food and clothes, or to your children's friends' homes, because kids in America had to be driven to playdates. That spontaneity, that freedom of Viljandi or Tartu was seven time zones away now. When you met with the other parents, you had to chat about sports or politics or work or the weather. It was nice to speak to them and yet unfulfilling. You had to learn to conceal your story, never talk about Estonia at all, or about what happened.

What happened?

It took a long time for the ache to wear off. I can't even say exactly what it was. Frustration with my own stupidity. Discomfort from those nosy, preachy people. Most people in America laughed when I told them about that night. Some of my closest friends were even *jealous* when they heard about the police and the tabloids.

"Wait, you were on the front page of a major newspaper?" my Filipino rapper friend in Los Angeles said. His real name was CJ, but he called himself Mista Cookie Jar. He had shoulder-length black hair and he was dressed in a zoot suit with white sunglasses.

"Yeah, but it was because I got in trouble with the police. You don't want to mess with the police."

"Who cares, bro? If you're on the front page, that means that people want to read about you. Damn it. How come cool stuff like that never happens to me, man?"

Me and Mista Cookie Jar. We were so tight in school. He was the one who taught me how to think like an artist, that creativity could save you. My gift seemed to be writing. One of my English teachers, a very sensuous older woman with long gray hair and clear blue eyes, even had a nickname for me then: F. Scott, like the great writer F. Scott Fitzgerald. "You have a way with words, young F. Scott." "This has the voice, F. Scott." "Whatever you do, keep on writing, F. Scott."

I don't know how other people see themselves or their roles in the world. Maybe they don't think about it so much. Maybe it doesn't matter. But as green and beautiful as it was out there on the coast, as much as I wanted to forget about what happened, all of that confusion and negativity, I knew that I was a writer, and that Epp was a writer, and we belonged in a place where we could be writers, where we could be fulfilled. A place at a corner table, in an old brick building, where we could spend a day seated by the window writing furiously, like F. Scott or Kerouac. Maybe have a good cappuccino.

You know what I mean?

I washed my hands in the sink, pausing again to read the story about the origin of the name Viljandi on the door. I came out into the bright light of spring that shone white through the great glass windows of the cafe, the sounds of jazz, the customers' voices. I paid my bill, and headed back to the table to write.

It's springtime in Estonia now, really springtime. There are few buds on the trees, but there is plenty of sunlight, and it catches on the faces of the red brick buildings of the Old Town. Wherever you go, you see people you know, and if you see them in this weather, then they are happy, but also a bit weary and aloof. They call it the "spring fatigue," the *kevadväsimus*.

When I first moved to Estonia and heard the term, I couldn't figure out what it meant. It seemed like spring was a glorious time. The snow was all gone, and you should skip down the street, singing. Now I know what the term means all too well. I pause to read the magazines at the kiosks that advertise home remedies for spring fatigue. What is this mysterious phenomenon? It feels like you have been holding your breath all winter, and then at last the birds come back and sing to you in the mornings, the days grow longer and longer, and then it hits you, comes over you like a cozy blanket and you feel as if you can at last just let it all go.

Some people in Estonia get frustrated by the spring fatigue because it slows them down and there is so much work to do. They want to run, sprint, but they can only walk, and slowly and deliberately at that. But I'm not bothered by it, as much as I yawn, as much as I stretch, because I am at last content in my life and content in my place. The other day I saw my old friend David in this very cafe, and we were asked to carry out a survey by a friendly young woman. "It's part of my master's thesis," she asked. "I hope you don't mind."

"Did *you* ever finish your master's paper?" David cocked an eyebrow at me.

"Nah," I yawned. "Still writing this damn book. Then the next one. And the next."

"But you love it, right?"

"Oh yeah. There's nothing else I would like to do, nowhere else I would like to be."

"That's good to hear."

We both filled the surveys out and I saw David jot down his age in the box marked *Vanus*, and then I thought for a moment and put mine. Thirty-five. "Goddamnit, I'm the oldest 35-year-old ever," I said. "Except for that Ramzan Kadyrov, you know, the president of Chechnya."

"Well, yes, we all have our own distinct paths in life," David said. "You still think about going back to the States? You were there for what? Nine months? That was a nice place you had on the coast. It was pretty when I came out to see you."

I shook my head. "Oh, it's not like I don't miss it. I could really go for a bowl of clam chowder right now. Some potatoes, green onions, salt and pepper, and some crackers."

David just smiled as he watched me drool over the idea of a bowl of soup.

"But I'm just so exhausted, David. I don't want to go anywhere."

He chuckled a bit.

"I'm serious. I've just moved too much, done too much. I just want to stay here, stay right here, with my wife, with my children, in my home. It used to be that whenever I got back from a business trip I could stay in Estonia for a few weeks and then I would start to get restless, those itchy legs you know, like I couldn't stay put or be happy."

"Oh, yeah, I have also been cutting way back on traveling. I did Japan and Brazil this year, and then other than a trip to Brussels in a few weeks that's it for me until summer."

"Really? You too? I came back here nine months ago and I haven't wanted to leave."

„But what about your biotech editing job?"

„I'm not doing it anymore."

„You aren't?"

„I'm only freelancing now, writing articles about things I care about."

„That's good to hear."

„You know, I just want to stay here, writing, to go home, maybe take a sauna, you know. Play with my children, kiss my wife, eat something, write something. That's it."

"There's nothing wrong with that," David shook his head back and forth a few times. "It's good to have something to do, to keep you busy, like writing. It's good to have a family and it's good to have a sauna. It's good to have a home. So keep on writing."

"Whatever you do, keep on writing, F. Scott."

I looked out the window for a moment, and saw Gea come walking down the sidewalk, pushing a stroller with her youngest son Samuel in it. Gea saw me and smiled and waved, and I tipped my head and waved back, with the sun in my eyes.

"You're right, David, you've always been right," I said. "It is good to have a home."